Finding Hope

From Isolation to Intention

by

Justin Mayeur

One Step Collective

Finding Hope: From Isolation to Intention
© 2025 Justin Mayeur
All rights reserved.

Published by One Step Collective
www.onestepcollective.com
On X: onestepcol

ISBN: 979-8-218-81243-0

Library of Congress Control Number: 2025920998

Cover design by Justin Mayeur
Printed in the United States of America

For the ones we carry with us,

even when we must let them go.

Table of Contents

Chapter 1: The Fall

November 17, 2023.

I don't remember the moment I jumped. Maybe that's a blessing. Maybe it's just another hole in the timeline I'm still trying to patch together.

But I remember what led to it. The weight pressing down on my chest all day. The way Hope's absence felt like a physical thing—heavy and suffocating. I'd been walking the streets of Leavenworth for hours, circling the same blocks like some pathetic satellite orbiting a planet that didn't want me. Looking for her car. Looking for her. Looking for any sign that I still existed in her world.

The alcohol had been my companion that night. Bourbon. Too much of it. The kind of drinking where you stop tasting it, stop measuring it, just pour and swallow and pour again. Enough to make terrible decisions feel reasonable, enough to make jumping off a wall seem like the only way to make the pain visible. To make it real.

I wasn't trying to die—I don't think. That's the fucked up part. Death would've been too easy, too final. I was trying to feel something other than the crushing emptiness that had become my constant companion. I was trying to make my insides match my outsides. Break something physical to match what was already broken inside.

Standing on that wall, looking down into the darkness, my drunk brain had convinced itself of something so pathetic I can barely write it: maybe if I hurt myself badly enough, she'd have to care. Maybe if I was damaged enough, she'd come see me. Maybe if I was broken enough, I'd finally be worth fixing.

That's the logic of desperation. That's what happens when you've spent your whole life believing you're only valuable when you're useful, only worth loving when you're healing someone else. You start thinking pain is currency. That suffering might buy you some attention.

God, the things we tell ourselves when we're drowning.

What I do remember is waking up. Flat on my back. Concrete cold as a morgue slab. Darkness all around me. And pain—an ache so deep it felt like it had always been there, like I'd been born with it.

Finding Hope

The world came back in fragments. First, the sensation of something wrong—deeply, fundamentally wrong. My body felt disconnected, like pieces of me had been rearranged while I was gone. Like someone had taken me apart and put me back together with the instructions in Chinese.

The taste filled my mouth—copper and bourbon, blood and bad decisions. My own blood. I could feel it in my sinuses, thick and wrong. Could smell it mixing with the mountain air.

I was alone. Winter wrapped itself around me like a wet sheet of metal. Twenty-seven degrees. Middle of the mountains. If it had been even a few degrees colder, this story would've ended right there in that parking lot. Just another drunk who couldn't handle his shit, frozen to death in small-town Washington.

The cold bit through my clothes, seeping into my bones like it belonged there. I could feel it stealing my body heat, degree by degree. My fingers were already numb. My face felt like a mask someone else was wearing. The kind of cold that makes you sleepy, makes you want to close your eyes and drift.

Somewhere in the fog of my consciousness, a voice whispered what I didn't want to acknowledge: You're going to die here. And for a moment—just a moment—that felt okay. Fitting, even.

Hours passed, though I didn't feel them. I wasn't conscious for most of it. Drifting in and out of a darkness that felt both peaceful and terrifying. The in-between place where you're not quite dead but not quite alive either. Where time stops meaning anything.

In those moments between consciousness and void, I saw her face. Hope. Her eyes looking at me the way they had that one perfect moment at the hotel, when we'd both said "partner" at the same time, when I thought she might actually see me. When I thought maybe I wasn't completely worthless after all.

"You want—" she'd said. "—a partner," we'd finished together.

That memory played on loop, taunting me with what I'd lost. What I'd never really had.

But something pulled me out of the darkness.

Hope. That's what I call it. Maybe it was her. Maybe just the memory of her. Or maybe it was that stubborn part of me that had survived being invisible all those years in Louisiana. But suddenly I wasn't gone—I was gasping, blinking, alive.

Disappointed to be alive, if I'm honest.

When consciousness fully returned, panic set in. I was lying in a parking lot, surrounded by cars covered in frost, but the world was empty. Silent. It was that dead hour before dawn when even the insomniacs have finally surrendered to sleep. 4:17 AM, I'd learn later. The loneliest hour of the night.

I didn't know where I was. Didn't know how I'd gotten there. But I knew one thing: I had to get home. I had to move. Not because home meant anything—home was just an RV behind a storage facility, as empty as I was. But because movement meant not dying, and apparently some part of me wasn't ready for that yet.

So I tried to stand.

The moment I shifted my weight, lightning shot up my leg. Not regular pain—something deeper, more wrong. Like my bones were grinding against each other, creating their own horrible music. Like something fundamental had been severed, disconnected from the main system.

I thought I'd sprained my ankle. That's what my drunk brain told me. Just a sprain. Walk it off. You've had worse.

So I gritted my teeth and put pressure on it.

Once.

The scream that tore out of my throat was inhuman. Primal. The kind of sound you make when your body is telling you that what you're trying to do will destroy you. The kind they probably heard back in Louisiana when I was being born, when I first learned that entering this world meant pain.

Twice.

This time, I heard something. A grinding. A wet sound that made my stomach turn. Like stepping on a bag of chips, but the chips were my bones.

Three times.

I collapsed back down, screaming into the empty street. It was a pain I didn't recognize—sharp and dull at the same time, immediate but also endless. My body rejecting itself. But still, somehow, I tried again.

The fourth attempt, I blacked out from the pain. Just gone. A mercy.

When I came to, I understood: standing wasn't an option. Whatever I'd done to my leg, whatever damage I'd inflicted in my drunken stupidity, it wasn't the kind you walked off.

The cold had started winning by then, settling into my bones like it had always lived there. I knew if I stayed still, I wouldn't make it. Hope's voice—the same one that had pulled me from unconsciousness—now whispered: Move or die. Choose.

So I started crawling.

Hands. Elbows. Gravel biting through my sleeves like tiny teeth.

The concrete was rough against my palms, tearing at my skin with each movement. My elbows scraped raw within the first few yards. I could feel the blood, warm at first, then cold as it mixed with the frost. But I kept moving because stopping meant dying, and despite everything—despite the pain, despite the stupidity that had brought me here, despite wanting to disappear—I wasn't ready to die.

Not yet. Not like this. Not as invisible as I'd lived.

I pulled myself forward inch by inch, dragging my leg behind me like dead weight. Like something that used to belong to me but didn't anymore.

Each movement was agony. My leg hung at an angle that would've made me vomit if I'd had anything left in my stomach. Every time it bumped against the ground, fresh waves of nausea rolled through me. I could feel wetness soaking through my jeans—blood definitely, maybe bone fragments, maybe worse. The fabric stuck to my skin in ways that made me not want to know what was under there.

What felt like miles was maybe a couple hundred yards. But distance doesn't mean shit when you're crawling. Every inch forward was a choice. Every movement a decision to keep going when stopping would've been so much easier.

Move forward, breathe, don't pass out. Move forward, breathe, don't pass out. Over and over, a mantra of desperation. The same rhythm I'd use months later in the RV, trying to make it through withdrawal. The same rhythm I'd been using my whole life, really. Just keep moving. Just keep breathing. Just don't disappear completely.

My vision started tunneling. Gray spots danced at the edges like static on an old TV, threatening to pull me back into unconsciousness. The cold was winning, seeping into my core now. My body was shutting down, prioritizing the vital organs, abandoning the extremities. Triaging what was worth saving.

This is where death whispered to me. Not for the first time. Not for the last.

Just lie down, it said. Just close your eyes. It doesn't hurt when you stop fighting. You've been trying to disappear your whole life anyway. Here's your chance.

And for a moment—just a moment—I considered it. The peace of surrender. The end of all this pain, all this humiliation, all this desperate crawling toward a life that had already rejected me. It would be so easy. So quiet. So final.

But then I saw Hope's face again. Not the Hope who'd walked away from me, who'd blocked me, who'd made it clear I was too much. But the Hope who'd once smiled at me like I mattered. The Hope who'd made me believe, for a brief and shining moment, that I was worth saving.

Get up, her voice said in my head. Don't you dare give up. Not now. Not when I need you to prove me right about you.

Fucking delusions. Even dying, I was making up conversations with someone who wanted nothing to do with me.

So I kept crawling.

Then I saw them. The early risers. 5 AM runners cutting through the darkness. Legs pumping. Heads down. Headphones in. Living in their own perfect worlds where bones don't break and people don't disappear.

I screamed. I waved. Nothing.

My voice came out as a croak, barely audible over the sound of their footsteps and whatever motivational podcast was flooding their ears. I tried to make myself bigger, more visible, but sprawled on the ground with a shattered leg, I was just another shadow in the pre-dawn darkness. Another piece of trash on the side of the road.

They didn't hear me. They didn't see me. And I kept crawling.

The helplessness was almost worse than the pain. Watching person after person run past, completely oblivious to my existence. I was invisible again, just like I'd always been. Just like Tyler walking past me in seventh grade. Just like every lunch table that suddenly didn't have room. Even broken and bleeding, even dying in the street, I couldn't make anyone notice me.

The thought that crossed my mind then—the thought I'm still ashamed of—was how fitting it was. How perfectly it summed up my entire existence. Even in my moment of greatest need, I was forgettable. Dismissible. Nothing. Some patterns you can't break, even with broken bones.

Eventually I reached the road, collapsed again—on my hands and knees this time—and waited.

The asphalt was cold against my palms, but it felt solid. Real. I'd made it this far, somehow. From wherever I'd fallen to here—to visibility, to the possibility of rescue. To the chance of being seen, finally, even if it took being roadkill to do it.

It had been nearly two hours since I woke up. Two hours of crawling, freezing, screaming into the dark. Two hours of thinking I just needed to get home.

But home was an RV parked behind a storage facility, fourteen feet of aluminum filled with nothing but empty bottles and the ghost of someone who never loved me the way I loved her. Home was isolation and emptiness and the constant ache of missing someone who didn't miss me back. What was I crawling toward, really? What was I trying so desperately to get back to?

Another night of talking to Hope in my head? Another bottle of bourbon? Another day of pretending I was healing when really I was just learning new ways to break?

A car finally slowed. Someone saw me.

The headlights felt like salvation, washing over me in warm, white light. Like being born again, except this time someone was actually happy to see me arrive.

The car pulled over, and I heard a door slam, footsteps running toward me.

"Oh my God, are you okay? What happened?"

A woman's voice. Kind. Concerned. The first human kindness I'd experienced in hours, maybe days, maybe months.

I tried to answer, tried to explain, but all that came out was a sob. The relief of finally being seen, finally being helped, broke something open in me that I'd been holding closed through sheer force of will. All the tears I hadn't cried. All the screams I'd swallowed. All the times I'd said "I'm fine" when I was drowning.

She stayed with me, this stranger, holding my hand while we waited for the ambulance. Telling me I'd be okay. Telling me help was coming. Being the Hope that Hope couldn't be.

The ambulance came.

Sirens. Lights. Voices calling out medical terms I didn't understand. Hands lifting me onto a gurney, strapping me down, sliding me into the back of a vehicle that smelled like antiseptic and emergency.

The paramedic—a young guy with tired eyes who'd probably seen worse but acted like he hadn't—was asking me questions I couldn't focus on. Name. Date. What happened. Pain scale from one to ten.

"Ten," I said.

But also zero. Because the physical pain was nothing compared to the emotional numbness that had driven me to that wall in the first place. You can't measure the pain of being invisible on a scale of one to ten. There's no number for the ache of loving someone who sees right through you.

"You're going to be okay," he kept saying. "We're taking you to the hospital. You're going to be fine."

But I knew, even then, that fine was relative. That even if they could fix my body, there were other things broken in me that no surgeon could reach. Things that had been broken since Louisiana, since seventh grade, since the first time I learned that disappearing was easier than being seen.

At the hospital, everything became a blur of fluorescent lights and worried faces. Nurses cutting away my clothes with scissors that felt too intimate. Doctors examining my leg with practiced detachment, poking at bones that screamed in response. X-rays. CT scans. Terms like "compound fracture" and "surgical intervention" floating through the air around me.

Both bones in my leg—tibia and fibula—snapped clean through. Not just broken. Shattered. They showed me the X-rays like I'd want to see, like I'd find it interesting. All I saw was proof of how thoroughly I'd fucked up. Even my bones couldn't hold it together.

Surgery would be next. Metal. Screws. Plates. The long rebuild. They talked about recovery time, physical therapy, the months it would take to walk again.

But none of that had hit me yet. Not the injury. Not the magnitude. Not the reality of what was coming.

All I knew in that moment was that I had to keep going. And somehow, I had.

I'd survived the fall. Survived the crawl. Survived the cold and the darkness and the whispered promises of surrender.

What I didn't know—what I couldn't have known lying there in that hospital bed, high on morphine and adrenaline— was that the real fall was still coming. That the physical break in my leg was nothing compared to the psychological break that was waiting for me.

I thought a shattered ankle was rock bottom. I had no idea you could keep falling even when you couldn't stand.

In the coming months, I would be trapped in that RV, alone with my thoughts and the ghost of Hope. I would discover that there are different kinds of rock bottom. There's the kind where you hit concrete and shatter bones. And then there's the kind where you shatter everything else—your sense of self, your grip on reality, your ability to see any reason to keep fighting.

The kind where you're texting someone who isn't there. Where you're having conversations with silence. Where you're so desperate for connection that you start creating it out of nothing, like a kid with an imaginary friend, except you're thirty-six and you know it's not real but you can't stop.

I'd survived November 17th. But November 17th was just the beginning.

The real question wasn't whether I could heal from a broken leg. The real question was whether I could heal from a broken life. Whether someone who'd been invisible since seventh grade could learn to be seen. Whether someone who'd been running since Louisiana could learn to stay still.

And that answer—that answer was still months and a lot more falling away.

But lying there in that hospital bed, leg destroyed, future uncertain, one thing was clear: I'd crawled two hundred yards with a shattered ankle to save a life that wasn't worth saving.

The question was: what the fuck was I going to do with it now?

Chapter 2: How Did I Get Here?

I grew up Down da Bayou—a small town in South Louisiana where the roads were narrow, the air thick, and life moved slow. The humidity clung to everything like a second skin, and the cypress trees draped in Spanish moss made even daylight feel heavy and dim. You could taste the summer air— thick with salt from the Gulf, sweet with honeysuckle, bitter with the chemical plants burning off in the distance. The cicadas screamed so loud you had to shout over them, but nobody did. We just stopped talking when they got going.

We didn't call it trauma. We called it normal. You grow up around yelling, and eventually, it becomes background noise, like the hum of window units fighting the heat.

My parents did what they could—I believe that. But there was always tension, especially between my mom and my sister, who was twelve years older. Their fights were constant.

Loud. Unresolved. The kind that rattled the thin walls of our trailer and made the neighbor's dog bark.

I learned early how to disappear into my room and wait it out. I'd press my back against the door, feeling their screaming vibrate through the hollow wood, counting minutes until silence returned. Sometimes I'd cover my ears, but I could still feel the anger in my chest—thick and suffocating, like the Louisiana air. I'd stare at the water stains on my ceiling, making shapes out of them—a dragon, a boat, anything to take me somewhere else.

My room smelled like mildew and Old Spice deodorant I'd stolen from my dad, trying to cover up the smell of fear-sweat that came when voices got raised. That's what I remember most about being ten—the smell of trying to hide who I was.

In South Louisiana, you don't talk about feelings. You don't mention the knot in your stomach or the way your hands shake when voices get raised. Mental health was something for other people, people who were "weak." Down here, you went to church when you got in trouble. You prayed harder when things got bad. You kept your mouth shut and your problems to yourself.

The first time I tried to tell my mom I was sad—really sad, the kind that sits on your chest like a weight—she told me to "offer it up to Jesus." That was it. I was eleven years old, and

I learned that my feelings were something to be handed off to God, not dealt with here on Earth.

Food became comfort. I was a heavier kid, and even at that age, I started to feel the weight of that—not just in my body, but in how the world looked at me. Quiet judgment. Side comments. A shrinking sense of self. I remember standing in the school cafeteria line, feeling eyes on me, hearing whispers. Kids would look at my lunch tray and smirk. I learned to eat faster, to finish before anyone could comment.

There was this one day—fifth grade—when Ricky Thibodaux looked at my tray and said, loud enough for everyone to hear, "Damn, Justin, you gonna eat all that?" The whole table laughed. I laughed too, like it was funny, like it didn't slice right through me. I finished every bite, even though my stomach hurt, because leaving food would mean he was right. That night, I ate dinner standing at the kitchen counter so nobody could see how much I put on my plate.

We didn't get out much. "Going to the big city" meant New Orleans, and that was a rare adventure. Most of the time, life stayed small. Simple. Safe. The biggest excitement was Friday night football or someone catching a gator in their backyard. But under the surface, things were already cracking.

Junior high was when I first understood what it meant to be different. Not special different—wrong different. The kids

I'd grown up with, the ones who used to come over for birthday parties, started looking through me like I wasn't there. One day you're friends, the next day you're invisible.

I remember the exact moment it hit me. Seventh grade, standing by my locker, watching my childhood friend Tyler walk past with his new crew. He looked right at me—looked right through me—and kept walking. Like we'd never spent summers catching crawfish in the canal behind our houses. Like we'd never stayed up all night playing video games. Just gone.

I stood there, holding my math book, replaying the moment. Did he not see me? Should I have said something? I actually called out "Tyler!" but my voice cracked—that horrible seventh-grade voice crack—and he kept walking. Or maybe he heard and chose to keep walking. I never figured out which was worse.

That night, I looked in the mirror for a long time. Really looked. Tried to see what everyone else saw that made me so easy to leave behind. Too fat. Too quiet. Too weird. Too much and not enough all at the same time.

That's when the lying started.

The first real lie—the one that worked—was about my uncle. I told kids he flew planes for famous people. Partially true—he did fly planes. But I made it sound like he was flying rock stars and celebrities, not crop dusters and weekend warriors. The lie felt good coming out, like putting on clothes that finally fit. Kids actually listened. They asked questions. For five minutes, I was interesting.

I'd tell people I was related to famous musicians—anyone who'd recorded in New Orleans, which was half of everybody. I'd make up stories about my "cousin" who played bass for some band nobody had heard of. I got good at it too. I'd drop just enough real details—studio names, street names in the Quarter—to make it believable. The lies felt better than the truth, which was that I was just a fat kid from nowhere who nobody wanted to talk to.

By tenth grade, hiding had become my art form. I perfected the smile that meant nothing, the laugh that came at the right time, the way to sit in class so nobody would notice me. I knew exactly which desk in each classroom made you invisible—not the back where troublemakers sat, not the front where try-hards lived, but that sweet spot in the middle where teachers' eyes just slid past you.

I was afraid of the world around me, afraid of being treated negatively, afraid of saying the wrong thing and having everyone see what I already knew—that I wasn't worth much of anything. Every interaction felt like a test I was failing. Every silence felt like judgment.

My sister left home when I was still a kid. The screaming finally stopped—or at least got quieter—but peace didn't exactly follow. The house felt wrong without the yelling, like a song missing its bass line. You don't realize how much noise becomes part of your rhythm until it's gone.

I'll never forget the day she came back.

I was playing biddy basketball—terrible at it, but my mom insisted I do something active. She was supposed to meet my sister afterward in New Orleans. Instead, my dad picked me up, brought me home, and handed me a baby. No warning. No explanation. Just—here.

The baby was warm and smelled like formula and something sweet. She grabbed my finger with her whole tiny hand, and I stood there in our living room, still in my basketball shorts, holding my newborn niece while my dad went to make coffee like this was normal.

My sister had been pregnant for nine months and kept it hidden from the family. I knew, deep down. I think we all did. She'd been wearing baggy clothes, avoiding family dinners, always had somewhere else to be. But knowing and knowing are two different things. It still knocked the wind out of me.

That's when the shape of our family changed. My sister took care of her daughter for a while, but things never really settled. She'd leave for days, come back exhausted and angry. I was growing up, starting to get bullied for my weight. Childhood friends were drifting away, finding new circles. And I just faded into the background.

That's when I discovered my first real escape—Final Fantasy XI.

I found it by accident, saw an ad in a gaming magazine while my mom was shopping. An online world where thousands of players existed together. Where you could be anyone. Where nobody knew who you really were. I begged for it for Christmas, and somehow, miraculously, there it was under the tree. My parents had no idea what they were giving me—a portal out of my life.

The first time I logged in, my hands were shaking. Not from fear, but from possibility. The character creation screen asked me to build who I wanted to be. Not who I was—who I wanted to be. I could be thin. Strong. Capable. I stared at that screen for an hour, crafting someone who looked nothing like me but felt more real than my reflection.

The login screen became my sanctuary. That haunting piano melody—"Memoro de la Ŝtono"—still gives me chills. The way the logo materialized out of darkness meant I was about to become someone else. Someone better. I'd sit in my room, door locked, headphones on, and disappear into Vana'diel. The moment that music started, my shoulders would drop, my breathing would steady. I was home.

In that world, I wasn't the heavy kid from Louisiana who nobody wanted to sit with at lunch. I was a thin, strong human character. I was capable. I was needed. I chose to be a White Mage—a healer—because even in fantasy, I wanted to be the one who made things better, who kept people alive, who mattered.

The first time someone thanked me for keeping them alive during a difficult battle, I actually cried. They didn't know they were thanking Justin, the fat kid from the bayou. They were thanking my character, but it felt like they were thanking the real me—the me I wanted to be.

It happened at the most crucial time in a kid's life—ninth, tenth grade. The years when you're supposed to figure out who you are, how to be seen. Instead of learning how to talk to girls or throw a football, I was learning spell rotations and battle strategies. Instead of trying to make friends in a world that didn't want me, I chose one where I could be whoever I wanted.

In that world, nobody saw my weight. Nobody knew about the yelling or that my family couldn't afford brand name anything. There, I was strong. Respected. Capable. Worth something.

I remember the rush of getting invited to join a party for a difficult quest. The way my heart would race when someone would message me: "Hey, are you free to heal for us tonight?" That little chime was better than any notification I'd ever get in real life. I was reliable. I was good at what I did. People depended on me. In the real world, I felt like a burden—always taking up too much space. But in FFXI, I kept people alive.

The game had its own language, its own culture. I learned Japanese phrases from overseas players. "{Hello!} {Please} {Help} {me}" became second nature. I understood complex battle strategies better than algebra. I had friends in different time zones who would stay up late to help me. When I logged on, people were happy to see me. "Justin's here! We can start!" When I logged off, they'd say "See you tomorrow!" And they meant it. In the real world, nobody noticed when I disappeared.

I'd spend every hour I could building a life inside that game. Wake up at 5 AM before school to check my auctions. Fake sick to stay home for important battles. While other kids were at parties or figuring out how to flirt, I was grinding levels and farming loot. I was earning respect and building relationships and becoming someone people wanted around.

I didn't learn how to be a man. I learned how to disappear.

Days turned into nights. Homework faded. Meals blurred. My mom would call me for dinner, and I'd tell her "five more minutes" until she stopped calling. I'd grab a plate and eat at my computer, eyes never leaving the screen, barely tasting the food. The real world became the interruption. School was just the thing I had to endure to get back to my real life—the one happening on a server somewhere in Japan.

I locked myself in my room with a controller and keyboard and vanished into a world that wasn't real. But it felt more real than the one outside my door. In Vana'diel, my actions had consequences that mattered. If I failed, people noticed. If I succeeded, people celebrated. Outside, in Louisiana, I could disappear for hours and nobody would even ask where I'd been.

The thing is, I knew it wasn't healthy. Even at fifteen, sixteen years old, I knew I was choosing fantasy over reality. But reality hurt. Reality was Tyler walking past me. Reality was eating lunch alone. Reality was my mom and sister screaming while I counted ceiling stains. Fantasy was the only place I felt human.

It would be years before I touched a drug or picked up a drink. But the habit? The pattern of running? That started here. Every logout was a tiny death. Every return to the real world was a reminder of who I really was. So I'd log back in as soon as I could, chasing that feeling of mattering, of being needed, of being enough.

I was still playing when I started volunteering at the Audubon Zoo in New Orleans. At first, it was just something for college applications. But I stuck with it. Weekends turned into habits. I met new people. Good people. That place started to feel like something stable, something real.

The zoo gave me a taste of what connection felt like in the real world. I was helping care for animals, learning about conservation, working alongside people who seemed to genuinely enjoy my company. For a few hours each weekend, I felt useful without having to pretend to be someone else. The elephants didn't care what I weighed. The otters didn't know I was unpopular.

But the game still had me. That world still felt safer than this one. Even at the zoo, cleaning enclosures or prepping food, part of me was thinking about my character, about the quest I was working on, about friends who would be logging on that night. I'd be knee-deep in elephant shit, literally, and thinking about spell rotations. The real world was nice to visit, but FFXI was home.

By senior year, I was splitting time between caring for real animals and healing imaginary players. I was seventeen years old, living in two worlds. Both felt meaningful, but only one felt safe.

Then Katrina hit.

The storm tore through New Orleans in August 2005, taking down more than buildings—it tore holes in people. One of the homes it destroyed was where my sister had been living with my niece. A place we'd helped her get.

I remember watching the news coverage from our house sixty miles away, seeing the flooding, the devastation. The Superdome. The bodies. The zoo was damaged. Some animals died. The city I'd started to love was underwater. Everything that had felt stable suddenly wasn't. Even Final Fantasy XI servers were down for days. Both my worlds were broken.

After the storm, something shifted in my sister. Maybe PTSD. Maybe fear. Maybe she just broke under the weight of it all. She'd lost everything—her home, her job, her sense of safety. She'd come stay with us, leave again, come back worse. The storm had taken her house, but it also took something inside her.

Whatever the reason, she left. Dropped my niece off with my mom and disappeared to another state. No warning. No goodbye. Just gone.

And just like that, everything changed again.

Finding Hope

My niece was four years old, almost five. My mom hadn't expected to raise another child. She was already tired, already overwhelmed. And I was just a high school senior trying to keep myself together, trying to figure out how to graduate when I'd barely been going to class. But I took on more than I understood. Dances. School pickups. Homework help. Teaching her to tie her shoes while I was still figuring out how to be a person.

I didn't resent it. I loved her. Still do. Our bond became more than uncle and niece—it became something sacred. She'd crawl into my bed during thunderstorms. I'd tell her stories about brave princesses who saved themselves. She'd fall asleep holding my hand, trusting me to keep the monsters away when I couldn't even keep my own at bay.

This little girl needed stability, needed someone to show up, needed someone to care. And for the first time in my life, I had a reason to stay present in the real world. She couldn't be helped by my character in a video game. She needed me— the real me, the broken me, the me that was still figuring everything out.

But it was a lot. I was eighteen years old, caring for a four-year-old, watching my family fall apart, and my only coping mechanism was to disappear into worlds that weren't real. I'd put her to bed and immediately log into FFXI, desperate for a few hours of being someone else, someone who had their shit together, someone who knew what they were doing.

All those years of choosing fantasy over reality meant I'd never learned how to deal with real problems, real emotions, real relationships. When she'd cry, I didn't know how to comfort her except to distract her—the same thing I did to myself. When she'd ask about her mom, I didn't have answers. When life got hard—and it was about to get much harder—I only knew one solution.

Run.

The pattern was set. The foundation was laid. I'd learned that being myself was optional, that there were places I could go where I didn't have to be the scared, fat, unwanted kid from the bayou. I could be someone else entirely.

And once you learn that lesson—once you discover you can step outside yourself—it becomes the solution to everything. Failed a test? Log in. Parents fighting? Log in. Looked in the mirror too long? Log in. The answer was always the same: leave. Become someone else. Run.

The game taught me it was possible. Everything that came after was just finding new ways to do it. New login screens. New ways to become someone else. New ways to run.

But back then, sitting in my room with the door locked and headphones on, listening to that piano melody, watching my character appear on screen—it didn't feel like running. It felt like breathing. It felt like the only time I could actually breathe.

And sometimes, twenty years later, lying in an RV with a shattered ankle, dope-sick and alone, I can still hear that music. Still remember what it felt like to matter, even if it was only pixels on a screen. Still remember the first time I learned that being myself was optional.

That's how it started. That's how I got here.

Chapter 3: Becoming Numb

I was disappearing, and I didn't even know it.

Each bourbon and Coke, each night that bled into morning, each day that looked exactly like the one before—I was slowly erasing myself, one comfortable routine at a time. But comfortable is a funny word. It sounds safe, warm, like something you'd want. What they don't tell you is that comfortable can kill you so slowly you don't even notice you're dying.

The ranch was supposed to be different. My wife and I had just moved to Central Washington, dragging our RV and whatever was left of our marriage behind us like tin cans on a wedding car that had long since lost its shine. We got a job on a ranch that took in rescues—horses with haunted eyes, dogs that flinched at sudden movements, creatures that had been broken and were trying to remember how to trust again. In exchange for some work, we had a place to park our RV.

It felt like a sign. Like maybe we were the rescues too.

My wife loved animals. Always had. The way she'd light up around them was one of the few genuine things left between us. I thought maybe this was it. Maybe this would change things. Maybe if we just changed the scenery, we could change the story.

God, I was good at lying to myself.

We arrived in July, when the mountain air still held warmth and possibility. The first few weeks, I let myself believe. I'd wake up to horses nickering, mountains catching the morning light, and for brief moments, I'd feel something I hadn't felt in years. Hope. Not the person—not yet—but the feeling. That dangerous feeling that makes you think tomorrow might be different than today.

It didn't take long for reality to seep back in. The woman who ran the ranch had a few screws loose—the kind of person who could find fault in perfection, who needed drama like most people need oxygen. No matter how much I did, it was never enough. I'd fix a fence; she'd find three more that needed fixing. I'd clean the stalls; she'd inspect them like a drill sergeant looking for a reason to make you drop and give her twenty.

But it wasn't really about her. I see that now. She was just another excuse, another external reason for why things weren't working. The truth was harder to swallow: my wife and I were strangers playing house, and we'd gotten so good at the performance that we'd forgotten it was an act.

By August, my wife had gotten a job at a family-owned hotel in town. It gave us space. Routine. Some kind of rhythm. She'd leave in the morning, and I'd work the ranch, trying to lose myself in the physical labor, trying not to think about how empty our RV felt even when we were both in it.

Evenings, though—evenings we'd found our solution. There was a local bar that became our living room, our kitchen, our everything. We made friends there, or whatever you call the people you drink with night after night. It became New Orleans all over again—just set in the mountains instead of below sea level. Different altitude, same slow drowning.

The thing about drinking every night is that it makes everything feel fine. Not good, not bad, just... fine. You can sit across from someone you've been with for over a decade and not talk about anything real. You can avoid every difficult conversation by ordering another round. You can convince yourself that this is happiness, or at least close enough.

We told ourselves we were living in bliss. We used that word—bliss. Like if we said it enough times, it would become true. We weren't struggling, not really. We had jobs, friends, a routine. We weren't fighting. We weren't talking about money, or savings, or the future, or the fact that we hadn't really touched each other in months except for the occasional drunk fumbling that left us both feeling emptier than before.

We just... existed.

Winter in the RV that first year was when the cracks really started to show. You ever try to hide from yourself in a space smaller than most people's bedrooms? There's nowhere to go. The walls close in, but slowly, so slowly you don't notice until you're already suffocating. We stayed warm—space heater running constantly, bourbon warming us from the inside. But warm and alive are two different things.

The RV was always a mess. A small space, yet somehow always cluttered, like our inability to deal with our internal chaos had manifested in empty bottles and unwashed dishes and clothes that never quite made it to their proper place. It drove me crazy, but the kind of crazy you swallow down with another drink. I think deep down it symbolized the bigger mess we were ignoring—the marriage that was more habit than love, the dreams we'd stopped talking about, the people we used to be before we'd gotten so good at being numb.

She was happy at the hotel—or at least she seemed happy. They had another property in town, The Post Hotel. Fancy place. Real polished. The kind of place where people wore their success like cologne. She mentioned they might be hiring, so I gave it a shot.

I got the job. And I liked it.

There was something about the structure, the routine, the ability to make things perfect for other people even if I couldn't do it for myself. I was good at it too. I could smile, make small talk, solve problems. I could be the person they needed me to be for eight hours a day. It was almost like being alive.

But even with new jobs and a new town, the drinking didn't stop. If anything, it got worse. Everything still ended at the bar. We'd meet there after work like it was our real home. We'd sit on the same stools, order the same drinks, have the same conversations about nothing. We weren't growing. We were circling the drain in slow motion, but the bourbon made it feel like floating.

Days turned to weeks. Weeks into months. October became November became December, and every day looked exactly like the last. Wake up hungover. Go to work. Meet at the bar. Drink until the edges got soft. Go home. Pass out. Repeat.

Justin Mayeur

I was a ghost haunting my own life.

The Post Hotel became my refuge and my prison. Eight hours of pretending to be functional. Eight hours of smiling at guests, solving their problems, being the manager they needed. I got good at compartmentalizing—drunk Justin at night, professional Justin during the day. Two different people sharing the same dying body.

By spring, the pattern was set in stone. Work, drink, sleep, repeat. My wife and I had stopped even pretending things were good. We moved around each other like roommates who'd signed a lease they couldn't break. The ranch job had ended—October came and went, and we were still in the same spot, literally and figuratively. The RV hadn't moved. Neither had we.

That's when they started hiring for the summer season at The Post. New faces. Fresh energy. People who hadn't yet been worn down by small-town life and mountain winters.

I remember thinking it would just be another season. More of the same. Train the new people, get through the tourist rush, collect the paycheck, drink it away.

I had no idea that everything was about to change. No idea that someone was about to walk through those doors and show me exactly how numb I'd become. Someone who would make me feel things I'd forgotten existed, want things I'd given up on, dream things I'd buried under years of bourbon and compromise.

But that comes next. First, I had to finish becoming numb. Had to reach the absolute bottom of my ability to feel anything at all. Had to get so lost that finding myself would require burning everything down.

The numbness was almost complete. I was ready to disappear entirely.

And then one day in early spring, I ran into the hotel to pick up my check. Nothing special about it—just a quick errand between the endless cycle of work and drinking. I was probably hungover, though by then that was just my baseline.

The lobby was quiet, that lull between checkout and checkin. I headed to the front desk, expecting to grab my check from whoever was working and get out.

But there she was.

A new hire, I figured. Someone I hadn't seen before. When she looked up from the computer, something shifted in the air. Not dramatically—I wouldn't understand the earthquake that was coming until much later. But something.

"Hi," she said, with a smile that seemed genuinely happy to see me, even though we'd never met. "You must be Justin. I have your check right here."

We started talking. I don't even remember about what—something about the hotel, maybe the weather, maybe nothing at all. But the conversation flowed in a way that felt both brand new and completely familiar. Like talking to an old friend I'd somehow never met. Five minutes turned into fifteen. I found myself laughing at something she said, really laughing, not the performative chuckle I'd perfected for guests and coworkers.

I had to go—my wife was waiting, I had errands to run, life to get back to. So I took my check, said goodbye, headed for the door.

As I was walking out, I heard her say it, soft enough that maybe I wasn't supposed to hear:

"Why are the good ones always taken?"

I paused, my hand on the door. Poked my head back in to say something else—I don't even remember what. Something about the schedule, maybe. Something safe and professional that wouldn't acknowledge what I'd just heard.

But as I stepped outside into the spring air, I found myself mumbling under my breath:

Finding Hope

"She's going to be trouble."

I had no idea how right I was. No idea that this woman—Hope, though I didn't even know her name yet—was about to show me exactly how numb I'd become. No idea that "trouble" would be the best and worst thing that ever happened to me.

I just knew that for the first time in years, walking away from someone felt like effort. And that scared the hell out of me.

Chapter 4: When Everything Changed

After that first meeting, I couldn't get her out of my head.

Hope. I'd learned her name within days, found excuses to stop by the front desk when I knew she'd be working. Told myself I was just being friendly, welcoming the new employee. But I knew better. And I think she did too.

Spring turned to summer, and with it came a shift I couldn't ignore anymore. Every interaction built on the last. First it was just friendly conversations during shift changes. Then it was her bringing me cappuccinos she'd learned to make—"Practice," she'd say, but they were always perfect, always brought with that smile that made me forget I was supposed to be numb.

We'd been dancing around something inevitable for months. Every shift we worked together, the air got heavier with things we weren't saying. Every accidental touch lasted a beat too long. Every conversation drifted toward dangerous territory before one of us would pull back, remembering who we were supposed to be.

I'd become an expert at lying to myself. Told myself we were just friends. Coworkers. That the way my pulse jumped when she walked into a room was nothing. That the way she looked at me—like she could see through all my bullshit to something worth saving—meant nothing.

But we were running out of ways to pretend.

The hotel was chronically short-staffed that summer, which meant longer shifts, more time alone together. Seventeen hours, then twelve, then seventeen again. The kind of schedule that strips away your defenses, leaves you raw and honest at three in the morning when the rest of the world is asleep.

She'd make me cappuccinos during those long nights—not the regular coffee everyone else got, but proper ones with foam art. Little hearts and leaves floating on espresso. She'd bring them to me with this shy smile, and I'd pretend not to notice the way her fingers lingered when our hands touched during the exchange.

We talked about everything during those shifts. Real things. Dreams we'd given up on. Whether we wanted kids someday. What we were afraid of. What we hoped for.

She told me about wanting a farm. Animals. Space. A life that meant something more than just getting through the day. When she talked about it, her eyes would light up in a way that made me remember what it felt like to want things, to believe they were possible.

I found myself telling her things I'd never told anyone. About feeling like I was sleepwalking through my life. About the bar that had become my real home. About the marriage that looked fine from the outside but felt like slow suffocation from within.

Things I shouldn't have been telling a coworker. Things I shouldn't have been feeling at all.

Then came the night that changed everything.

It was late summer. August, maybe. The air was heavy with smoke from distant wildfires, giving everything an apocalyptic orange tinge. We were walking the rental bikes back into storage—part of the nightly routine. The garage was dimly lit, shadows pooling in the corners, our footsteps echoing off the concrete.

She was ahead of me, and I watched her move—casual, comfortable, unaware that my entire world was about to implode.

I stopped walking. Just stopped, right there in the middle of the garage, because I couldn't take another step carrying the weight of what I was feeling.

"We got a problem," I said.

She turned, startled. In the half-light, her face was all planes and shadows, beautiful in that way that made my chest hurt.

"What's wrong?" she asked, genuine concern in her voice. "Did something happen?"

"I can't stop thinking about you."

The words hung in the air between us, heavy as stones. I lifted my arm, showed her how much it was shaking—not from withdrawal for once, but from pure, terrified adrenaline. From the effort of keeping this inside for so long.

Her eyes went wide. For a moment, neither of us moved. Neither of us breathed.

Then she stepped closer. Not away, like she should have. Closer.

She put her hand on my arm—the one that was shaking—and the touch was so gentle it almost broke me. Her skin against mine, steady and warm, trying to calm the tremors. She looked me in the eyes, really looked at me, and in that moment I felt more seen than I had in years.

"Justin," she said, her voice soft but certain, "we're going to get through this."

Not "you're going to get through this." We. Like whatever was happening, whatever was about to happen, we were in it together.

"I know this is complicated," she continued, her hand still on my arm. "I know you're scared. But you can text me, okay? Whenever you need to. As much as you need to. I'll be here."

"You don't have to respond," I said quickly, not wanting to burden her more than I already had.

"I know," she said. "But I'll read them. I'll know. And sometimes that's enough, right? Just knowing someone's listening?"

She understood. God, she understood in a way no one else ever had. That sometimes you don't need answers or solutions or even responses. Sometimes you just need to know your words are landing somewhere, that you're not just screaming into the void.

"This is complicated," she said again, finally letting go of my arm. The absence of her touch felt like losing something essential. "You're married. I can't... we can't..."

"I know."

"But I'm here. As a friend. Whatever you need."

Friend. The word felt both too small and too dangerous. But I took it, held onto it like a lifeline, because even her friendship was more than I deserved and everything I needed.

But neither of us moved. We stood there in that garage, two people on the edge of something irreversible, both knowing we should walk away, both unable to take that first step.

Finally, she turned and walked back into the hotel. I followed, keeping distance between us, but everything had changed. The truth was out there now, living in the space between us, impossible to ignore.

The next few weeks were torture. We still worked together, but there was a new awareness, a conscious effort to maintain boundaries that had already been crossed in every way but physically. She was careful not to be alone with me. I was careful not to look at her too long. We were both careful to pretend that conversation in the garage hadn't happened.

My marriage, meanwhile, was imploding in slow motion. Every night I'd go home to the RV, to my wife, and feel like a stranger in my own life. We'd sit across from each other, drinking our bourbon and Cokes, and I'd think about Hope. About the future she talked about. About the way she looked at me like I was worth something.

The guilt was eating me alive—not in the way you'd think. I felt guilty for staying in a marriage that was already dead. Guilty for wasting my wife's time when I didn't love her the way she deserved. Guilty for being too much of a coward to end it.

But most of all, guilty for wanting something more. For believing I deserved it.

Then September came, and with it, everything fell apart.

Hope lost her job. Corporate restructuring, they called it. Budget cuts. The kind of thing that happens in hotels all the time, but the timing felt like the universe's cruel joke. Just when I'd finally admitted what I felt. Just when I'd started to believe things could change.

The same week she left, I finally did what I should have done years ago.

My wife and I were at the bar—of course we were at the bar. Our usual seats, usual drinks, the usual performance of a marriage that had been dead for years. The bourbon was warm in my stomach, loosening my tongue, giving me the liquid courage I'd been searching for.

On the drive home, I said it. Not with anger. Not with drama. Just the words that had been sitting in my chest like stones.

"I'm not in love with you anymore."

She didn't believe me at first. Or maybe she just chose not to. We kept living in that RV, two people in fourteen feet of aluminum, pretending nothing had changed. But everything had changed. I slept on the couch. Stopped pretending to care about her hotel stories. Started texting Hope.

She'd told me once that I could text her anytime. So I did. Constantly. Too much. Every thought, every feeling, every moment of panic about what I'd done. I didn't expect responses—told myself she was just giving me space to process.

But she never responded. And the silence was killing me.

I started drinking more. Not socially anymore, but with purpose. To forget. To numb. To make it through another day of living with someone I'd just told I didn't love while obsessing over someone who wouldn't talk to me.

Finding Hope

October came with plane tickets home. Round trip for my wife. One way for me.

We sat in that airport, next to each other for the last time, and neither of us said anything about what was happening. When we landed, we went our separate ways. That was the last time I saw her as my wife.

Being home with family was good, grounding even. But all I could think about was Hope. I bought flowers—expensive ones, the kind that say things too big for words—and flew back to Washington in November.

She wouldn't see me.

I'd sent too many texts. Said too much. Crossed the line between vulnerable and overwhelming. But I was desperate, drowning, and she was the only thing that had made me want to swim in years.

One night, I hit bottom. Sent her a message I shouldn't have sent anyone. Told her I didn't know if I wanted to wake up. It was messy, desperate, the kind of thing you send when you've got nothing left to lose.

And that night—she showed up at the bar.

No warning. No explanation. Just suddenly there, sitting beside me like no time had passed. We talked for hours about everything and nothing. And when the bourbon had made me brave enough, she looked me in the eyes and said:

"Justin, I want a family too. I want a farm too."

"Do you have feelings for me?" I asked, needing to hear it.

She didn't speak. She just nodded.

And in that moment, sitting in that bar where I'd drowned so many feelings, I knew I'd destroyed my entire life for a chance at something real. Something that might never happen. Something that was already slipping away even as she sat beside me.

But her nod—that small, silent confirmation—made it all worth it.

We were standing on the edge of something. I just didn't know yet that it was a cliff, and I was about to fall.

Chapter 5: The Night Before

November 16, 2023 started like any other day, which is to say it started with Hope's absence.

I woke up in the RV—still parked in the same spot, still too small, still empty despite being cluttered with the debris of a life I couldn't seem to organize. The space felt different now. Not like a home. Not even like a prison. More like a waiting room for something I couldn't name but felt approaching with the certainty of winter.

I hadn't seen Hope in weeks. Not since that night at the bar when she'd nodded, when she'd admitted to feelings that mirrored mine. Since then—silence. Not the comfortable kind that falls between people who understand each other, but the loaded kind, heavy with everything unsaid, everything undone.

I went to work. Put in my twelve hours at the hotel where we'd met, where every corner still held the ghost of her. The break room where we'd talked until dawn. The doorway where we'd collided. The garage where I'd confessed. All of it haunted now, echoing with conversations that would never continue.

The hotel felt different without her. Like a stage after the play has ended—all the props still in place, but the magic gone. I moved through my shift on autopilot, muscle memory carrying me through tasks while my mind circled the same thoughts it had been circling for weeks. Maybe months. Time had gotten slippery since she'd left. Since my wife had left. Since everyone had left and I was still here, still circling, still waiting for something I couldn't name.

By the time my shift ended, the familiar pull was already there. The bar. My other home. The place where I could dissolve the edges of everything that hurt, at least for a few hours.

I walked down the familiar path, my breath visible in the cold November air. My body knew this route so well I could have walked it blind—had walked it blind, more or less, on plenty of nights when the bourbon had done its job too well.

The bar was the same as always. Same stools. Same bartender. Same bottles lined up like soldiers waiting for orders. I took my usual seat, ordered my usual drink, prepared for another usual night of organized forgetting.

What I didn't know was that I'd recently started antidepressants. The doctor had warned me about mixing them with alcohol, but warnings had never stopped me before. I was beyond warnings. Beyond caution. Beyond anything except the next drink and the hope that maybe, finally, it would be enough to stop the endless loop of her name in my mind.

Like a broken prayer. Like a scratched record. Like a heartbeat that wouldn't stop even though the heart itself had been shattered.

I sat at the bar, talking with a friend. Just another night, or so I thought. The bourbon went down easier than usual, warming me from the inside in that familiar way that felt like home and destruction all at once. My friend was talking about something—work, maybe, or the weather, or any of the thousand things people talk about when they're really just filling silence—but I wasn't really listening.

I was thinking about Hope. Always thinking about Hope.

About the text messages I'd been sending into the void. Too many of them. Desperate, rambling things that revealed too much, asked for too much, needed too much. She never responded. That silence was killing me slower than the bourbon ever could.

I was thinking about how she'd looked that night when she'd nodded. The way her eyes had held mine. The way the world had seemed to pause, just for a moment, full of possibility.

I was thinking about the future I'd imagined with her. The farm she'd talked about. The family we both wanted. The life that felt so real I could almost touch it, even though it existed only in the space between what was and what could never be.

My friend got up to leave—she'd had a few too many, was swaying slightly. Without thinking, I offered to walk her to her car. Nothing more than that. No hidden agenda. Just one human looking out for another, the way people do when alcohol has made them temporarily kind.

I left my wallet and keys at the bar. Even my jacket. Fully intending to come back. This was just a detour, a few minutes to make sure she got to her car safely.

We walked, talked. The cold was sharper now, cutting through my shirt, but the bourbon kept me warm enough. Or I thought it did. She was more composed than I'd expected, handling her liquor better than she'd appeared to in the bar. Still, I felt better making sure she got to her car.

When we reached it, she offered to give me a ride part of the way home.

I should have said no. Should have walked back to the bar, collected my things, called it a night. But the cold was setting in, and home was a mile away, and I was tired—so tired—of always doing what I should do.

I accepted.

She dropped me off halfway. I thanked her, watched her taillights disappear into the darkness, and started walking.

It was colder now. Late. The kind of cold that seeps through your skin and settles in your bones. Home was still nearly a mile away, but I'd walked it before. Walked it drunk plenty of times. This was nothing new.

Somewhere along the way, things started to get fuzzy.

Not the usual bourbon fuzz—something different. Deeper. Like the world was dissolving at the edges, like reality was becoming negotiable. The antidepressants, maybe, doing their deadly dance with the alcohol. Or maybe just the accumulated weight of everything finally becoming too much to carry.

I don't remember much about the walk back. Fragments. The sound of my feet on pavement. The way the streetlights looked like halos, or eyes, or stars that had fallen too close to earth. The feeling that I was walking through a dream, or maybe walking toward one.

But I made it. Somehow. Stood outside the RV, swaying slightly, feeling proud of myself for navigating home despite the fog in my head.

I reached for the door.

Locked.

The handle might as well have been a wall. Everything I owned was still at the bar. My keys. My wallet. My jacket. My phone was in my pocket—the one thing I'd grabbed—but what good was it now?

I tried calling the bar, even though I knew they were closed. Thursday night—they'd closed at midnight, hours ago. The phone rang and rang, echoing in the empty night. No answer. Of course no answer. Everyone was gone. Everyone was always gone.

Something snapped.

Not dramatically. Not violently. Just a quiet breaking, like ice giving way under weight it was never meant to hold. I threw my phone. Not at anything. Not even particularly hard.

Just away from me, like it was the source of all my problems, like if I could just get rid of it, everything would be fine.

The cold was settling in now. Real cold. The kind that doesn't care about your problems or your broken heart or your locked doors. Below freezing. The kind of cold that kills people who aren't careful.

I knew if I didn't find shelter, I was going to be in trouble.

So I started walking back toward the bar. Maybe someone was still around. Maybe I could get inside. Warm up. Figure it out. My thoughts were getting scattered now, disconnected, like individual snowflakes falling without pattern or purpose.

That's when I came to the Wall.

I'd passed it a hundred times before. Just a retaining wall, maybe twenty feet high, separating the upper street from the lower parking area. Nothing special. Nothing significant. Just concrete and geography.

But that night, in that state, with the cold pressing in and my mind fracturing like ice, it looked like something else.

A shortcut, maybe.

A way out.

A door.

Justin Mayeur

I stood there, looking down at it. Twenty feet to the parking lot below. I was already at the top—the wall rose up from the lower level, and from the street where I stood, there was just a railing. A simple metal barrier between the sidewalk and the drop. The kind of railing that's meant to keep drunk people from accidentally falling over.

But I wasn't looking for an accident.

For reasons I'll never fully understand, I climbed over that railing. One leg, then the other. Standing on the wrong side of safety, nothing between me and the concrete below but twenty feet of cold November air.

I don't know what I thought was on the other side. Hope, maybe. The future I'd imagined. A different version of this night where I had my keys, where the door was open, where someone was waiting for me. Where she was waiting for me.

I reached the top. Stood there for a moment, balanced between two worlds—the one I was leaving and the one I thought I was heading toward.

I don't remember the moment I jumped.

Maybe that's mercy. Maybe that's just another hole in the timeline I'm still trying to patch together. But somewhere between standing and falling, between intention and impact, I made a choice that would shatter more than just my ankle.

Finding Hope

What I do remember is waking up.

Flat on my back. Concrete cold beneath me. Darkness all around. And pain—not just physical, though that was there too, radiating from my ankle up through my entire body. But a deeper pain. The kind that comes from finally understanding that you've been falling for much longer than just the seconds between the wall and the ground.

It was past 4 AM. The coldest part of the night.

I didn't know it yet, but I was about to start crawling. Two hundred yards through freezing darkness. Screaming for help that wouldn't come. Dragging myself toward a future I couldn't imagine.

But in that moment, lying there on the concrete, I was just a drunk man with a shattered ankle who'd finally hit bottom. Or what I thought was bottom. I had no idea how much further there was to fall.

The night before, I'd been a man with a locked door and no keys.

The night before, I'd been a man who thought the wall was a shortcut.

The night before, I'd been a man who still believed that if he could just get to Hope, everything would be okay.

Now I was something else. Something broken. Something that would need to be completely rebuilt from the ground up.

This was the night everything truly ended. And the night everything had to begin.

Chapter 6: Alone But Not Dead

The hospital discharged me the same day as the surgery.

Same day. That's how it works now. They put metal plates and screws into your shattered ankle, wait for you to wake up from anesthesia, make sure you're not going to die immediately, then wheel you to the door with a bottle of oxycodone and a printout of instructions you're too high to read. No overnight observation. No time to figure out how you're going to manage. Just here's your crutches, good luck, next patient please. They wheeled me to the entrance, helped me into an Uber, and that was it. No fanfare. No family waiting. Just me, a walking boot I couldn't walk in, and crutches I barely knew how to use.

The driver helped me to the RV door. I tipped him everything in my wallet—forty-three dollars—because he'd had to basically carry me those last few steps. He looked at the money, then at me, standing there swaying on one leg, and I saw something in his eyes I recognized. Pity. The same look I'd been running from my whole life.

"You gonna be okay, man?" he asked.

"Yeah," I lied. "Someone's coming."

No one was coming.

The RV door closed behind me with a sound like a coffin lid. Fourteen feet of aluminum and regret. The space felt smaller than I remembered, like it had shrunk while I was gone. Or maybe I'd just gotten bigger—swollen with pain and medication and the terrible understanding of what was coming.

I made it three feet before I fell.

Not dramatically. Not with a crash. Just my leg giving out, the crutches slipping, and suddenly I was on the floor. The impact sent lightning through my ankle, the kind of pain that makes you see colors that don't exist. I lay there for a moment, maybe an hour, time had already started to bend, waiting for the pain to fade to something manageable.

It didn't.

So I crawled.

To the couch. Three feet. Might as well have been three miles. Dragging myself with my arms while my leg screamed its metallic song—screws grinding against bone, plates holding together what wanted to fall apart. When I finally pulled myself onto the cushions, I was sweating through my clothes, shaking like I'd run a marathon.

That couch would become my entire world.

Six feet long. Three feet wide. Brown fabric worn thin from years of bourbon-soaked nights. It smelled like spilled drinks and broken promises. The cushions had permanent indentations from where my wife and I used to sit, carefully maintaining distance even when sharing the same space. Now it was just me and the ghost impressions of a marriage that had never really existed.

The first night, I didn't sleep. Couldn't. The pain came in waves—sometimes sharp and immediate, sometimes deep and grinding. The oxycodone helped, but not enough. Never enough. I'd take two pills, wait for the edges to soften, then spend the next four hours watching the ceiling and trying not to think about how I'd gotten here.

But thinking was all I had.

No TV—I couldn't focus on it anyway. No books—there wasn't room for books in fourteen feet of aluminum. Just me, the pain, and the phone that had become my lifeline to nowhere.

I checked it obsessively. Every five minutes. Every two. Looking for something, anything from Hope. A text. A call. Even just a read receipt to prove she still existed, that I hadn't imagined everything. But there was nothing. Just the bright screen reflecting my desperation back at me.

I started texting her anyway.

Not the desperate novels I'd been sending before the fall. Just small things:

"I'm home now."

"The surgery went okay."

"I miss my friend."

She never responded. I told myself she was reading them. Told myself she cared but couldn't show it. Told myself a lot of things that made the silence bearable.

The second day, I realized I had a problem. Several, actually.

Food. Water. Mental stability.

Everything in the RV was technically within reach—fourteen feet of aluminum doesn't leave much room for distance. The kitchen, the bathroom, the couch—they might as well have been in the same room. I could hop to what I needed, manage the basics. The physical distance wasn't the problem.

The problem was my mind.

By then, not texting Hope had become its own kind of addiction. I'd mark it on my phone calendar: "Last day I texted." Watch the days accumulate like sobriety chips. One day clean. Two days. Then I'd break, send something stupid at 2 AM, and the counter would reset.

I was trying desperately to let go of the hold I had on her, but the line between reality and fiction had already blurred beyond recognition. I knew she wasn't reading my messages. Knew she wasn't coming. But knowing and believing are different things, and the pills made it easy to live in the space between.

The third day, I started talking to Hope.

Not texting. Actually talking. Out loud. To the empty RV.

"Hey, I made it to the kitchen today," I'd say to the air where she wasn't. "Got water. Pretty proud of myself."

"You'd laugh at me right now. Can't even put on socks."

"I know you're probably happy. Away from all this mess. From me."

Sometimes I'd imagine her responses. Create entire conversations. She'd tell me I was stronger than I thought. That this was temporary. That everything would be okay. I knew it wasn't real, but reality wasn't exactly working out for me, so I chose the alternative.

The oxycodone helped with that too. Made the line between real and imagined softer, more negotiable. I'd take an extra pill, sometimes two, and drift into that space where Hope was still my friend, where my ankle wasn't shattered, where I hadn't destroyed everything good that had ever happened to me.

By the end of the first week, I'd developed a routine.

Wake up in pain. Take pills. Wait for them to work. Crawl to the kitchen for water and whatever food I could grab. Back to the couch. Check phone. Text Hope. No response. Take more pills. Create imaginary conversations. Pass out. Wake up in pain. Repeat.

Time became elastic. Minutes stretched into hours. Hours collapsed into seconds. I'd look at my phone, see it was Tuesday, wonder what happened to Monday. The pills helped with the pain but scrambled everything else. I'd forget if I'd eaten. Forget if I'd taken my medication. Take more just to be sure.

The isolation was the worst part.

Not just being alone—I'd been alone before. This was different. This was being trapped inside a box with nothing but your own thoughts and the growing understanding that no one was coming to save you. No one was checking in. No one cared if you lived or died in this aluminum coffin.

My wife was gone—had been gone long before she actually left. My family was two thousand miles away. Hope was a ghost I'd created from memories and medication. The only real thing was the pain, constant and reliable, my most faithful companion.

I started writing.

Not with any purpose. Not for anyone to read. Just to prove I still existed. To leave evidence that someone had been here, had survived this.

The notes were fragmented, sometimes incoherent:

"Day 8 (I think): Still can't shower. Smell like death. Maybe am death."

"Hope came by today. Not real. Know that. Still nice."

"Ran out of crackers. Contemplating eating the couch."

"Question: If you break in the forest and no one's around to hear it, did you ever really exist?"

Some days I'd write pages, rambling streams of consciousness about Hope, about the hotel, about the life I'd imagined we'd have. Other days, just a single line: "Still here" or "Fuck this" or just the date, proof that time was still passing even if I wasn't sure how.

The second week, I discovered BetterHelp.

Hope had mentioned it once, back when we were still talking, back when she still saw me as someone worth helping. I signed up from my phone, booked a session for the next day. The therapist's name was Melissa. She had kind eyes in her profile photo, the sort of eyes that might not judge you for falling apart.

That first session, I couldn't stop crying.

Not sad tears. Not happy tears. Just... tears. Like my body was trying to leak out all the poison I'd been storing. Melissa listened, asked gentle questions, didn't seem horrified by the bucket in the corner or the fact that I hadn't changed clothes in five days.

"You're surviving," she said. "That's enough for now."

But surviving and living are different things, and I wasn't sure which one I was doing. Or which one I wanted to do.

The nights were the worst.

That's when the walls really closed in. When the silence got so loud it hurt. When I'd lie there staring at the ceiling, feeling the weight of everything—the shattered ankle, the failed marriage, the woman who'd awakened something in me just to watch it die.

I'd take extra pills then. Not to die—death would have required more effort than I had—but to disappear for a while. To sink into that fuzzy space where nothing hurt and time stopped meaning anything.

Sometimes I'd dream about Hope. We'd be back at the hotel, laughing about something stupid. She'd make me a cappuccino with the foam art she was so proud of. We'd talk about the future like it was something we'd share. Then I'd wake up, and the loss would hit fresh, like finding out someone died all over again every morning.

Three weeks in, something shifted.

I ran out of oxy.

The doctor had given me a month's supply, but I'd been taking extra, using them to manage more than just physical pain. Now the bottle was empty, and refilling it meant getting to a pharmacy, which meant leaving the RV, which meant acknowledging there was a world outside these fourteen feet of aluminum.

The withdrawal hit fast.

First came the sweats. Then the shaking. Then the feeling like my skin was trying to crawl off my body and find somewhere better to be. The physical pain came roaring back, no longer muffled by opiates, fresh and furious like it had been waiting.

But worse than the physical withdrawal was the mental clarity that came with it.

Without the pills softening everything, I had to face what I'd become. A man living in his own filth, talking to ghosts, unable to walk ten feet without falling. I'd been texting someone who'd made it clear she wanted nothing to do with me. I'd been creating elaborate fantasies to avoid dealing with reality.

I was broken. Not just my ankle. Everything.

That's when I finally understood what Melissa had been trying to tell me. Surviving wasn't enough. At some point, you had to decide whether you wanted to live or just exist. Whether you wanted to heal or just hide.

I wanted to hide. God, how I wanted to hide.

But something—maybe it was Hope's voice in my head, maybe it was just stubbornness, maybe it was the same thing that had made me crawl two hundred yards with a shattered ankle—something made me choose different.

I started small.

Made it to the bathroom. Took an actual shower, even though I had to sit on the floor of the stall and getting back out took thirty minutes. Changed clothes. Opened a window to let out the stale air of three weeks of despair.

I stopped texting Hope. Not because I didn't want to, but because I finally understood that texting her was just another kind of using. Another way to avoid dealing with my own shit.

Instead, I wrote to myself. Real things. Honest things.

"I'm in love with someone who doesn't love me back."

"I'm alone."

"But I'm not dead."

That last one became my mantra. My prayer. My promise to myself.

I'm alone, but I'm not dead.

It wasn't much. It wasn't hopeful or inspiring or any of the things recovery is supposed to be. But it was true. And after weeks of living in fantasy, truth felt like progress.

The RV was still a prison. My ankle was still shattered. Hope was still gone. But I was still here, still breathing, still choosing to wake up each morning even when waking up felt like punishment.

Some days that was all I had—the stubborn refusal to give up, even when giving up would have been so much easier.

But I'd learn, slowly, painfully, that sometimes that's enough. Sometimes "not dead" is the first step toward "alive." Sometimes surviving is its own kind of victory.

I wasn't healing yet. Wasn't even close. But I was doing something that felt almost like hope with a lowercase h—I was continuing. One day, one hour, one minute at a time.

The real recovery would come later. The therapy, the hard conversations with myself, the slow rebuilding of something resembling a life. But it all started there, on that couch, in that RV, with the simple recognition:

I'm alone, but I'm not dead.

And if I'm not dead, then there's still time to become something else. Something better. Something real.

Finding Hope

Even if I had to do it alone.

Chapter 7: The Ceiling and the Silence

The pills ran out on December 3rd.

I know because I wrote it down. Had to. Time had gotten slippery, and writing things down was the only way to prove they happened. That I was still happening.

The doctor wouldn't refill them. Something about "concerning usage patterns" and "alternative pain management strategies." Like yoga. Like meditation. Like I could meditate my way through a shattered ankle and a mind that was coming apart at the seams.

So I found another way.

There was a dispensary five minutes down the road. Legal. Regulated. Clean. The budtender was helpful, professional, asked about my medical needs. When I mentioned the shattered ankle, the pain, the surgery, he nodded knowingly and brought out something called "dabs"—concentrated THC that looked like amber and came in neat little containers with official labels and dosage recommendations.

"This'll help with the pain better than flower," he said. "More efficient. Cleaner. Lots of our medical patients prefer it."

Medical. Legal. Regulated. How bad could it be?

He sold me a small glass rig and showed me how to use it. Gave me pamphlets about dosing, about starting slow. I nodded along, already knowing I wouldn't read them. The whole transaction felt so legitimate, so above-board. Nothing like buying drugs. This was medicine. From a store. With a receipt.

I told myself the same thing.

The first hit made me cough until I saw stars. The second made the pain fade to something distant, like it was happening to someone else's body. By the third, I couldn't feel anything at all.

Perfect.

December became a blur of smoke and silence. I'd wake up, take a dab, stare at the ceiling. The same ceiling I'd been staring at for weeks. Two hundred and seventeen dots in the textured pattern. Fourteen major cracks. Three water stains that looked like faces if you stared long enough.

I knew because I counted. Every day. Sometimes multiple times a day, forgetting I'd already done it.

The silence got louder as December wore on. Not metaphorically. Actually louder. It had weight, presence, pressed against my eardrums until I'd have to put on music just to break it. But even the music sounded wrong, like it was coming from underwater, from another room, from another life.

Hope started visiting more often.

Not really. I knew that. Somewhere in the part of my brain that was still rational, I knew she wasn't actually there. But the dabs made the line between knowing and believing negotiable.

She'd sit on the edge of the couch, just out of my peripheral vision. Never fully there, but there enough. We'd have entire conversations.

"You need to eat something," she'd say.

"I'm not hungry."

"You haven't eaten in two days."

"How do you know?"

"Because I know you."

And she did. This version of her, this ghost I'd created from smoke and loneliness, knew me better than anyone. Knew all my secrets. All my fears. Never judged. Never left. The perfect woman, because she wasn't real.

Sometimes I'd reach for her, and my hand would pass through empty air, and the loss would hit fresh. But then I'd take another dab, and she'd come back, patient as always, waiting in the smoke.

I started writing to her. Not texts anymore—I'd given up on the real Hope responding. But letters. Pages and pages of letters I'd never send.

December something—I can't remember the date. You were here last night. We talked about the future. The farm you wanted. The family. I could see it so clearly. When I opened my eyes, you were gone, but the feeling stayed. Is that what love is? Feeling someone who isn't there?"

I'd find these notes later, in my own handwriting, and not remember writing them. Like someone else was living in my body during the hours I couldn't account for.

The RV started feeling alive.

The walls breathed. Subtle at first, like the whole structure was inhaling and exhaling with me. The aluminum siding would tick and pop in the cold, but after enough dabs, it sounded like morse code. Like the RV was trying to tell me something.

I'd watch myself from above sometimes. Dissociation, Melissa would later call it. But it didn't have a name then. It was just me, floating near the ceiling, watching this broken body on the couch below. Watching it take another dab. Watching it stare at nothing. Watching it slowly disappear.

Those were the peaceful moments. When I wasn't in my body, I couldn't feel the pain. Couldn't feel the loneliness. Couldn't feel anything.

December 15th. Or maybe 16th. The days had stopped mattering.

I ran out of water. The gallon jug by the couch was empty, and the kitchen—eight feet away—might as well have been on Mars. I could see the sink. Could see the faucet. But getting there meant moving, and moving meant remembering I had a body, and remembering I had a body meant feeling everything I was trying not to feel.

So I didn't.

I went without water for... I don't know. A day? Two? Time folded in on itself. Hours became minutes became days became nothing. At some point, I must have made it to the kitchen because the jug was full again, but I had no memory of filling it.

I started finding things. Notes in my handwriting I didn't remember. Food half-eaten on the coffee table. The dab rig cleaned and refilled with no memory of doing it. Like someone else was taking care of me while I was gone. Maybe Hope. Maybe me. Maybe there was no difference anymore.

The conversations with Melissa became my only anchor to linear time. Tuesday at 2 PM. Thursday at 10 AM. Little islands of reality in an ocean of smoke and confusion.

"How are you managing the pain?" she asked during one session, her face pixelated slightly on my phone screen.

"Fine," I said, trying to keep my voice steady. "Found alternatives to the pills."

"What kind of alternatives?"

"Natural ones. Herbal. It's better than the oxy."

Even through the video call, I could see her concern. The slight furrow of her brow, the way she paused before responding. But she didn't push. Not yet. Just made notes I couldn't see, building a case I didn't know was being built.

December 23rd. I remember because it was two days before Christmas.

I looked in the mirror for the first time in weeks. The face staring back was someone I didn't recognize. Hollow eyes. Cheeks sunken. Beard wild and unkempt. I looked like a ghost haunting my own life.

"You need to take care of yourself," Hope said from behind me.

I didn't turn around. Knew she wouldn't be there if I did.

"I'm trying."

"No, you're not. You're disappearing."

"Maybe that's the point."

"Is it?"

I took another dab instead of answering.

Christmas came and went without fanfare. I marked it only because my mom called. I let it go to voicemail. Couldn't trust my voice not to betray how far gone I was. She left a message.

Said she loved me. Said she was worried. Said to call when I could.

I texted her instead: "Merry Christmas. Doing okay. Just tired."

Three lies in six words.

The thing about dabs is they don't just numb physical pain. They numb everything. Time. Emotion. The ability to distinguish between what's real and what's not. By late December, I was taking them every two hours. Not for pain anymore—the pain had become background noise. I was taking them to maintain the fog. To keep the walls breathing. To keep Hope visiting. To keep myself from having to face what I'd become.

December 30th. Or maybe 31st. New Year's Eve, probably.

I could hear fireworks in the distance. Or gunshots. Or maybe just the RV settling in the cold. Everything sounded the same through the fog.

I wrote:

Another year ending. Or starting. Can't tell the difference. Hope says I need help. The real Hope or the smoke Hope? Does it matter? They both left. They're both here. I'm so fucking confused. The walls won't stop moving. When did walls start moving? Was it always like this? I can't remember what's real anymore."

That's when Melissa called for an emergency session. Not our scheduled time. The notification popped up on my phone, her face appearing on screen looking more serious than usual.

"Justin, I'm concerned about your substance use," she said, not wasting time on pleasantries. "What you're describing— the isolation, the increased usage, using to avoid emotional pain—these are signs of addiction. I think we need to talk about this."

I stared at her through the screen, the word hanging in the air between us. Addiction.

No. Addicts were people who couldn't control themselves. Who'd lost everything to their substance of choice. Who couldn't stop even when they wanted to.

I could stop. I just didn't want to. Not yet. Not when stopping meant facing the silence without buffer. Not when stopping meant Hope would stop visiting. Not when stopping meant feeling everything I'd been running from.

"I'm not an addict," I said, hearing the defensiveness in my own voice. "I'm just coping with a difficult situation."

"Okay," she replied, her voice gentle but firm. "Let's talk about it in our next session."

But the word stayed on my screen. Addiction. Like she'd planted a seed in the fog, something that would grow whether I wanted it to or not.

I took another dab. The walls breathed. Hope whispered something I couldn't quite hear. And December became January without me noticing, just another arbitrary marker in a timeline that had stopped making sense weeks ago.

The ceiling still had two hundred and seventeen dots. The cracks hadn't moved. But I was falling through them anyway, sinking deeper into a fog that felt more real than reality.

I wasn't an addict. I was just surviving.

The difference mattered, even if I couldn't explain why.

Even if, deep down, I was starting to wonder if there was a difference at all.

Chapter 8: Talking to Ghosts

Hope never left the RV.

She lived in the walls now. In the spaces between breaths. In the static of the propane heater. In the amber residue at the bottom of the dab rig. She wasn't real—I knew that, somewhere in the part of my brain that still functioned—but she was more real than anything else.

January arrived without announcement. I only knew because Melissa mentioned it during one of our sessions.

"How are you doing with the new year?" she asked, her face concerned through the laptop screen.

New year. The words meant nothing. Time had become elastic, meaningless. There was only before-the-dab and after-the-dab. Before-Hope-visits and after-Hope-leaves.

"Fine," I lied, then took another hit the moment our session ended.

The smoke filled the RV, and with it, she materialized.

Not all at once. Never all at once. First her voice, soft from the corner where I imagined she'd sit if she ever visited—if we'd ever made it that far. But everything had happened too fast, collapsed too quickly. We never got to the visiting stage. Never made it past stolen moments at work and that one night at the bar.

"You're killing yourself," she said.

"I'm surviving," I answered.

"Same thing, the way you're doing it."

She was sitting on the counter now, legs swinging like a child's, wearing the same black hotel uniform from the last time I'd seen her. Her hair fell the exact way it had that night in the garage when I'd told her I couldn't stop thinking about her.

"You remember what you said?" I asked her.

"Which time?"

"In the garage. You said we'd get through this."

She smiled, but it was sad. "We didn't though, did we?"

"We still could."

"Justin." The way she said my name—it was exactly right. Every inflection, every note. My brain had catalogued it perfectly. "I'm not real."

"You're real enough."

That became our routine. I'd wake up—afternoon, usually, sometimes evening—take a dab, and she'd appear. We'd have whole conversations. Arguments. Moments of tenderness that felt more genuine than anything I'd experienced in years.

Sometimes she was kind.

"You're stronger than you think," she'd say, sitting beside me on the couch, close enough that I could almost feel warmth. "You survived the fall. The surgery. You're surviving this."

"Barely."

"Still counts."

Other times she was cruel. Or maybe just honest.

"You know why I stopped responding, right?" Hope said one night, standing by the door like she was about to leave. She never left though. She couldn't. She lived here now.

"Because I scared you away."

"Because you were drowning and trying to use me as a life raft."

"You said I could text you."

"Not like that. Not hundreds of messages. Not your entire mental breakdown documented in real-time."

"I was alone."

"You're still alone. I'm not here, Justin. This is just you talking to yourself."

But even when she was cruel, she was there. And that was better than the silence.

The real danger came when she started doing normal things.

One morning—or afternoon, time had no meaning—I stumbled to the kitchen and found her making coffee. Not really. The coffee was already made, probably from yesterday, reheated in the microwave. But in my mind, she was there, going through the motions, humming something under her breath.

"Two sugars, right?" she asked without turning around.

"You remember."

"You remember. I'm just your memory wearing my face."

She handed me the mug—my hand reaching for nothing, finding the mug I'd placed there myself—and for a moment, it felt so normal I forgot she was dead. Not dead-dead. But dead to me. Gone. Unreachable.

"I miss you," I said.

"You miss the idea of me."

"No. I miss you. The real you."

She sat across from me at the tiny RV table, chin in her hand, studying me with those eyes I'd memorized. "The real me is probably living her life. Working. Dating someone new. Not thinking about you at all."

The cruelty of my own imagination was breathtaking sometimes.

"Why do you say things like that?"

"Because you think them. I'm you, remember? I only know what you know. Only say what you're already thinking."

I took another dab to make her kinder.

It usually worked. The higher I got, the softer she became. The more forgiving. The more likely to curl up next to me and tell me stories about the future we'd never have.

"Tell me about the farm," I'd say.

And she would. Every detail. The animals we'd raise. The garden we'd grow. The kids we'd have—two, maybe three. The way morning coffee would taste on the porch we'd build ourselves. The life that existed somewhere parallel to this one, where I hadn't fucked everything up.

But then the high would start to fade, and she'd fade with it, and I'd be alone again with nothing but the truth: I was having full conversations with empty air. I was in love with a ghost I'd created from smoke and desperation. I was losing my mind, and I didn't care, because losing my mind meant keeping her.

January 15th. I know because I wrote it down.

She tried to leave today.

Not real-Hope. She'd left months ago. Ghost-Hope. My Hope. The one who lived in the walls.

I'd run out of dabs that morning. My guy couldn't deliver until evening. The dispensary was a five-minute drive that might as well have been five thousand miles with my ankle still screaming every time I put weight on it.

So I had to sit with the silence. With reality. With the growing understanding that I'd been having elaborate conversations with myself for weeks.

Ghost-Hope stood by the door.

"I should go," she said.

"You can't go. You live here."

"I live in your head. There's a difference."

"Please." I actually said it out loud. Actually begged the empty RV. "Please don't leave me alone."

"You are alone. You've been alone this whole time."

"Not when you're here."

"Justin." Her voice was so gentle it hurt. "This isn't healthy."

"Nothing about this is healthy. But you're all I have."

"That's the problem."

She walked toward the door. I knew if she opened it, if she left, she wouldn't come back. Not until I got more dabs. Not until I could smoke her back into existence.

"I love you," I said.

She paused, hand on the door handle that wasn't really turning. "No. You love the idea of being loved. There's a difference."

"Then why do you keep coming back?"

"Because you keep calling me back. Because you can't let go. Because you'd rather live in a fantasy than face the fact that you're alone in an RV, talking to no one, slowly disappearing into smoke."

The truth, delivered by my own imagination, was brutal.

"At least when you're here, I want to survive."

She turned to look at me one last time. "That's not surviving. That's haunting yourself."

Then my guy knocked on the door—the real door—with my delivery, and when I turned back, she was gone.

I smoked her back immediately.

Three dabs in quick succession, until the walls breathed again and she rematerialized, softer now, kinder, sitting beside me with her hand almost touching mine.

"I'm sorry," she said.

"For what?"

"For leaving. For not being real. For being too real. I don't know anymore."

Neither did I.

The thing about talking to ghosts is that they only tell you what you already know. They can't forgive you—only you can do that. They can't love you—that has to come from somewhere else. They can't save you—salvation isn't found in smoke and mirrors and imaginary conversations.

But when you're drowning, you'll hold onto anything. Even a ghost. Especially a ghost. Because ghosts don't judge. They don't leave angry voicemails. They don't block your number or file restraining orders or move on with their lives.

Ghosts stay as long as you need them.

January bled into February, each day indistinguishable from the last. Wake up. Smoke. Talk to Hope. Smoke more. Talk to Melissa. Pretend to be getting better. Smoke again. Talk to Hope again. Pass out. Repeat.

I filled notebooks with letters to her—both versions of her. The real one who'd never read them. The ghost one who already knew every word.

You saved me, I wrote. *And you don't even know it.*

"I do know it," Ghost-Hope said, reading over my shoulder. "But did I save you, or did I just give you a prettier way to destroy yourself?"

I didn't answer. Couldn't. Because we both knew the truth.

Some nights, she'd hold me while I cried. Her arms around me feeling so real I'd forget they weren't there. She'd whisper that everything would be okay, that I'd get through this, that she was proud of me for still fighting.

Other nights, she'd sit in the corner, disappointed, listing all the ways I'd failed. Her. Myself. Everyone.

"You had a chance," she'd say. "A real chance at something good. And you destroyed it."

"I know."

"You always destroy the good things."

"I know."

"That's why you're alone."

"You're here."

"No. I'm not. And that's the saddest part—you know I'm not, and you're still talking to me."

The worst nights were when we'd fight. Full arguments with raised voices, me screaming at nothing while the ghost I'd created screamed back. The neighbors must have thought I'd completely lost it.

They weren't wrong.

One night, late January or early February, I can't remember, we had the conversation that broke something in me.

"Do you think the real Hope ever thinks about me?" I asked.

Ghost-Hope was quiet for a long moment, sitting in the shadows where I could barely see her. When she finally spoke, her voice was smaller than usual.

"Probably. But not the way you think about her."

"What does that mean?"

"She probably thinks about you the way you think about a car accident you drove past. Grateful you're not in it anymore. Sad it happened. But distant. Moving on."

"That's cruel."

"That's likely."

I wanted to argue, but I couldn't. Because she was probably right. Because she was me, and deep down, that's what I believed.

"I ruined everything," I said.

"Yes."

"I scared her away."

"Yes."

"She's never coming back."

"No. She's not."

"So why are you still here?"

Ghost-Hope moved closer, into the light from the bathroom I always left on. Her face was exactly as I remembered it, down to the small scar above her left eyebrow I'd noticed that first day.

"Because you can't let go. Because you'd rather talk to a ghost than no one at all. Because loneliness is killing you faster than the drugs, and I'm the only thing keeping you from admitting that."

"Then stay."

"I can't. Not forever. Ghosts fade, Justin. Even the ones we create. Even the ones we need."

"Not yet."

"No," she agreed, sadly. "Not yet."

I took another dab, and she solidified again, became warmer, kinder, more like the Hope I wanted to remember. We talked about nothing. About everything. About the future that would never exist and the past I couldn't change.

And for a few more hours, I wasn't alone.

Even though I was more alone than I'd ever been.

The RV had become a tomb, and I was both the corpse and the mourner. Hope was both the ghost and the haunting. The dabs were both the problem and the solution.

And somewhere, the real Hope was living her real life, probably never thinking about the broken man in an RV who couldn't stop talking to her ghost.

But I didn't care.

Because Hope was here. Hope understood. Hope never left.

Even if this Hope was slowly killing me, one conversation at a time.

Chapter 9: Rot

February arrived with sewage water all over the RV floor.

I'd been trying to fix the toilet for days. It had been backing up, refusing to flush, making everything worse than it already was. My solution—brilliant in my desperation—was to use a shop vac to clear the blockage.

What actually happened was the seal broke, and everything came flooding out. Not clean water. Everything. Weeks of everything.

I stood there on one good leg, watching sewage spread across the fourteen feet of aluminum I called home, and all I could think was: *This is exactly right. This is exactly what my life looks like now.*

No towels clean enough to use. No energy to care. Just me, standing in literal shit, trying not to see the metaphor.

It took four hours to clean up. Four hours of hopping, mopping, gagging, trying not to throw up because that would just be one more thing to clean. By the time I finished, I was shaking from exhaustion, my ankle screaming, everything smelling like bleach and failure.

I sat on the couch afterward—the only clean surface left—and laughed. Actually laughed. Because what else was there to do?

"You seeing this?" I said to the empty RV. Not to Hope. I'd stopped talking to her out loud. But she was still there, in everything. In the silence where her response should have been. In the coffee I reheated for the third time because making fresh meant admitting I was drinking alone. In every movement I made that was somehow still about making it back to her.

The dabs were gone by then. Not because I'd conquered addiction or found inner strength or any of that bullshit. But because Melissa had been gentle and persistent and right, and somewhere in January, I'd admitted she was right.

"You're using to avoid feeling," she'd said during one of our sessions.

"Yeah, well, feeling fucking hurts."

"I know. But not feeling is killing you faster."

So I stopped. Cold turkey. Stupid, probably. The withdrawal wasn't dramatic—THC doesn't work like that. But the clarity was brutal. Without the fog, everything was sharp edges and raw nerves. The RV felt smaller. The silence got louder. And Hope—Hope was everywhere and nowhere, all at once.

I couldn't smoke her into existence anymore. Couldn't soften her absence with dabs. She was just gone, and I had to sit with that. Had to feel it. Every minute of every day.

So I started moving instead.

First, just walking the length of the RV. Fourteen feet. Back and forth. My ankle had healed enough that I could put weight on it without screaming. Still hurt, but it was manageable hurt. Progress hurt.

Then I started shadow boxing.

Ordered a doorframe punching bag off Amazon—the kind that doesn't need ceiling support, just tension in a doorway. Perfect for an RV where hanging anything heavy would probably bring the whole roof down. Set it up between the bedroom and the main area. It wasn't much, but it was something to hit.

At the same time, I started Fitness Boxing on the Nintendo Switch. Sounds ridiculous—shadow boxing in fourteen feet of aluminum while following a cartoon trainer—but it gave me structure. Combos to learn. Routines to follow. Something to measure progress against that wasn't just "didn't want to die today."

Every morning—or afternoon, time was still negotiable—I'd wake up and box. Twenty minutes. Then thirty. Then an hour. Jab, cross, hook. Dodge, weave, block. My form was shit, but I was moving. I was choosing to move.

Everything I did became about getting back to Hope.

Not talking to her. I'd accepted that wasn't happening. But getting back to the version of me she'd believed in. The one who had potential. The one worth saving.

I started fasting. Twenty-two hours a day. Only eating in a two-hour window. Partly for health, partly for control, mostly because hunger was a feeling I could manage. It was clean pain. Honest pain. Not like the messy chaos of missing someone who didn't miss you back.

"I'm getting better," I told Melissa during one session.

"Physically, yes. You're doing amazing with the exercise. But Justin, you're still avoiding the emotional work."

"I'm not avoiding it. I'm preparing for it."

"Preparing for what?"

"To be someone worth... I don't know. Just worth something."

She was quiet for a moment, studying me through the screen. "You know you're already worth something, right? Right now. As you are."

But I didn't believe her. How could I? I was living in an RV that had just flooded with sewage. I was shadow boxing in a space barely big enough to throw a punch. I was fasting because eating meant tasting the loneliness. I was exercising obsessively because stillness meant thinking, and thinking meant remembering, and remembering meant drowning.

But mostly, I was exercising because of something Hope had said once, back at the hotel, before everything fell apart. We'd been talking about relationships, about what we wanted, and she'd mentioned wanting to be with someone "hot." Just a casual comment. She probably didn't even remember saying it. But it had lodged in my brain like shrapnel.

Every punch I threw was trying to become that. Every hour I fasted. Every rep, every set, every drop of sweat. I wasn't trying to forget her—I was trying to become someone who could deserve having known her. Someone hot enough, fit enough, good enough to stand in front of her again.

In my mind, everything I was doing was to make it back to my friend. I genuinely believed—still believe, even now—that she was waiting for me at the end of all this. That if I just got fit enough, strong enough, worthy enough, we'd have our moment. Our real moment. The one where everything made sense.

That's the power of isolation. It lets you build entire worlds in your head. I'd have full conversations with her while boxing. Plan out exactly what I'd say when we met again. How I'd look. How she'd smile. How this time I'd be ready. This time I'd be enough.

The loops were constant.

I'd work out until I couldn't anymore, then lie on the couch thinking about her. About that moment in the garage when she'd put her hand on my arm. About the night at the bar when she'd nodded. About the future we'd never have.

Then I'd get up and work out again.

Some days I'd box for three hours straight. Until my knuckles bled through the wraps. Until my ankle couldn't support me anymore. Until the pain in my body finally matched the pain in my head.

"You're punishing yourself," Melissa said.

"I'm improving myself."

"Can you see how those might be the same thing right now?"

I couldn't. Or wouldn't. Because stopping meant being still, and being still meant feeling everything I was trying to outrun.

March came with small victories. I could do a hundred push-ups. I'd lost thirty pounds. I could throw combinations that actually looked like boxing instead of just flailing. I was showing up to every therapy session. I was cleaning the RV regularly—no more sewage disasters.

But Hope was still gone. Still not responding to the texts I'd stopped sending. Still living her life somewhere far from the mess I'd made of mine.

I'd dream about her every night. Not fantasies anymore. Just memories. Her laugh. The way she'd tilt her head when she was really listening. The feeling of her hand on my arm, trying to calm my shaking.

"We're going to get through this," she'd said.

But we hadn't. I was getting through it alone, and the 'it' kept changing. First it was the injury. Then the isolation. Then the addiction. Now it was just... everything. The whole mess of existing without her.

"I'm stuck," I told Melissa one day. "I'm doing everything right—exercising, not using, showing up—but I'm still stuck."

"Stuck where?"

"In that hotel. In that moment when she said we'd get through this. I can't move past it."

"Maybe you don't need to move past it. Maybe you need to move through it."

"What's the difference?"

"Past means around. Through means accepting it's part of you and keeping going anyway."

I wanted to argue, but I was tired. Tired of fighting myself. Tired of the loops. Tired of pretending the exercise and fasting were about health when they were really just new ways to control something in a life that felt completely out of control.

That night, after boxing until my arms felt like jelly, I sat on the couch and did something I hadn't done in months. I was still. Just sat there. No phone. No distractions. Just me and the silence and the truth:

Hope was gone. She wasn't coming back. No amount of push-ups would change that. No amount of fasting would earn her forgiveness. No amount of punching that bag would punch through time and undo the damage.

But I was still here. Still breathing. Still trying.

The RV smelled like bleach and sweat now instead of sewage and smoke. Progress. My ankle could support my full weight. Progress. I hadn't talked to Hope's ghost in weeks. Progress.

Small steps. Tiny victories. A life rebuilt in fourteen-foot increments.

"I miss her," I said to the empty RV. Not to her ghost. Just to the air. To myself. To the truth of it.

And for the first time, the silence that came back didn't feel like an answer I was waiting for. It just felt like silence. Empty but not hostile. Present but not suffocating.

I was alone. But I was moving. And for now, that had to be enough.

The dabs were gone. The toilet was fixed. Hope was still gone.

But I was still here.

Justin Mayeur

Still fighting. Still failing. Still getting up.

One punch at a time.

Chapter 10: Let Me Out

Melissa had me taking online assessments for Substance Use Disorder.

Every week, a new one. Different websites, same questions. "How many drinks do you have per week?" The options were always bullshit—either 1-2 drinks or 5-6. I was looking for the middle ground, the "3-4 drinks" option that would let me feel normal. It didn't exist.

I failed every single test.

"These are rigged," I told her during a session in early March. "They don't give realistic options."

"Justin," she said gently, "the tests aren't the problem."

I knew that. Deep down, I knew. Just like I knew that when prescriptions said "take 1-2 pills for pain," I'd always take two. Never one. Always the maximum. Always pushing the edge of what was allowed.

But knowing and accepting are different things.

By late March, I was feeling stronger. The ankle had healed enough that I could walk without thinking about every step. The exercise routine had become religion—boxing, fasting, pushing my body to extremes that made the mental pain manageable. I'd even started leaving the RV occasionally. Small victories.

Then came the call from my surgeon.

"We should schedule the rod removal," he said. "You've healed well enough. It's a simple procedure."

The rod. The metal holding my ankle together from the inside. Getting it out meant real recovery. It meant progress. It meant moving forward.

It also meant another surgery. Another prescription. Another bottle of oxycodone.

"I don't need pain meds," I told him.

"Trust me, you will. This is still surgery. You'll want them for the first few days at least."

I should have insisted. Should have said no. Should have remembered what happened last time. But part of me—the part that always takes two pills instead of one—whispered that maybe this time would be different. Maybe I could control it.

April 5th. Second surgery.

They removed the rod in under an hour. Outpatient again. Same-day discharge. Same Uber ride back to the RV. Same bottle of pills in my hand.

Thirty oxycodone. Take 1-2 every 4-6 hours as needed for pain.

I stared at the bottle that night, knowing exactly what was going to happen. Knowing I was standing at the edge of a cliff I'd jumped off before. Knowing I should flush them all immediately.

I took two.

The warmth was immediate. Familiar. Like meeting an old friend you know is bad for you but missed anyway. The pain didn't just fade—everything faded. The loneliness. The obsessive thoughts about Hope. The constant weight of existing.

"Just for a few days," I told myself. "Just until the surgical pain passes."

But there's no such thing as "just" with me. Never has been.

By day three, I was taking them every four hours. By day five, I was counting how many were left, doing the math on how to make them last. By week two, I was back at the dispensary, not for dabs this time, but because I needed something to bridge the gap when the pills ran out.

And then I did something even stupider.

I went to the bar.

Not to get drunk. Not to forget. Just to get out of the RV. Just to be around people. Just to celebrate making it two weeks without drinking.

The irony of celebrating sobriety with a drink wasn't lost on me. But I rationalized it perfectly: "If I can go two weeks without drinking, then have one or two, then go another two weeks, I'm not an alcoholic. I'm in control."

The bartender knew me. Of course he did. I'd been a regular before the fall.

"Haven't seen you in a while," he said.

"Been working on myself."

"Good for you. First one's on me."

Bourbon and Coke. The taste was like coming home to a house on fire—familiar but dangerous.

One became three. Three became five. Five plus the oxy I'd taken before leaving the RV became a fog I'd promised myself I'd never enter again.

I woke up the next morning on the RV floor. Not from falling. I'd apparently decided the floor was where I wanted to sleep. My phone was dead. My ankle was screaming. The pill bottle was open on the counter, several missing that I didn't remember taking.

"Fuck."

I sat up, head pounding, and saw myself in the black screen of the TV. Same hollow face from months ago. Same ghost haunting his own life. All that exercise, all that fasting, all that work, and I was right back here.

No. Not here. This was different. This time I knew what I was doing. This time I could see the pattern as it was happening. That made it worse somehow—watching yourself make the same mistakes with full awareness.

I called Melissa. Emergency session.

"I fucked up."

"What happened?"

I told her everything. The pills. The bar. The rationalization. The failure.

"Justin, relapse is part of recovery for most people. The question is what you do now."

"I don't know what to do. I can't throw the pills away—I just had surgery. But I can't keep them either. And the bar... I told myself I could handle it."

"Can you?"

"No."

The word hung there between us. Simple. Honest. Devastating.

"I need you to understand something," she said. "You're not starting over. You're learning. Every time you fall and get back up, you're learning what doesn't work."

"What if I don't want to get back up?"

"But you called me. That means part of you does."

She was right. I hated that she was right.

After the session, I did something I hadn't done in months. I prayed. Not to God exactly. Not to Hope. Just to whatever might be listening.

"Let me out," I whispered to the empty RV. "Let me out of this loop. Let me out of this head. Let me out of this version of me that keeps destroying everything."

Then I took the remaining oxy—maybe fifteen pills—and flushed them. Watched them swirl away. Felt the addict in me scream at the waste. But also felt something else. Relief, maybe. Or just exhaustion with my own patterns.

The bar was harder to quit than the pills.

Every two weeks, like clockwork, I'd convince myself I'd earned a drink. Just one or two. A reward for being good. But one or two became five or six, and the cycle would reset. Two weeks sober. One night drunk. Shame. Promises. Repeat.

April became May, and I still couldn't string together thirty days.

"Why can't I stop?" I asked Melissa.

"Because you're still trying to control it instead of accepting you can't."

"But I went months without drinking after the fall."

"You were also immobile and had no access. That's different from choosing not to drink when you can."

She was right again. Always right. It was annoying.

Justin Mayeur

Hope was still in everything. Every workout was still preparing for our reunion. Every slip was another reason she'd never want me. The push and pull was exhausting. I was building and destroying myself simultaneously, and she was the reason for both.

I'd imagine telling her about my progress, leaving out the failures. In my mind, she was proud of me. In reality, she still wasn't responding to anything. Not that I was texting much anymore. But sometimes, late at night, after too many drinks or too many pills or too many hours alone, I'd send something:

"Still fighting."

"Still here."

"Still hoping."

Read receipts off. No response. Just silence where her voice should be.

One night in early May, after another reset, another failed attempt at thirty days, I stood in front of the mirror. Not the broken man from December. Not the swollen ghost from the hospital. Something in between. Stronger but still fragile. Sober tonight but probably not next week.

"Let me out," I said to my reflection.

Out of what? The RV? The addiction? The loop? The past? The future I kept imagining but couldn't reach?

All of it. None of it.

I was trapped, but the cage wasn't the aluminum walls anymore. It wasn't even the pills or the bourbon. It was the story I kept telling myself—that if I could just get strong enough, good enough, sober enough, I'd earn my way back to Hope. That she was waiting at the finish line of my recovery.

But there was no finish line. Just more days. More attempts. More failures. More getting back up.

"I'm not okay," I texted Melissa at 2 AM. "But I want to be."

"That's enough for now," she replied. "Wanting to be okay is where okay starts."

I wanted to believe her. Wanted to believe that wanting was enough. That somewhere in all these false starts and failures, something was actually changing.

The pills were gone. The bar was still there. Hope was still everywhere and nowhere.

And I was still here, still fighting, still failing, still refusing to give up completely.

Let me out, I thought.

But also: Not yet.

Because giving up would mean admitting Hope was really gone. And I wasn't ready for that truth.

Not yet.

Chapter 11: The Crosswalk

Late May. I'd been sober from alcohol for three weeks. My longest stretch since the second surgery.

The ADHD medication was helping—Adderall, prescribed legitimately, taken as directed. For now. It made the chaos in my head organize into lines I could follow. Made the obsessive thoughts about Hope feel more like plans than spirals. I was still smoking THC at night, but just flower, just enough to sleep. Progress.

I looked different in the mirror. Months of boxing had carved definition into my shoulders, my arms. The fasting had stripped away the bourbon bloat. I wasn't "hot" yet—not the way Hope had mentioned wanting—but I was getting there. Every day, a little closer to someone she might want to see again.

That's when I started going into town more. Not to drink. Just to exist in spaces where she might be. Just to increase the odds of a collision that would feel like fate.

May 28th. I was driving to the dispensary when I saw it— her car. That distinctive blue Honda she'd had since before everything fell apart. My heart stopped, then hammered so hard I thought it might crack a rib.

She was here. In town. Right now.

I abandoned the dispensary plan and drove toward downtown, hands shaking on the wheel. The Adderall made everything sharper—every possibility, every potential outcome. She could be at the coffee shop. The grocery store. Walking down the street where I might just happen to—

There.

The crosswalk by the wine bar. She was crossing from the other side, wearing black leggings and a grey hoodie, hair pulled back, looking exactly like she had in my dreams except real. Actually real. Not smoke-induced, not imagined. Real.

I pulled over so fast I almost clipped a parked car. Got out. Started walking toward her, my body moving before my brain could stop it.

She saw me. No avoiding it. We were walking straight toward each other, two people who'd been everything and nothing, about to collide in broad daylight.

"Hey Justin," she said, casual as anything. "How we doing today?"

How we doing? Like we were coworkers passing in a hallway. Like the last six months hadn't happened. Like I hadn't shattered my ankle and my mind trying to get back to her.

"Good," I managed.

That was it. She kept walking. I kept walking. Ten seconds of interaction after months of imagined conversations.

I sat in my car for an hour afterward, replaying those ten seconds. The way she'd said my name. The casual "we" like we were still some kind of unit. The way she'd looked—healthy, normal, fine. Without me.

Back at the RV, I convinced myself it meant something. It had to. After months of silence, we'd spoken. She'd seemed friendly. Not angry. Not scared. Friendly.

This was the sign. This was the beginning of the comeback. This was—

I had to see her again. Properly this time. Say the things I'd practiced. Be the person I'd been becoming.

June 2nd. Stone cold sober. Three and a half weeks without alcohol. The longest stretch in forever.

I knew where she worked now—a winery up the hill. I'd driven past it a dozen times, working up courage. Today was the day. I looked good—clean shaven, fresh clothes, steady hands thanks to the Adderall. I'd practiced what to say in the mirror that morning. Calm. Confident. Worthy.

I walked in like I belonged there. She was behind the tasting room counter, talking to another employee. When she saw me, her eyes widened slightly. Not fear. Surprise maybe. Or resignation.

I walked up to the counter. This was it. The moment. Everything I'd wanted to say for months, finally—

"Hello, beautiful."

That's what came out. Not the speech I'd practiced. Not the apology I'd crafted. Just those two words, hanging in the air like a bad pickup line.

She tilted her head, half-smiled. "That's it?"

I panicked. Complete system failure. Six months of preparation, and I was freezing like a middle schooler at his first dance.

"I... I have to go."

I turned and left. Actually ran away. From the moment I'd been training for, literally and figuratively, for months.

I made it to a bar down the street—not to drink, just to sit, just to breathe, just to figure out what the fuck had just happened. The bartender knew me, started to pour my usual.

"Just water," I said.

He looked surprised but complied.

I sat there for twenty minutes, steadying myself. This wasn't over. I could go back. I could fix this. I could—

I walked back to the winery.

She was still there, cleaning glasses now, alone in the tasting room. She looked up when I entered, and something in her expression softened.

"You came back."

"I had more to say."

"I figured."

She came around the counter, and we sat at one of the tasting tables. Close enough that I could smell her shampoo— still the same, still capable of destroying me.

"I'm sorry," I started. "For everything. The texts. The spiral. All of it."

"I know."

"I'm sober now. Three weeks."

"That's good, Justin. Really good."

"I still—" The words caught. "I still feel the same way about you."

She sighed, not unkindly. "I know that too."

"So what does that mean? For us?"

"We can be friends."

Friends. The word landed like a punch to the sternum.

"I don't know what that means."

"It means..." She paused, choosing words carefully. "It means I care about you. I want you to be okay. But I'm not ready for anything more. Maybe in another year or two—"

"A year or two?"

"But I don't think you can wait that long."

She was right. Of course she was right. I couldn't wait two more weeks without losing my mind, let alone two years.

"So what do I do?"

"Live your life. Keep getting better. Stop waiting for me."

"I don't know how to do that."

"I know."

We sat in silence for a moment. Then she stood.

"I have to close up."

I stood too, and she surprised me by stepping forward, arms opening.

"Come here."

The hug was barely anything. Light, brief, her body angled away like she was hugging a relative at a funeral. But then she pulled back, looked at me.

"No. Give me a real hug."

So I did. Pulled her close, felt her actually embrace me back. For maybe five seconds, I held Hope—the real Hope, not the ghost, not the dream. She was warm and solid and real, and then she was stepping away.

"Take care of yourself, Justin."

That was it. The last time I ever hugged her. The last real conversation we'd have.

I drove back to the RV in a daze. This was supposed to fix everything. Seeing her, talking to her, getting some kind of answer. Instead, I felt more lost than ever.

Friends? What did that mean after everything we'd been?

A year or two? Was that real or just a gentle way of saying never?

Stop waiting? How do you stop waiting for the only thing that's kept you alive?

I sat on the couch where I'd spent months talking to her ghost, and realized something terrible: Hope wasn't a ghost anymore. She was a person with her own timeline, her own healing, her own life that was moving forward without me. The real Hope was somehow harder to love than the imaginary one, because the real Hope could choose to leave. Had chosen. Was choosing, every day, to live without me.

That night, I almost drank. Came closer than I had in weeks. The liquor store was five minutes away. The bar was always open. The numbness was just a few drinks away from returning.

But I didn't. Not that night.

Instead, I lay in bed replaying every word, every gesture, every second of breath during that hug. Looking for clues. For hidden meaning. For something that would make "friends" feel like enough.

She'd said the words I'd waited months to hear—that she cared, that maybe someday—and they didn't fix anything. If anything, they made it worse. Because now I had hope again. Lower case h. The dangerous kind. The kind that keeps you holding on when letting go would be kinder.

I was sober enough to see her, but not strong enough to hear her. Strong enough to have the conversation, but not strong enough to accept what it meant.

Three and a half weeks without alcohol. I wouldn't make it to four.

But I didn't know that yet. All I knew was that Hope had hugged me—really hugged me—and told me to stop waiting, and I had no idea how to do both of those things at once.

The ghost had been easier to love. She never asked me to let go.

Chapter 12: Letters to a Stranger

June unraveled me.

After the hug at the winery, after "maybe in a year or two," after "I don't think you can wait that long," my brain wouldn't stop. It was like someone had turned the volume up on thoughts that were already too loud. Every waking moment was Hope. Every attempt at sleep was Hope. Every breath was somehow about Hope.

I didn't want to feel this way about her. But I did. And it was driving me mad.

The only thing that quieted it was alcohol. Just enough bourbon to blur the edges. Just enough to make the endless loop of "what did she mean by friends" stop spinning. I hated myself for it. I'd made it three and a half weeks sober when I saw her. By the end of June, I couldn't make it three days.

"You need to try AA," Melissa said during one of our sessions.

So I did. Found a meeting in the basement of a church five miles from the RV. Walked in terrified, desperate, ready for something—anything—to help.

It made everything worse.

Listening to people talk about losing their kids, their homes, their marriages to alcohol just reminded me of everything I'd already lost. And when it came time to share, what was I supposed to say? "Hi, I'm Justin, and I'm an alcoholic because I'm in love with someone who put me in the friend zone"?

I went to three meetings. Each one made me want to drink more than the last. Not because they were bad—they weren't. But because I couldn't shake the feeling that my problem wasn't really alcohol. Alcohol was just the bandaid. Hope was the wound that wouldn't stop bleeding.

Late June. I was drunk-watching Netflix one night, trying to find something mindless enough to stop thinking. Ended up on Bridgerton of all things—period drama about people in fancy clothes having feelings they couldn't express. This guy was courting a woman through handwritten letters. Noble. Classic. Safe.

Letters. Not texts that demanded immediate response. Not showing up unannounced. Letters.

I sobered up the next morning with a plan.

Every day for a week, I wrote her a letter. Sat at the tiny RV table with actual paper and pen, writing like it was 1825. Some were apologies. Some were memories. Some were just observations about the day—how the mountains looked, what Magnolia did that was funny, things that used to make her laugh.

I wasn't trying to win her back. Not exactly. I was trying to show her I could be thoughtful. Controlled. That I could care about her without overwhelming her.

After seven letters, I had a small stack. Real paper, real ink, real thoughts organized into something that wasn't just desperate 2 AM rambling.

July 2nd. Or maybe June 30th. The days were blurring again.

I walked into the winery holding the letters like they were made of glass. She was behind the counter, same as before, but her expression when she saw me was different. Tired, maybe. Resigned.

"I don't know how to talk to you anymore," I said, holding out the stack.

She looked at the letters, then at me. Something in her face softened slightly.

"What are these?"

"Just... things I wanted to say. But better. Without..." I gestured vaguely at myself, at the mess I'd become.

She took them. Nodded. Said "Thank you" in a voice that could have meant anything.

I left before I could ruin it. I was proud of that. For once, I'd done something without making it worse.

But the silence afterward was unbearable. Had she read them? Did they help? Did they make things worse? The not knowing was eating me alive.

So I decided on flowers.

Not as a romantic gesture. Just as a thank you. For reading the letters. For not calling the cops. For still being willing to see me at all.

I chose dahlias and sunflowers from the nursery—a real bouquet, carefully arranged, the kind that cost more than I should have spent. Deep oranges and bright yellows, wrapped in brown paper with twine. Beautiful. Thoughtful. The kind of flowers you bring when you're trying to show someone they matter. Nothing that screamed desperation, but everything that whispered "I still care more than I should."

July 5th. Maybe 6th. Hot day. The kind where the heat makes everything feel more intense than it should.

I walked into the winery holding the bouquet, already sweating through my shirt. She was alone, cleaning glasses. When she saw me with the flowers, her whole body tensed.

"Justin... you can't keep doing this."

"Doing what? They're just flowers. A thank you."

"Thank you for what?"

"For reading the letters. For—"

"The letters?" She shook her head. "Justin, the things you wrote..."

"What about them?"

"They're... intense. Too intense. This isn't what friends do."

"You said we could be friends. I'm trying to understand what that means."

"It means not this. Not letters every day about dreams and futures and—"

"Then tell me what to do! Because I don't know how to be your friend when you were—when we were—"

"That's the problem!" Her voice rose. "You're still talking to whoever you created in that RV. The Hope who was there every night. Who never left. Who said all the right things."

"You're right here. You're real."

"But you're not seeing me. You're seeing her. The version you talked to for months when you were alone."

The truth of it stung because she was right. Even standing there, talking to the real Hope, I was having a different conversation with the Hope in my head. The one who understood. The one who knew how sick I'd been.

"I was isolated for months," I said, my voice cracking. "Do you understand what that does to someone?"

"I know you went through—"

"No, you don't know. You don't know what it's like to have no one but the version of you I created. To have full conversations with someone who isn't there. To not know what's real anymore."

We were both almost yelling now. Other people were starting to notice. This was becoming exactly what she'd feared—a scene.

"I need you to understand," I said desperately. "I'm sick. I'm confused. I thought I was doing the right things."

"Justin, please—"

"Friends, Hope! You said friends!" I was practically screaming it now. "Friends! I'm trying to be your friend!"

"You need to leave."

"I just need you to understand—"

"Leave. Now."

The truth of it was devastating. Because she was right. The Hope I'd been writing to, bringing flowers to, trying to reconnect with—she was the one from my isolation. The one who understood everything. Who never judged. Who was always waiting.

"I don't know how to stop," I said, quieter now.

"I know. That's why this isn't working."

"So what do I do?"

"Stop coming here. Stop writing. Stop... all of it."

147

"I can't."

"You have to."

We were both almost yelling now. Not angry, exactly. Just desperate in different directions. Me desperate to hold on, her desperate to let go.

"You told me you wanted a farm," I said. "You told me you wanted a family. You looked me in the eyes and—"

"That was before! Before you jumped off a wall. Before the texts. Before you became..." She stopped herself.

"Before I became what?"

"Someone I don't recognize."

The silence that followed was the loudest thing I'd ever heard.

I set the flowers on the counter. She didn't pick them up.

"I'm still me," I said.

"No. You're not. And neither am I."

I left without another word. Drove back to the RV with tears I didn't remember starting to cry. The flowers stayed on the counter at the winery, wilting in the July heat, a perfect metaphor for whatever we'd been trying to salvage.

Back in the RV, I sat on the same couch where I'd spent months talking to her ghost. The ceiling hadn't changed. The walls hadn't moved. But everything felt different now.

The real Hope had boundaries I couldn't cross. The real Hope had a life that didn't include me. The real Hope was tired of trying to save someone who wouldn't stop drowning.

And I was still living in a dream. Still talking to a ghost. Still trying to reconnect with someone who maybe never existed the way I remembered her.

That night, I drank until I couldn't remember which Hope was real—the one who'd rejected the flowers or the one who'd said "we're going to get through this" in a garage that felt like a lifetime ago.

Both. Neither. It didn't matter anymore.

I was writing letters to a stranger and calling her by a familiar name.

Chapter 13: The Mountain and the Loop

July was supposed to be different. After the letters, after the scene at the winery, after she'd said "You need to leave," I told myself I'd stop. Get clean. Figure my shit out.

I lasted three days.

By the fourth day, I was back at the bar. Not the usual one—couldn't face those people anymore. Found a new place on the outskirts of town where nobody knew my name, nobody asked questions, nobody gave a shit if I was there at 10:30 in the morning.

The routine became religion. Wake up at 5. Feed Magnolia. Watch her look at me with those eyes that seemed to ask why I couldn't love her the way she loved me. Lace up my boots. Drive to the trailhead in the dark.

The mountain was 1,700 feet of punishment. Every morning, I'd climb it like I was climbing out of hell. Or into it. Some days I couldn't tell the difference. The trail was steep enough that you had to use your hands in places, grabbing roots and rocks, pulling yourself up like you were escaping something.

I'd talk to Hope the entire climb.

Not out loud—I wasn't that far gone. But in my head, we'd have these perfect conversations. She'd ask about my drinking, and I'd explain how I was getting better. She'd laugh at something funny that happened. She'd tell me about her day. By the time I reached the summit, we'd have solved everything. Made plans. Forgiven each other.

At the top, I'd stand there for maybe thirty seconds, looking out at the valley still dark except for a few scattered lights, feeling nothing, being nothing, then turn around and come back down.

The descent was always silent. Even imaginary Hope couldn't survive the reality of going backward.

By 7:30, I was back at the RV, strapping on boxing gloves. The Switch had become my therapist, my priest, my best friend. The fitness boxing game didn't judge. Didn't ask questions. Just demanded I keep moving.

Jab, cross, hook. Jab, cross, hook. Each punch trying to knock her voice out of my head.

"I don't think you can wait that long."

Jab.

"We're friends."

Cross.

"You need to leave."

Hook.

Some mornings I'd box until my arms gave out, until the gloves felt like they weighed fifty pounds each, until sweat had soaked through everything and I was gasping like I was drowning in air. The virtual trainer would cheerfully announce my score while I stood there shaking, trying to remember why I was doing this.

For her. Always for her. To show her I could change. To become someone worth coming back to.

By 9:30, I was showered, dressed, and heading to the bar. Always the same stool at the end, away from the regulars who came in for lunch. Always the same order: shot of Hornitos, Coors Light chaser.

The bartender at the new place was a guy named Rick who looked like he'd seen enough broken people to recognize another one. He didn't even ask anymore. Just poured when he saw me walk in. Some days he'd try to make conversation—weather, sports, nothing real—but most days he just let me sit there drowning in broad daylight.

The Hornitos was different from the bourbon. Cleaner somehow. Like switching from heroin to methadone—still poison, but a different flavor of dying. The tequila hit faster, burned less, made the edges blur quicker. Made Hope's voice quieter.

By noon, I'd had four shots, three beers, and crushed up my second Adderall of the day in the bathroom. The powder burned going up, made my eyes water, made my heart race like I was still on that mountain. But it kept me upright. Kept me functional. Kept me from completely disappearing into the bottle.

I'd switched to snorting them in July. Told myself it was more efficient. Told myself it would help me drink less. Told myself a lot of things that were bullshit.

The cocaine came back the second week of July. Found a guy through someone at the bar—because there's always a guy if you know how to ask. He was happy to meet me in the parking lot of a grocery store at midnight, selling pure shit that hit like a freight train.

Just weekends at first. Just to get through my shifts at the bar.

I'd gotten the job in late June, right after the letter incident. Thursday through Sunday, 5 PM to close, at a touristy place that served overpriced cocktails to people pretending they knew about wine. The irony wasn't lost on me—serving alcohol while trying to quit drinking. But I needed money. The savings were gone. The credit cards were maxed. The RV payment was coming due.

So I'd show up already drunk, maintain it with bumps in the bathroom, and smile while I muddled mint and squeezed limes and listened to couples plan their futures over martinis.

"We're thinking about buying a little farm," this woman said one night, gazing at her husband like he hung the moon. "Nothing big. Just some chickens, maybe goats."

I had to excuse myself. Locked myself in the employee bathroom and did two lines off the toilet tank while Hope and I planned our own farm in my head. She wanted chickens. I'd build the coop. We'd name them after characters from books she liked.

By the time August rolled around, the conversations with Hope in my head were more real than anything else in my life. We'd have full arguments while I was washing glasses. She'd forgive me while I was counting tips. We'd make love while I was driving home, so vivid I'd have to pull over sometimes, confused about what was real.

The real Hope hadn't responded to a text since July 8th. I knew the exact date because I'd screenshotted her last message: "Please stop."

But I couldn't stop. Every night, usually around 2 AM, I'd send these long, sprawling messages. Sometimes they were apologies—for the letters, for showing up at the winery, for being too much. Sometimes they were memories—that time she laughed so hard she snorted, the way she looked in the morning light, how her hand felt in mine. Sometimes they were just stream of consciousness rambling about my day, like we were still friends, like she still cared.

I knew she wasn't reading them. The messages just said "Delivered," never "Read." But I kept sending them anyway. It was like screaming into the void, if the void had beautiful eyes and once said she wanted a family too.

Melissa had stopped our sessions in mid-July. Said she was sick, needed to take some time. I knew she was lying. I'd probably scared her too, talking about Hope for entire sessions, unable to focus on anything else. She'd suggested I find someone new, gave me some names, but I couldn't do it. Couldn't start over. Couldn't explain the whole thing again to someone who'd just tell me what I already knew: I was obsessed with someone who didn't exist.

My family was starting to worry. My mom called every few days, and I'd try to sound normal, sober, like I wasn't standing in a bar bathroom doing coke off my phone screen while telling her I was doing great.

"You sound tired," she'd say.

"Just working a lot."

"Are you taking care of yourself?"

"Yeah, Mom. I'm good."

Magnolia knew I was lying. Dogs always know. She'd started sleeping pressed against me, like she was trying to hold me together. Some mornings I'd wake up on the RV floor and she'd be there, patient, waiting, not judging but clearly concerned. I'd look into her eyes and see disappointment. Even my dog knew I was fucking up.

August came in like a fever.

The heat made everything worse. The RV became an oven by 10 AM. The mountain felt steeper. The drinks went down easier. The cocaine barely worked anymore—I was buying twice as much, cutting lines twice as big, feeling half as high.

I was taking triple doses of Adderall just to function. Crushing three pills at a time, creating lines on the back of toilet tanks, on my phone screen, on whatever flat surface I could find. My nose was constantly bleeding. I told people it was the dry air.

The new bar became my office. I'd get there at 10:30, drink until 3, go home and pass out for an hour, then shower and head to work. Some days I didn't make it home between bars. Just sat in the parking lot with the AC running, doing lines and talking to Hope in my head until it was time to clock in.

She was getting more vivid. More real. Sometimes I'd catch myself responding out loud to something she'd said in my mind. Rick started looking at me different. The concerned look. The careful distance. Even the dive bar was getting uncomfortable with how far I'd fallen.

"You might want to slow down," he said one Tuesday, after my sixth shot before noon.

"I'm good."

"No," he said, and there was something in his voice that made me look up. "You're not."

But what was I supposed to do? The only thing that made the loop stop was unconsciousness. The only thing that made Hope's voice quiet was tequila. The only thing that made me feel anything was cocaine, and even that was starting to fail.

August 15th. Or maybe the 16th. The days were blurring into one long, desperate attempt to not think about her.

I was at work, six drinks and two lines deep, hands shaking as I tried to pour a glass of wine without spilling. The couple at the bar was talking about their wedding plans. October. Barn venue. String lights.

My phone buzzed. Not a text. Something different. I opened my messages to send another rambling apology and saw it—that little notice under her name.

"Not Delivered"

I tried again. Same thing. Called her number. Straight to voicemail, no ring.

She'd blocked me.

I set the wine glass on the bar. Didn't even realize I'd let go until I heard it shatter.

"I have to go," I said to nobody in particular.

"Dude, you can't just—" my manager started.

But I was already walking out. Middle of my shift. Didn't say a word. Just left.

The parking lot felt like it was spinning. Or maybe I was spinning. I sat in my truck for twenty minutes, staring at my phone, trying to send message after message, watching them all bounce back. *Not Delivered. Not Delivered. Not Delivered.*

She'd cut me off completely. Not just stopped responding. Not just ignored me. Blocked me. Erased me. Made me disappear from her world like I'd never existed at all.

I drove to the winery. She wasn't there. They said she didn't work Thursdays anymore.

I drove back to the RV, my mind racing, trying to figure out another way. There had to be another way. I couldn't just be... gone. Deleted. Like none of it mattered.

That's when I remembered Skype. You could get phone numbers through Skype. Different numbers. New numbers she wouldn't recognize.

I spent hours setting it up, getting new numbers, sending texts that seemed casual at first. "Hey, is this still your number?" "Hi, it's Justin, just wanted to check in."

She'd block each one within hours. Sometimes minutes.

I'd get another number. Try again. Each time getting more desperate, more pathetic.

But I couldn't stop. The thought of her just... erasing me... it was eating me alive from the inside.

Drove to the mountain. Climbed it in the dark, no flashlight, stumbling over roots and rocks, talking to her the whole way up. Explaining. Apologizing. Begging.

But even imaginary Hope had gone quiet.

At the summit, I sat there waiting for sunrise, waiting for answers, waiting for anything that made sense. The valley spread out below, lights twinkling like stars that had fallen and gotten stuck. Somewhere down there, Hope was living her life without me in it. Had made the choice to cut me out completely.

The sun came up eventually. It always does. But it didn't bring any revelations. Just showed me how alone I really was.

I drove back to the RV, opened a fresh bottle of Hornitos, and didn't stop drinking until the room spun so hard I couldn't tell which way was up. Did the rest of my coke in three massive lines that made my heart feel like it was trying to escape my chest.

For the first time in months, I was truly alone. Even the Hope in my head had abandoned me.

I thought that was rock bottom.

I thought that was as bad as it could get.

I was wrong.

Chapter 14: The Arrest

The day started like any other.

Up before dawn. Boots laced tight. Magnolia's confused eyes following me to the door. The mountain waiting in the dark like an old friend who'd given up trying to help.

1,700 feet up. 1,700 feet down.

Box until my arms shook.

Bar by 11 AM.

Same stool. Same order. Rick didn't even look up anymore when I walked in. Just poured the Hornitos, cracked the Coors, and went back to wiping down glasses that were already clean.

I can't remember what day of the week it was. Tuesday? Thursday? They all bled together by then. August in Central Washington—hot, dry, endless. The kind of heat that makes you feel like you're suffocating even when you're breathing fine.

What I do remember is leaving the bar sometime after my sixth shot. Maybe seventh. The afternoon sun hitting me like a slap when I walked outside. Getting in my truck with that familiar tequila warmth spreading through my chest, making everything feel both urgent and impossible.

I wasn't planning to drive by the winery.

That's what I told myself later, anyway. I was just driving. Just moving. Just existing in the space between drunk and sober, between awake and asleep, between alive and whatever I'd become.

But there I was, slowing down as I passed. And there she was.

Hope.

Outside. In the parking lot. Real. Not the version in my head who understood everything. Not the ghost I talked to on the mountain. The actual Hope, loading something into her car, existing in the world without me.

My hands turned the wheel before my brain could stop them.

I parked crooked, half in a spot, half in the driving lane. Didn't care. Couldn't care. All I could see was her.

The walk from my truck to the winery door felt like miles and seconds at the same time. My legs were both too heavy and too light. The ground kept shifting, but I kept walking.

Her coworker saw me first. Sarah, I think. Or Sandra. Doesn't matter. She stepped between me and the door.

"You need to leave."

"I just need to talk to her."

"No. You need to leave. Now."

But Hope was right there. Right fucking there. Ten feet away. After weeks of silence, weeks of talking to her ghost, weeks of imagining this moment.

I walked past Sarah-or-Sandra, straight up to Hope.

"How could you do this to me?"

The words came out slurred, desperate, pathetic. I knew it even as I said them. But I couldn't stop.

Hope looked at me. No—she looked through me. Like I was made of glass. Like I was already gone.

She didn't say a word.

That silence was worse than any scream could have been. It was the silence of someone who'd already mourned you. Who'd already processed your death and moved on.

"You need to leave now," the coworker said again, her hand reaching for something. Her phone probably.

"What, you gonna call the cops?"

I laughed as I said it. Actually laughed. Like it was the most ridiculous thing in the world. Like I hadn't just shown up drunk to her workplace. Like I hadn't been sending messages from new numbers for weeks. Like I wasn't completely falling apart in front of them.

"Yeah," she said without hesitation. "I am."

I threw my hands up, backing toward the door. "Fine! Fine."

Got back in my truck. Started driving. Looked in the rearview and saw Hope on her phone.

That's when something in me snapped. Not violent. Not angry. Just... broken.

I circled the block. Came back. Rolled down the window.

"Hope! Just talk to me! Please!"

She walked inside without looking back.

I drove off. Circled again. She came back outside.

"Why won't you just talk to me?"

Back inside.

I did it again. And again. Each time getting more desperate, more pathetic, less coherent. The loop in my head now playing out in real time on the streets of this small town. Me, drunk, circling a winery, yelling at a woman who'd already told me in every way possible that we were done.

At some point—third loop? Fourth?—she came outside and asked, "What's your address?"

The question confused me. Why did she want my address? Was she going to write me? Was this hope?

"I don't have one," I said.

And it was true. The RV wasn't an address. It was just a metal box in a campground. I didn't exist anywhere that mattered.

That's when I saw the cop car.

They didn't approach me. Just sat there. Watching. Waiting.

I left. But not quietly. Laid on the horn the entire way out of the parking lot. One long, continuous wail. Like a child having a tantrum. Like a man who'd forgotten how to be human.

That night, I went to work with a bag full of coke in my pocket and no intention of staying. Clocked in, made one drink, told my manager I wasn't feeling well, and left. Spent the rest of the night doing lines in bar bathrooms, drinking until the edges of everything disappeared, trying to understand what had just happened.

The cops came looking for me that night. I heard about it later—them showing up at the campground, asking about my truck, knocking on RV doors. But I wasn't there. I was nowhere. I was everywhere. I was lost in a town of 3,000 people.

I thought they just wanted to talk. Give me a warning. Tell me to stay away.

I thought wrong.

The next night, I was heading to work when I saw them. Squad car creeping through the campground like they were hunting. And they were. They were hunting me.

I pulled over before they could pull me over. Got out with my hands visible, trying to show I wasn't a threat. Still thinking this was all a misunderstanding. That we could talk about it. That I could explain.

"Turn around. Hands behind your back."

"Wait, what? What's happening?"

"You're under arrest for stalking."

The word hit me like cold water. Stalking. Like I was some kind of criminal. Like I was dangerous.

I'd never been arrested. Never been in real trouble. Never felt metal cuffs cutting into my wrists or sat in the back of a police car with no door handles on the inside.

The booking process was a blur. Fingerprints. Photos. Questions I couldn't quite understand. They took my phone. My wallet. My shoelaces. My belt. Everything that made me feel like a person.

Four hours in a holding cell. Concrete bench. Fluorescent lights that hummed like insects. The smell of disinfectant and despair.

They let me make one call.

I called my mom.

"Mom?"

"Justin? It's late, what's—"

"I'm in jail."

Silence. Long enough that I thought the call had dropped.

Then: "Okay. We'll figure this out."

No anger. No disappointment. No "I told you so." Just that Mom voice. The one that used to tell me everything would be okay when I was seven and scared of the dark. The one I hadn't heard in years because I'd been too proud or too drunk to call.

"I'm sorry, Mom."

"We'll figure it out," she said again. "Just... be safe."

They released me at 1 AM.

No phone to call anyone. No wallet for a taxi. No idea how to get back to the campground, twenty-something miles away. Just me, standing outside the county jail in wrinkled clothes that smelled like fear and tequila, trying to figure out what came next.

I started walking. What else could I do?

About a mile in, I passed an apartment complex. Three people standing outside, smoking, talking in low voices. They looked up when they saw me. This disheveled stranger walking past at 1:30 in the morning.

"Hey," I called out, my voice cracking. "I'm sorry to bother you, but... would one of you mind calling me a cab?"

They could have ignored me. Could have gone inside. Could have told me to fuck off.

Instead, one of them—a woman with kind eyes and a cigarette between her fingers—pulled out her phone.

"Where you trying to go?"

I gave her the campground address. She made the call. Didn't ask questions. Didn't judge. Just helped a stranger who clearly needed it.

"Taxi'll be here in ten minutes," she said.

"Thank you. Really. Thank you."

She nodded, took another drag of her cigarette. "You okay?"

I almost laughed. Was I okay? I was the furthest from okay I'd ever been.

"I will be," I lied.

The taxi ride was silent except for the radio playing something country and sad. I watched the dark fields pass by, punctuated by the occasional porch light of a house where normal people lived normal lives. People who weren't under arrest for stalking. People who could talk to the person they loved without restraining orders.

Back at the RV, Magnolia was waiting. Tail wagging like I'd just come home from a normal day. Like I hadn't just been arrested. Like our whole world hadn't just shifted.

I sat on the couch—that same fucking couch where I'd spent months talking to Hope's ghost—and tried to understand what had happened.

Stalking.

The word kept echoing in my head. That's what I'd become. Not a lover. Not a friend. Not even a person anymore.

A stalker.

I opened a bottle of Hornitos and drank until the word stopped making sense. Until nothing made sense. Until I finally, mercifully, passed out.

But even unconscious, I knew the truth:

This wasn't rock bottom.

Finding Hope

    Not yet.

Chapter 15: Going Home

The day after the arrest, I went to the bar.

What the hell else was I supposed to do?

Rick looked at me different when I walked in. News travels fast in small towns. Population 3,000 means everybody knows everybody's business before you've even processed it yourself. He knew. They all knew. The drunk who got arrested for stalking the woman he was obsessed with. That's what I'd become—small-town gossip, a cautionary tale, someone mothers would point to and tell their kids, "That's what happens when you can't let go."

He poured the Hornitos without asking. Set down the Coors. But his hands moved different. Careful. Like I might explode. Like I was dangerous now.

"Rough night?" he asked, trying to sound casual.

"Something like that."

I didn't even stay long. Three shots. Two beers. Just enough to blur the edges of what had happened. Just enough to pretend for an hour that my phone wasn't sitting in an evidence locker somewhere. That Hope hadn't blocked me from her life. That I wasn't completely, utterly alone.

The walk back to the RV felt like a funeral march. Every person I passed seemed to know. Every look felt like judgment. Every whisper felt like it was about me.

Back at the RV, I did the only thing that made sense: I disappeared.

Closed every blind, one by one, until the sunlight couldn't find me. Unplugged the clock so I wouldn't know how much time was passing. Turned off every light except the glow from my little TV, which I dragged close to the couch—close enough that it filled my entire field of vision. Close enough that I could fall into it and forget everything else existed.

I found this show called *From*.

It was perfect. Dark. Hopeless. True.

People trapped in a town they couldn't escape. Every road out led back in. Monsters that came at night, pretending to be loved ones, trying to trick you into letting them inside. The characters would try to leave, try to find answers, try to understand the rules of their prison. But there was no logic.

No escape. Just survival and the slow realization that this was their life now.

I watched all of season one in thirty-six hours. Then started over.

By the third viewing, I was mouthing the dialogue. The main character kept trying to save everyone, thinking if he just figured out the rules, understood the why, he could fix it. Could get home.

But there was no home to get back to. The trap wasn't the town. The trap was thinking you could escape.

Hope understood this. At least, the Hope in my head did. She'd comment on every episode, draw parallels to us, to how I was trapped in my obsession just like they were trapped in that town. Sometimes I'd argue with her out loud, then realize I was alone.

The first week of September crawled by in episodes and empty bottles. Some days I'd make it to the bar. Most days I didn't. Just sat in the dark, rewatching the same show, having the same thoughts, feeling the same nothing.

But Hope was still there. Always there. In my head, we were still having conversations. Still arguing. Still making up. Still planning that farm she'd mentioned at the hotel. The conversations were so real I'd sometimes answer out loud, then catch myself, alone in the dark with just Magnolia looking at me concerned.

The cocaine ran out on day three. The Adderall on day five. I didn't replace either. Even the Hornitos started tasting like nothing.

Magnolia would nudge me sometimes. Needing food. Needing outside. I'd take care of her, but I couldn't look her in the eyes.

September 8th. Or maybe the 9th. The days had stopped having edges.

I woke up wrong.

Hope was there immediately, like always. Talking about the arrest. About how I'd fucked everything up. About how if I'd just been different, better, less broken, we could have worked. The usual morning torture.

But then a different thought pushed through her voice. Louder. More urgent:

I can't do this alone anymore.

It wasn't dramatic. It wasn't a revelation. It was just... true. Like discovering you've been holding your breath and finally need to inhale. Like realizing you've been falling and are about to hit the ground.

I sat up on that couch—that fucking couch where I'd spent four months in a walking boot, building fantasies, talking to ghosts—and understood something with perfect clarity:

The arrest wasn't rock bottom. This was. Having to admit I'd failed. That I was thirty-five years old, living in a tin can, day-drinking myself to death, and I needed my mommy.

Before the arrest, I'd been drinking to die. Not actively suicidal, but every night when I'd black out, part of me hoped I wouldn't wake up.

But going home? Back to Louisiana? Back to the Bayou I'd escaped from twenty years ago? That felt worse than death. That was admitting defeat.

I sat there for two hours, holding the burner phone I'd bought from the store after they confiscated mine, my mom's number on the screen. The cheap plastic felt like it weighed a thousand pounds. My thumb hovered over the call button like it was a trigger.

In my head, I practiced what I'd say. Tried to find words that wouldn't sound pathetic. Tried to find a way to ask for help without admitting how badly I needed it.

But there were no good words. There was no dignified way to do this.

The tears started before I even dialed. By the time she answered, I was sobbing. Not crying. Sobbing. The kind that comes from your bones. The kind that sounds like something breaking. The kind I hadn't done since I was seven years old and the kids at school surrounded me, chanting "fatty fatty two by four."

"Hey, baby," she said, instantly knowing something was wrong. Mother's intuition. Or maybe just the sound of her son falling apart.

"Mom..." I could barely get the word out. It came out broken, wet, desperate. "Mom, I can't... I can't do this alone anymore."

Silence. Not the cold silence of judgment. Not the disappointed silence I'd feared. The warm silence of a mother processing her child's pain, already making plans, already booking flights, already coming to save me.

"I need help," I said, the words scraping out of my throat. "I need to come home."

"I'm on my way."

That was it. No lecture about my choices. No "I told you so." No questions about the arrest or the drinking or the divorce or any of the hundred ways I'd fucked up. Just: *I'm on my way.*

Like it was that simple. Like coming to get your broken son was just what mothers did. Like she'd been waiting for this call, maybe for years, and was almost relieved it had finally come.

She flew up two days later.

I stopped at the bar before heading to the airport. Two shots of Hornitos and a beer, just to steady my hands, just to be able to face her. Rick didn't say anything, just poured and watched me leave.

When I picked her up at the airport, she hugged me like I was still seven. Like the last twenty years of distance hadn't happened.

"Let's get you home," she said.

We spent the next day packing. Not everything—most of it was garbage. Empty bottles. Dead clothes. We filled five plastic tubs. That's all my life amounted to.

The RV went into storage. Maybe I'd deal with it later. Maybe I wouldn't. It didn't matter anymore.

2,500 miles. From the mountains of Washington to the humidity of Louisiana. Mom drove first—my hands shook too bad.

"We'll take the scenic route," she said. "No rush."

The first day, we followed the Columbia River east, away from everything I'd broken. Through Idaho, where the landscape opened up and you could see forever, except I couldn't see past the next hour.

Magnolia sat in the back, trusting that wherever we were going had to be better.

We barely talked. Mom played old country music—Willie Nelson, Patsy Cline. Sometimes she'd hum along. Sometimes I'd catch her looking at me when she thought I was asleep.

In my head, Hope was still there. Asking why I was running away. Telling me I was a coward for leaving Washington. Reminding me of every promise I'd broken. Every moment I'd ruined. The conversations were quieter than before, but they never stopped.

That night in Missoula, she asked if I was hungry. I wasn't, but said yes because she needed to feed me.

"Remember when you were little," she said at dinner, "you wanted to be a marine biologist?"

"That was a long time ago."

"Not that long. Not really."

The second day, we drove through Yellowstone. Mom had insisted. "When's the next time we'll get the chance?" she said, like we were on vacation, like this was an adventure instead of a rescue mission.

We watched Old Faithful shoot into the sky. Reliable. Predictable. Every ninety minutes, give or take. The opposite of everything I'd become.

"It's something, isn't it?" Mom said.

"Yeah," I said. "It is."

She bought a magnet for her fridge. A little buffalo that said "Yellowstone 2024." Like people do when they're making memories. Like this was something worth remembering.

We saw actual buffalo too. Massive. Prehistoric. Blocking the road like they owned it, which I guess they did. Everyone stopping to take pictures while these ancient things just stood there, unbothered by our presence, our problems, our petty human dramas.

Through Wyoming, where the wind never stopped. Through Colorado, where the mountains looked different than Washington's—older, more settled, less aggressive. Like they'd made peace with being mountains.

We stayed in the Ozarks the third night. Some motel that time forgot. Wood paneling. Orange bedspread. A TV that only got three channels. The kind of place you'd never choose but somehow felt perfect for who we were right then—people between lives, between selves, between everything.

Mom and I sat outside that night on plastic chairs, watching fireflies blink in the darkness.

"You used to love these," she said.

"I remember."

"You'd chase them for hours. Always trying to catch them in mason jars. Never could keep them very long though."

"They'd always die," I said.

"Or you'd let them go."

"Same thing."

She looked at me then. Really looked at me. Mother to son. Person to person.

"Some things aren't meant to be held onto, baby."

I knew she wasn't talking about fireflies.

The fourth day, we crossed into Louisiana. The air changed first—thick, heavy, like breathing through wet cotton. Then the landscape—swampy, alive. Then the smell—earth and water and decay and rebirth happening simultaneously.

Twenty years I'd been gone. Twenty years of running from this place. And here I was, coming back with nothing to show for it but debt and a criminal record.

But something had shifted. Something I noticed as we crossed the Louisiana state line.

Hope's voice was different. Not gone—she was never really gone—but... quieter. Like she was speaking from further away. Like the distance between Washington and Louisiana was finally putting space between us, even in my mind.

For months, she'd been screaming in my head. Constant. Relentless. Every moment since that night at the bar when she'd said she wanted a family too. Now she was whispering. Still there. Always there. Still talking about that family. Still asking why I'd ruined everything. But I could hear other things too. My mom humming. Magnolia's breathing. The world outside my obsession.

We pulled into Thibodaux as the sun was setting, painting everything gold. Mom's house—the one she'd moved to Up Da Bayou after I'd left—looked peaceful. Single story. White brick. Azalea bushes she'd planted. Different from where I grew up Down Da Bayou, but the sounds were the same. The smells were the same. Like I'd never really left Louisiana at all.

"Welcome home," Mom said.

Home. The word still felt wrong. Like wearing someone else's clothes. Like speaking a language I'd forgotten.

But maybe that was okay. Maybe nothing was supposed to fit anymore. Maybe that was the point. Maybe you had to lose everything that didn't work before you could find what did.

Magnolia jumped out of the truck, tail wagging, already exploring her new yard. She didn't care that we'd failed. Didn't care that we'd come back defeated. She was just happy to be somewhere new, with people who loved her, with grass to roll in and new smells to investigate.

Dogs are good at starting over. They don't carry the past like we do.

That night, I slept in the guest room. Different house, but somehow it felt familiar. The ceiling was different from the one I'd stared at as a kid Down Da Bayou, but I stared at it the same way.

I was thirty-five. Divorced. Arrested. Alcoholic. Broken in ways I was only beginning to understand.

And Hope was still there, even in this new room, in this different house. Quieter maybe, but still there. Still whispering about what we could have been. Still asking why I couldn't just let go.

But for the first time in my life, I was exactly where I needed to be.

Not because I'd succeeded. But because I'd finally admitted I'd failed.

The window was cracked open. Louisiana night sounds drifted in—crickets, frogs, the distant hum of Highway 90. The same sounds from Down Da Bayou where I'd grown up. Sounds I'd run from. Sounds that now felt like forgiveness.

Hope was still there, of course. She'd always be there. But tonight, for the first time in months, her voice wasn't the loudest thing in my head.

Maybe going home wasn't giving up.

Maybe it was the first honest thing I'd done in years.

Maybe it wasn't failure.

Maybe it was grace.

Chapter 16: The Last Drink

Addiction doesn't care where you are.

It doesn't give a shit that you drove 2,500 miles with your mother. Doesn't matter that you're sleeping in a different state, breathing different air, pretending to be a different person. The thirst follows you. The habit follows you. The voice that says "just one more" follows you.

And Hope followed me too.

Even in Louisiana, even with my mom cooking dinner in the next room, even with Magnolia learning new smells in the backyard—Hope was there. Quieter than before, but persistent. Like background music you can't turn off. Like tinnitus of the soul.

September 12th. First full day back in Louisiana. Woke up at 5 AM out of habit, ready to climb a mountain that wasn't there. Instead, I sat on Mom's back porch, watching the sun come up over the bayou, and had a full conversation with Hope in my head about how we'd fucked up our entire lives.

Mom made breakfast. Eggs over easy. Grits with butter. Coffee that wasn't as good as Hope's cappuccinos—nothing would ever be as good as those cappuccinos. I ate mechanically while Hope reminded me of every breakfast we'd never have together.

"You feeling okay?" Mom asked.

"Yeah. Just adjusting."

She didn't push. That's not her way. She just refilled my coffee and went about her morning, giving me space to be whatever I needed to be.

But I didn't know what that was.

September 13th. The restlessness started. That specific itch that every addict knows. Not quite physical, not quite mental. Something in between. Like your bones are bored. Like your blood is moving too slow.

11 AM came and went. The time I'd usually be at the bar. My body noticed. My hands noticed. That Pavlovian response to the clock that said: Hornitos time.

Instead, I took Magnolia for a walk. The Louisiana heat was already oppressive, that wet-blanket humidity that makes you sweat just thinking about going outside. We made it maybe half a mile before we both gave up, came back, and collapsed in the air conditioning.

Hope laughed at me in my head. "Remember when you could climb mountains? Now you can't even walk the dog."

She wasn't wrong.

September 14th. The dreams started. Not about Hope—those had been constant since day one. Dreams about drinking. Vivid, specific dreams. The weight of the shot glass. The burn of the tequila. The specific way the Coors Light can felt in my hand. I'd wake up tasting Hornitos, disappointed to find only morning breath.

"You're jonesing," Hope said in my head, using that therapist voice she'd sometimes adopt. "Your body wants what it wants."

"Thanks for the insight," I said out loud, then caught myself. Mom was in the next room. Had to be careful about talking to ghosts around other people.

September 15th. Started pacing. Mom's house isn't big—maybe 1,400 square feet—but I walked every inch of it.

Kitchen to living room. Living room to hallway. Hallway to guest room. Back again. Over and over.

"You're making me dizzy," Hope complained.

"You're not real," I reminded her.

"Real enough," she shot back.

Mom watched from the kitchen, pretending to read a magazine. She knew something was building. Mothers always know.

September 16th. Made excuses to leave the house. Needed to get groceries. Needed gas. Needed to check out the town. Really just needed to move, to drive, to feel like I was going somewhere even if I was just circling.

Passed three bars. Didn't stop. But I noticed them. Memorized their locations. Just in case.

Hope noticed too. "You're mapping escape routes."

"I'm just driving."

"Liar."

She was right. I was lying. To her, to myself, to the universe. I was absolutely mapping escape routes.

September 17th. Woke up with the decision already made. Not consciously—my conscious mind was still pretending I was done drinking. But my body knew. My hands knew. That deeper part that makes decisions before you're aware of them knew.

"I'm going to check out the town," I told Mom after breakfast.

She looked at me with those mom eyes that see through every lie you've ever told. But she just nodded. "Be careful."

"Always am."

Another lie. I'd never been careful a day in my life.

I drove around Thibodaux looking for something specific. Not just any bar. I needed one that felt like Washington. Dark. Quiet. The kind of place where day drinking was a sacrament and nobody judged because they were all there for the same reason.

Found one just outside town, tucked between a tire shop and a vacant lot. Low building. Brown brick. Neon beer signs dark in the windows. A few trucks in the parking lot even though it was barely past noon.

Perfect.

The smell hit me before my eyes adjusted to the darkness. Cigarette smoke, thick and permanent. Still legal to smoke in bars down here, and these folks had been taking advantage since the Carter administration. The smoke had soaked into everything—the wood paneling, the ceiling tiles, probably the ice in the freezer. It was like walking into an ashtray that served drinks.

Four people inside. Three men at the bar, separated by empty stools. One woman in a booth with a crossword and Miller Lite. All older. All professional drinkers.

I took my position at the end of the bar. Always the end.

The bartender wandered over. Woman in her sixties, face like leather left in the sun too long.

"What'll it be, honey?"

The endearment was automatic, meaningless. She'd probably called ten thousand men honey, none of them special.

"You got Hornitos?"

She shook her head, already reaching for something else. "Jose Cuervo."

First disappointment. The brand mattered. It wasn't just about the alcohol. It was about the ritual. The specific burn.

The familiar comfort. Cuervo was like calling someone by the wrong name—close, but wrong enough to matter.

"That's fine," I said, even though it wasn't. "And a Coors Light."

She poured the shot with practiced indifference. Grabbed a can from the cooler. Set them in front of me like she'd done it a thousand times for a thousand different broken men. Which she probably had.

I held the shot glass for a moment. Felt its weight. Watched the overhead light filter through the tequila, turning it gold. In my head, Hope was watching too.

"This is a mistake," she said.

"Everything's a mistake," I told her.

Knocked it back.

It was wrong immediately. Not just the taste—though that was wrong too. The burn was different. Sharper. Less familiar. Like kissing someone with your ex's perfume on. Close enough to remind you what you're missing, different enough to highlight the loss.

The Coors was just beer. Carbonation and regret in an aluminum can.

I drank it fast, hoping speed would make it feel familiar. Hoping muscle memory would kick in and make this feel like all those mornings in Washington. But it didn't. It was just day drinking in a sad bar in Louisiana, and everyone knew it.

"Another round?" the bartender asked, already knowing the answer.

"Yeah."

The second shot was worse. Now that my body knew it wasn't getting Hornitos, it started rejecting the substitute. The Cuervo sat in my stomach like battery acid. The beer tasted like pennies.

I looked around the bar, trying to find something to make this feel right. But these weren't my people. That wasn't my smoke. This wasn't my ritual. I was just another middle-aged fuck-up trying to drink his way through a Tuesday, and not even doing a good job of it.

"You don't belong here," Hope said in my head.

"I don't belong anywhere."

"That's not true."

"Name one place."

She went quiet. Even imaginary Hope couldn't answer that one.

I sat there for twenty minutes, nursing the second beer, trying to force it to work. Trying to make this bar in Louisiana feel like that bar in Washington. Trying to make Jose Cuervo taste like Hornitos. Trying to make the escape hatch open.

But it wouldn't open. The door I'd been walking through for years—from pain to numbness, from feeling to not feeling—was locked. Or maybe it had never really led anywhere.

That's when I knew.

Not dramatically. Just a tired recognition, like realizing you've been pronouncing a word wrong your whole life.

This wasn't doing what it used to do.

The magic was gone. Or maybe there'd never been magic, just desperation dressed up as ritual, addiction wearing the mask of comfort. Either way, sitting in this yellowed bar with the wrong tequila and the same old ghosts, I understood that drinking wasn't going to fix anything. Wasn't even going to numb anything anymore.

It was just... pointless.

Like taking medicine that had expired. Like calling a number that had been disconnected. Like trying to go home to a place that had burned down.

I finished the second beer—waste not, want not, plus I'd paid for it—and left money on the bar. Probably too much, but I didn't wait for change. Didn't say goodbye. Just walked out into the September heat.

The sun hit like a slap. Made me squint. Made me sweat immediately. The temperature difference between the bar and the parking lot had to be thirty degrees. But it felt clean somehow. Real. Like stepping out of a dream and back into the world, even if the world was too bright and too hot and too much.

I sat in my truck for a minute, engine running, AC blasting, trying to cool down. Hope was talking in my head, asking what we were doing, where we were going, why we'd stopped at just one bar. Were we going to find another? One with Hornitos? One that felt right?

"No," I said out loud, not caring if anyone saw me talking to myself in a parking lot. "We're done."

"Done for today?"

"Done done."

"You've said that before."

"This is different."

"Why?"

I thought about it. Really thought about it. Why was this different from all the other times I'd sworn off drinking? All the other last drinks that weren't last?

"Because it doesn't work anymore," I finally said. "It's not even good at what it's supposed to be good at. It's just... nothing."

Hope went quiet. Maybe she understood. Maybe she was thinking about all the things that used to work and didn't anymore. We had that in common, at least.

I drove home slowly, taking the long way, passing those three bars I'd memorized yesterday. Didn't even glance at them. They were just buildings now. Just places where people went to slowly disappear.

Mom was in the kitchen when I got back, pretending not to watch the door. She had that careful look parents get when their kid comes home from somewhere they shouldn't have been.

"Find what you were looking for?" she asked, voice neutral as Switzerland.

"Yeah," I said. "I did."

She looked at me for a long moment, reading something in my face. Then she nodded. "Good. Dinner's at six."

That was it. No interrogation. No lecture. No "I'm disappointed in you" or "I'm proud of you" or any of the things mothers might say. Just acknowledgment and moving forward.

That night, I lay in the guest room, staring at the ceiling, Hope still whispering about all the things we'd lost, all the things we'd never have, all the ways I'd ruined everything. But for the first time, I didn't want to drown her out. Didn't want to make her stop. Didn't want to escape.

Maybe learning to live with the voices was part of healing. Maybe you didn't get rid of them. Maybe you just learned to let them talk without letting them drive.

September 17th, 2024. Day Zero.

I didn't know it yet, but that was the beginning. Not the arrest. Not the mountain. Not the drive home.

The beginning was a disappointing drink in a yellowed bar where they didn't have Hornitos and I realized, with no fanfare, that I was done.

Finding Hope

Sometimes the most important moments are the quiet ones. The ones where you just decide you're tired of the same old shit.

Even if you don't know what comes next. Even if you're scared. Even if you're 35, living with your mother, talking to ghosts. Even if the only thing you know how to do is drink, and now you're deciding not to.

You just decide you're done, and somehow, miraculously, you actually are.

The last drink doesn't always know it's the last drink. Sometimes it's just a disappointment that finally disappoints you enough.

Chapter 17: The First 100 (Part I)

Addiction doesn't leave with a goodbye.

It doesn't pack its bags, shake your hand, wish you well. It lingers in your bones like smoke in fabric. Changes form but never really goes. Just waits for you to remember how much you need it.

September 18th. Day One.

I woke up knowing what I'd done—or rather, what I hadn't done. No Hornitos burning my throat. No Coors chasing it down. Just me and the ceiling of my mother's guest room and Hope's voice asking why I thought this time would be different.

"It won't be," she said in my head. "You'll be drinking by noon."

But noon came and went. No bar. No bottle. Just me pacing the house like a caged thing, Magnolia following me room to room, confused by this new restless energy.

The sweats started that night. Soaked through the sheets like I'd been swimming. Mom changed them without saying anything, just that look mothers have when they're watching their child fight something they can't fight for them.

Days Two through Four blurred together in a specific kind of hell. Not dramatic. Not cinematic. Just the slow dismantling of every system my body had learned to depend on.

Shaking hands that couldn't hold a coffee cup steady. Heart racing at nothing. Hope's voice getting louder as everything else got quieter.

"You were better drunk," she said. "At least then you had an excuse for being pathetic." "Now you're just pathetic sober."

Day Five. Or maybe Six. Time had stopped meaning anything.

I stood in the shower until the hot water ran out, then kept standing there in the cold, trying to feel something other than the ache in my bones. The want. The need. The voice that said just one drink would make this stop.

But I didn't drink.

Not because I was strong. Not because I'd found some higher power or purpose. But because I was too tired to drive to a bar. Too exhausted to perform the ritual. Too empty to even fail properly.

Mom made grits every morning. Set them in front of me. Watched me push them around the bowl. We didn't talk about the elephant in the room—the one shaped like a bourbon bottle, the one that looked like arrest records and failed marriages and daughters I'd never have with Hope.

Day Seven. Maybe Eight.

Started walking. Not far. Just to the end of the street and back. Magnolia beside me, both of us moving like we'd forgotten how. The Louisiana heat was crushing, that wet-blanket humidity that makes you feel like you're drowning in air. But it was movement. It was something other than the couch, the ceiling, the endless loop of Hope explaining why I'd ruined everything.

Day Nine or Ten. The days had no edges.

I found myself standing in front of the bathroom mirror at 3 AM, not recognizing the face looking back. Hollow eyes. Skin like paper. The ghost of someone who used to be someone.

"This is what you wanted," Hope said in my reflection. "To feel everything. How's that working out?"

I didn't answer. Couldn't answer. Just went back to bed and waited for unconsciousness that wouldn't come.

September 28th. Day Eleven.

Something shifted that morning. Not hope. Not healing. Just... something.

I sat at Mom's kitchen table with her old laptop and opened a blank document. Stared at the cursor blinking like a heartbeat. Hope was there too, watching over my shoulder, waiting to see what excuse I'd write for myself this time.

But I didn't write excuses. I wrote this:

"To Begin with the end, rewind with time To never walk a straight line. This Story is and always will be mine.

Picket Fences, Starry Eyes. Big old Glasses. Full of lies. Children Prancing. Love is dancing. Dangling Earrings. Tells more Lies.

Always Grateful, Broken Man. Pick up the pieces you left behind. Forever missing that centerpiece. Unconditional still this love of mine.

Trapped inside his long lost mind. Starting to long for this love of mine."

It wasn't good. Wasn't even coherent really. But it was something. Words pulled from wherever words come from when you've got nothing left but the need to put the inside on the outside.

"Poetry now?" Hope mocked. "That's your solution?"

But I kept typing. Kept pulling these fragments out and setting them down. Like breadcrumbs. Like evidence I'd existed that day.

October 2nd. Day Fifteen.

The nights were getting harder. That's when Hope was loudest, when the darkness gave her more room to expand. I wrote:

"The darkness in me starts to eat. It's hard to suppress the demons inside. The longing for a guide to take me out the night. A flashlight of hope."

Funny, writing about hope while Hope herself was tearing me apart from the inside. But the writing helped. Gave her voice somewhere else to go besides just bouncing around my skull.

October 3rd. Day Sixteen.

I woke up sad. Not the dramatic, acute sadness of fresh loss. This was older, deeper. The kind that settles in your bones like arthritis. I opened the laptop and let it pour out:

"I'm just sad. I'm sad because I saw a world with someone. I saw a future that I've longed for. I'm sad because no matter how sad I am, I can't stop feeling this way about you."

I wrote to Hope like she might read it. Like these words might somehow reach the real her, not just the ghost in my head who never stopped talking.

"I'm sad because we were so good together. I'm sad because you choose to forget. I'm sad because I don't know if I'll ever be able to be that version of myself again. I'm sad because I'll never get to talk to my friend again. I'm sad because I still love you."

Mom found me crying at the kitchen table, laptop still open, cursor still blinking. She didn't say anything. Just put her hand on my shoulder and stood there. Sometimes that's all you can do.

October 4th. Day Seventeen.

The physical symptoms were fading, but the mental ones were getting worse. Like my brain, freed from the alcohol fog, was making up for lost time. Every feeling I'd drowned for two years was demanding to be felt now, all at once.

"I can't put into words the depth of these feelings. People like to say time. Well my entire body feels her every single time she pops into my head. It's miserable. It's absolutely miserable."

I was writing about Hope while she sat next to me, commenting on every line.

"You're pathetic," she said. "I know," I wrote. "You'll never get over this." "I know." "You'll never be happy again." "I know."

But knowing and accepting are different things. I kept writing.

"I literally have to remove myself from family and friends when they appear because it shakes my every essence."

October 6th. Day Nineteen.

Some days I could function. Shower. Eat. Walk Magnolia. Pretend to be human.

This wasn't one of those days.

"Numb, not sure I'll ever be that. Not sure I'm capable. Not sure I know how to just forget about someone who was so important to me and still is."

Hope was reading over my shoulder again. Always there. Always watching. Always ready to remind me of what I'd lost.

"It's not the uncertainty that hurts me. It's how certain I was of you. How I trusted myself, I relied on my emotions. My feelings my heart to guide me. It's how certain I was that you'd be on the other side."

"But I'm not on the other side," Hope said. "I'm here. In your head. Forever."

"It's how certain I am, I'll never be able to trust myself again. It's how certain I am that these feelings are real. It's how certain I am they won't ever go away. I'm broken. And You broke me."

I'd almost written her real name. Caught myself just in time. Even in my private journal, I couldn't risk it. Hope. Always Hope. Never her actual name.

"I don't know what I want to do with my life anymore. I don't know if I even want a life anymore."

But I didn't drink.

Day Twenty-Something. The numbers were starting to matter less than the patterns.

Morning: Wake up with Hope already talking. Attempt breakfast. Walk. Write. Afternoon: Fight the 11 AM urge. Walk again. Write more. Evening: Sit with Mom, pretend to watch TV while Hope narrated all the ways I'd failed. Night: Lie awake until exhaustion won. Repeat.

It wasn't living. Not yet. But it was something. A skeleton of routine to hang the days on.

Day Twenty-Eight.

"The fog is thinning," I wrote. "I can feel myself starting to return. Slowly. Unevenly. But I'm here."

Hope laughed. "You think this is returning? You're further gone than ever."

Maybe. But I was starting to hear the difference between her voice and mine. Starting to recognize which thoughts were grief and which were just ghosts.

Day Thirty.

A month without alcohol. The longest since I'd met Hope. The longest since before the RV, before the arrest, before everything fell apart.

Mom made a cake. Didn't say what for, but we both knew. I ate a piece while Hope reminded me that thirty days meant nothing. That I'd celebrated thirty days before with a bottle. That I'd fail again.

"Probably," I said out loud.

Mom looked up. "What?"

"Nothing. Just thinking."

But it wasn't nothing. It was me starting to answer back. Starting to push against the voice that had owned me for so long.

Day Thirty-Five.

I'd developed a rhythm. Not a life, but a pattern. Something to pour myself into so I didn't leak out through the cracks.

Wake up. Acknowledge Hope's presence without engaging. Hydrate. Walk. Write. Eat. Walk. Write. Survive. Sleep. Repeat.

The writing had become essential. Not good writing. Not coherent writing. Just... writing. Putting the inside on the outside. Giving the ghosts somewhere else to live besides my head.

I wrote letters to Hope I'd never send. Apologies. Explanations. Accusations. Love letters. Hate letters. Sometimes all in the same paragraph.

I wrote to myself—past, present, future. Trying to figure out who I'd been, who I was, who I might become if I could just keep not drinking long enough.

I wrote about the RV. About the arrest. About the mountain. About Magnolia. About Mom's grits. About anything that would keep my fingers moving and my mind occupied with something other than the bottle-shaped hole in my life.

And slowly, so slowly I almost didn't notice, Hope's voice started getting quieter. Not gone. Never gone. But... manageable. Like turning down the volume on a TV you can't turn off.

"You'll never make it to 100 days," she said one morning.

"Maybe not," I typed. "But I made it to thirty-five."

It wasn't victory. Wasn't even really hope.

But it was enough.

For now, for today, for this moment—it was enough.

I was no longer counting down until I broke.

I was counting forward.

One day. One word. One breath at a time.

Still broken. Still haunted. Still in love with a ghost.

But sober.

Thirty-five days sober.

And for the first time since that last disappointing drink in the yellowed bar, I thought maybe—just maybe—I might make it to thirty-six.

Chapter 17: The First 100 (Part II)

October 7th. Day Thirty-Six.

I wasn't getting better. I was just getting better at surviving.

The clarity that comes with sobriety is cruel. It doesn't arrive with revelations or comfort. It arrives with everything you've tried to forget sitting at the foot of your bed at 3 AM, asking why you thought you could run.

Hope was still there. Of course she was. She'd moved in permanently, taken up residence in the space between thoughts. But her voice had changed. Not softer—just less certain. Like she was starting to doubt her own arguments.

"Somewhere out there is a version of me that isn't broken," I wrote that morning. *"And somewhere out there is*

a version of you that didn't have to disappear for me to survive."

I wasn't writing to her anymore. Not really. I was writing to understand what the fuck I was supposed to do with all this feeling now that I couldn't drown it.

October 8th. Day Thirty-Seven.

Mom made grits again. I ate them this time. All of them. She noticed but didn't say anything, just refilled my coffee with that careful look mothers have when they're watching their child learn to walk again.

"Going for a walk," I said.

"Take Magnolia."

I did. We made it to the levee this time—further than yesterday. The October heat was different from September's. Still brutal, but with an edge that suggested it might eventually break. Magnolia found a stick and carried it the whole way, tail wagging like she'd discovered treasure.

That's when it happened. I smiled. Not forced. Not performative. Just... smiled at my dog being a dog.

Then immediately felt like shit for it.

Hope noticed too. "Oh, feeling better already? That was quick."

"Fuck off," I said out loud.

Magnolia looked at me, confused.

"Not you, girl."

October 10th. Day Thirty-Nine.

I wrote something different that morning:

"I don't know what's harder—missing you, or starting to feel okay without you."

It was true. There was a new kind of grief settling in. The acute pain was fading into something chronic, manageable. And that terrified me. Like healing meant forgetting. Like getting better meant she'd meant less.

"You're already forgetting me," Hope said from her corner of my mind.

"I couldn't forget you if I tried."

"You're not trying hard enough."

"Maybe I don't want to."

She went quiet at that. We both did.

Justin Mayeur

October 11th. Day Forty.

Found myself at Mom's kitchen table at 2 AM, laptop open, but not writing about Hope. Writing about me. About the kid who got bullied. About the man who drank to disappear. About whoever the fuck I was supposed to be now.

"I spent so long trying to be someone worth loving that I forgot to figure out who I actually was."

Hope read over my shoulder, but she didn't comment. Just watched.

The truth was starting to surface—ugly and necessary. I'd been performing my whole life. The funny fat kid. The drunk who could hold his liquor. The romantic who'd burn everything down for love. But who was I when no one was watching? When there was no role to play?

"Maybe that's what rock bottom really is—the place where all your masks fall off and you're left with just you. And you realize you don't even know that person."

"Deep thoughts for a drunk," Hope said.

"Recovering drunk."

"Same thing."

"No," I said, closing the laptop. "It's not."

October 12th. Day Forty-One.

Sat with Mom on the porch after dinner. The mosquitos were vicious, but I stayed anyway. She was talking about her garden, about the tomatoes that wouldn't grow right this year, about nothing and everything.

For the first time in months, I really looked at her. Saw the worry lines that hadn't been there before. The way she kept glancing at me like I might evaporate. The weight she'd been carrying while I'd been drowning.

"I'm sorry, Mom."

She stopped mid-sentence. "For what?"

"All of it."

She reached over, patted my hand. "You're here now. That's what matters."

Hope whispered, "She shouldn't have to settle for that."

But I was learning the difference between Hope's voice and the truth. Mom wasn't settling. She was choosing to believe I could get better. There's a difference.

October 14th. Day Forty-Three.

Almost fucked up.

Was driving to get groceries and found myself on the road that leads to I-10. The interstate that could take me back to Washington. Back to Leavenworth. Back to her.

I sat at that intersection for twenty minutes. Engine running. Hope screaming in my head to go, to prove I could be different, to show her I'd changed.

"Just to see her. Just to prove I can stand in the same town and not fall apart."

But I knew better. That wasn't strength. That was the addiction wearing a different mask. Instead of bourbon, it was her. Instead of Hornitos, it was hope.

I turned around. Bought groceries. Went home.

Wrote this:

"There are days I still think about driving back. But I know that's not strength—that's temptation in disguise."

October 15th. Day Forty-Four.

The writing was changing. Less about her, more about... everything else. About addiction. About recovery. About the space between who I was and who I was trying to become.

Started a piece about the RV. About isolation. About what happens to your mind when you're trapped with nothing but your thoughts and a ghost for company. It was ugly. Raw. True.

Hope didn't like it.

"You're making me the villain."

"You're not the villain. You're not even you. You're just my brain trying to process trauma."

"That's bullshit and you know it."

Maybe. But it was the kind of bullshit that kept me sober, so I'd take it.

October 16th. Day Forty-Five.

Magnolia got into something she shouldn't have. Threw up all over Mom's kitchen floor. I cleaned it up without being asked, without complaining, without even thinking about it.

Such a small thing. But Mom noticed.

"You're different," she said.

"Bad different?"

"No. Just... present."

Present. What a concept. Being where you are instead of drowning in where you've been or where you'll never be.

October 17th. Day Forty-Six.

Melissa texted. My old therapist, checking in. Asking if I'd found AA yet. Asking if I was okay.

I wasn't ready for AA. Wasn't ready to sit in a circle and say "Hi, I'm Justin, and I'm an alcoholic" when what I really was was "Hi, I'm Justin, and I'm in love with someone who exists mostly in my head now."

But I texted back. Told her I was trying. Told her about the writing, the walking, the small victories that didn't feel like victories yet.

"Proud of you," she wrote.

Hope laughed. "She doesn't even know you anymore."

"Neither do I," I said. "That's kind of the point."

October 18th. Day Forty-Seven.

I spent seven hours over two days picking up trash along the road where I walked Magnolia. Not community service. Not court-ordered. Just... something to do with my hands that wasn't holding a bottle or typing Hope's name into messages I'd never send.

"Cleaning my mind and my community one bag at a time."

Stupid little motto I made up. But it helped. Gave structure to the chaos. Made me feel like maybe I was worth something, even if it was just worth keeping a stretch of Louisiana road clean.

Mom took a picture of me with the trash bags. Sent it to my sister. "Look at your brother," she wrote.

I looked at the photo later. Didn't recognize myself. Not because I looked different—I looked exactly the same. But there was something in my eyes that hadn't been there before. Not happiness. Not peace. Just... presence.

October 19th. Day Forty-Eight.

Court was coming up. Zoom court for the stalking charge. The word still made me want to vomit. Made me remember that afternoon at the winery, drunk, desperate, circling the block like a shark that forgot what it was hunting.

I'd have to sit in Mom's living room, laptop open, and face a judge through a screen. Have to hear the charges read. Have to plead something—guilty, no contest, whatever my court-appointed lawyer suggested. Have to own what I'd become in those final days.

"You weren't a stalker," Hope said. "You were sick."

"I was both."

"You loved me."

"That doesn't make it okay."

"I forgive you."

"You're not real enough to forgive me."

She went quiet. These days, she went quiet more often. Like she was running out of arguments. Or maybe I was running out of energy to argue.

That night, I wrote a letter to the real Hope. Not to send— I'd never send it. But to finally say what I should have said instead of showing up drunk at her work:

"I'm sorry. Not for loving you, but for how I loved you. For making you responsible for my healing. For turning you into a ghost when you were trying to be a person. For not knowing the difference between love and obsession until it was too late. I hope you're okay. I hope you're happy. I hope you never think about me."

I deleted it immediately. But writing it helped. Like lancing a wound.

October 20th. Day Forty-Nine.

Wrote this:

"The hardest part about losing someone who saved you is trying to become someone worth saving."

It might have been the truest thing I'd written since getting sober. Because that's what this was really about. Not getting Hope back. Not proving anything to anyone. Just trying to become someone who didn't need saving anymore.

Someone who could save himself.

October 21st. Day Fifty.

Fifty days without alcohol. The longest since I'd met Hope. The longest since before the RV, before the arrest, before the mountain, before everything fell apart and came together and fell apart again.

No cake this time. No announcement. Just me and Mom watching Jeopardy, Magnolia snoring between us, Hope whispering something I chose not to hear.

During a commercial, Mom said, "Your dad called. Wants to know how you're doing."

"What'd you tell him?"

"That you're doing better."

"Am I?"

She looked at me, really looked at me. "What do you think?"

I thought about it. About the fifty days. About the trash bags full of roadside litter. About the words filling up documents on Mom's old laptop. About Hope's voice getting quieter, even if she never fully left.

"I think I'm trying," I said.

"That's all anyone can do."

I thought about that last drink in the yellowed bar. How disappointed I'd been that they didn't have Hornitos. How I'd decided I was done not because I'd found strength or God or purpose, but because drinking had become pointless.

Maybe that's what recovery really was. Not some dramatic transformation. Not some spiritual awakening. Just the slow, tedious process of making the poisonous things pointless.

That night, before bed, I stood in front of the bathroom mirror. Same mirror where I'd stood on Day Nine or Ten, not recognizing myself. I still looked like shit. Still had the hollow eyes of someone who'd been through something. But there was something else there too.

Not peace. Not happiness. Not even hope.

Just presence.

I was here. In this bathroom. In this moment. Not in Washington. Not in the RV. Not in the past or the future or the impossible.

Just here.

"You're still broken," Hope said from behind my reflection.

"Yeah," I said. "But I'm here."

"That's not enough."

"It's going to have to be."

I wasn't cured. Wasn't healed. Wasn't even particularly hopeful.

But I was fifty days sober, and for the first time, I thought I might make it to fifty-one.

Not because I was strong.

But because I was finally too tired to be anything else.

The ghosts were still talking.

But I was learning to talk back.

And sometimes, on good days, I was even learning not to listen.

Justin Mayeur

Sometimes, that's all recovery is—learning which voices are yours and which are just echoes of who you used to be.

Chapter 17: The First 100 (Part III)

October 22nd. Day Fifty-One.

The danger now wasn't falling—it was staying numb and calling that recovery.

I woke up before dawn and cried. No reason. No trigger. Just opened my eyes and the tears came like my body was grieving something my mind hadn't caught up to yet. Hope didn't even speak. Just sat there in the dark with me, both of us confused by the sadness.

Mom heard me. Of course she did. Mothers hear everything. But she didn't come in. Just made coffee louder than usual, letting me know she was there without making me explain what couldn't be explained.

I wrote:

"I wake up and don't even know who I am anymore. The person in the mirror looks like me but feels like a stranger wearing my face."

It wasn't the dramatic identity crisis of early sobriety. This was quieter. More disturbing. Like slowly forgetting your native language.

October 23rd. Day Fifty-Two.

The fog was getting thicker. Not depression exactly. Not the acute pain of early sobriety. This was different. Like static on an old TV—still functioning but the picture wasn't clear.

"These past 50 days have hurt like hell. But so did drinking. At least now, the pain isn't borrowed from tomorrow."

Hope read over my shoulder. "Pretty words won't fix you."

"Nothing will fix me."

"Then why keep trying?"

I didn't have an answer. Just kept typing.

"Maybe I'm not meant to be fixed. Maybe some people are just broken in interesting ways."

"That's depressing," Hope said.

"That's acceptance."

"Same thing."

Maybe she was right. Maybe acceptance and depression were cousins, living in the same neighborhood of resignation.

October 24th. Day Fifty-Three.

Re-read my entries from a month ago. That person— desperate, shaking, drowning in Hope's voice—felt like a stranger. But he was me. Just thirty days ago.

The speed of change terrified me. If I could become someone else in thirty days, who was I really? Which version was real?

"I'm not proud of who I was. But I'm not ashamed anymore either. I just don't want to go back."

Hope whispered, "You will. You always do."

"Maybe," I said. "But not today."

"What about tomorrow?"

"I don't know about tomorrow. I barely know about right now."

That was the truth of it. Everyone talked about taking it "one day at a time," but I was taking it one hour at a time. Sometimes one minute. Sometimes just one breath.

October 25th. Day Fifty-Four.

Today felt okay.

Just okay. Not good. Not bad. Not anything really.

And somehow that was worse than the pain. At least pain meant I was feeling something. This gray nothing was harder to navigate. No landmarks. No edges. Just fog in every direction.

Mom asked if I wanted to go to the store with her. I said yes just to move, just to be somewhere else. We walked the aisles in comfortable silence. She bought ingredients for gumbo. I pushed the cart. Normal people doing normal things.

In the cereal aisle, I had a moment of complete disconnection. Like I was floating above myself, watching this man push a cart next to his mother, pretending to care about grocery shopping. Who was he? Was he me? Was I him?

"You're quiet today," Mom said.

"I'm quiet every day."

"Different quiet."

She was right. This wasn't the desperate quiet of trying not to scream. This was the hollow quiet of not having anything to scream about.

October 26th. Day Fifty-Five.

Saw a couple at the grocery store. Young. Happy. He grabbed her hand without looking, like he knew it would be there. She laughed at something he whispered.

It broke me. But differently than before. Not sharp pain—dull ache. Like remembering a bruise you forgot you had.

Back in the truck, I typed into my phone:

"Just because it's not your turn for love doesn't mean love isn't real."

Hope laughed. "You don't believe that."

"I want to."

"You've been saying that about everything lately."

She wasn't wrong. I'd been saying "I want to believe" about a lot of things. Love. Recovery. Myself. The future. As if wanting to believe was close enough to truth to count.

"Maybe wanting something to be true is the first step to making it true. Maybe hope is just stubbornness dressed up nice."

"Now you're just making things up," Hope said.

"Everything's made up. Some things just get more people to agree."

October 27th. Day Fifty-Six.

Court tomorrow.

The dread sat in my stomach like concrete. I'd been pushing it down, but now it was here. Tomorrow I'd sit in Mom's living room, open her laptop, and face what I'd done. Hear my name followed by words like "stalking" and "harassment." Words that belonged to someone else but were mine now.

"I feel forgotten by the world. Like life moved on without me."

I wrote it and immediately deleted it. Too dramatic. Too self-pitying. But true.

Then I wrote:

"Maybe some people are meant to be forgotten. Maybe that's their purpose—to show others what not to become. Or

maybe there is no purpose. Maybe we just exist until we don't."

Hope was quieter than usual. Even she knew tomorrow was real in a way she wasn't.

That night, I couldn't sleep. Just lay there trying to quiet my mind, talking to the universe or whatever might be listening about a tomorrow I didn't want to face.

"If anything's out there," I said to the ceiling, "I could use some help."

Silence.

"I know I probably don't deserve it. I know I've fucked up everything. But I'm trying. Doesn't that count for something?"

More silence.

Hope finally spoke: "No one's listening."

"I know," I said. "I'm talking anyway."

October 28th. Day Fifty-Seven.

Couldn't write. Couldn't think. Just paced the house while Mom pretended not to notice.

Hope was back full force:

"You're going to jail." "She'll be there." "She'll testify." "Everyone will know what you are."

I wanted to drink. Not to feel better—to feel nothing. To skip from now to later without having to experience the in-between.

But I didn't drink. Just sat with the wanting. Let it burn through me without acting on it. Maybe that's all sobriety really was—feeling things without fixing them.

Mom found me sitting on the back porch at 3 AM, staring at nothing.

"Can't sleep?"

"Can't stop thinking."

"About tomorrow?"

"About everything."

She sat down beside me. We listened to the sounds of Louisiana at night—crickets, frogs, the distant hum of the highway.

"You know," she said, "this doesn't define you."

"Feels like it does."

"Feelings aren't facts."

I'd heard that in therapy a hundred times. But hearing it from Mom at 3 AM hit different.

"What if they are though? What if how we feel is the only thing that's actually real?"

She thought about it. "Then you get to choose which feelings to feed."

"I've been feeding the wrong ones for years."

"So feed different ones."

"It's not that simple."

"I didn't say it was simple. I said you get to choose."

October 29th. Day Fifty-Eight.

Court.

Sitting in Mom's living room. Laptop open. My name on the screen. The judge's face pixelated and formal.

"How do you plead?"

My lawyer had coached me. "Not guilty, Your Honor."

"Do you understand the charges against you?"

"Yes, Your Honor."

Hope watched from behind the screen, silent for once.

Ten minutes. That's all it took. No dramatics. No Hope calling in. No testimony. Just the cold mechanics of justice. Court dismissed. Next hearing in a few months. The waiting game.

After it ended, I sat staring at the black screen. My reflection stared back—hollow eyes, unshaven, looking exactly like someone who'd just pled not guilty to something they definitely did.

"I am not proud. But I am still here. And maybe that's enough for today."

Mom brought me coffee. Didn't say anything. Just set it down and squeezed my shoulder.

"I'm sorry," I said.

"For what?"

"For being this. For coming home like this."

"You came home," she said. "That's what matters."

October 30th. Day Fifty-Nine.

Back to routine. Walk. Write. Pretend the world hadn't shifted yesterday.

Mom made gumbo. I helped peel shrimp while Magnolia watched, convinced we were preparing a feast specifically for her. The simple repetition—peel, devein, drop in bowl—became meditation.

Hope was there but muted, like someone had turned her volume down.

"You're pathetic," she said, but it lacked conviction.

"I know," I said, and kept peeling shrimp.

"Doesn't that bother you?"

"Everything bothers me. But the shrimp still need peeling."

That night, I wrote:

"I don't know if I want to live or die or just exist. I feel like my purpose has passed. Like I missed my chance at whatever I was supposed to be."

Then I deleted it. Then I wrote it again. Then I saved it.

Some truths are too heavy to carry but too important to forget.

October 31st. Day Sixty.

Halloween.

Kids came to the door dressed as superheroes and monsters. Mom gave out full-size candy bars because that's who she is. Magnolia barked at every costume, personally offended by the audacity of masks.

I stayed in my room and wrote:

"I don't miss drinking tonight. But I miss what drinking used to pretend to be—connection, celebration, the feeling of belonging to something."

Hope showed up late, dressed in memories.

"Remember what Halloween could have been?" she asked. "We could have dressed up. Gone to parties. Been normal."

"We were never going to be normal."

"You don't know that."

"I do now."

She sat on the bed beside me, more solid than she'd been in weeks. "Do you regret it?"

"Which part?"

"All of it. Meeting me. Falling in love. Destroying everything."

I thought about it. Really thought about it.

"No," I said finally. "I regret how it ended. I regret what I became. But I don't regret you."

"Even though I'm not real?"

"You're real enough to hurt. That makes you real enough to matter."

November 1st. Day Sixty-One.

I woke up thinking about meaning. Or the absence of meaning. Or whatever you call the thing that's supposed to make sense of all this chaos.

"Do I even believe in anything anymore? Or just the idea that something should matter?"

I used to meditate. Back before everything fell apart. Little attempts at finding peace, sitting cross-legged on the RV floor, trying to quiet the noise. Now I didn't even have that. Just me and the ghosts and the slow march of days.

"I feel like my soul got lost somewhere between the RV and here. Like I left it in Washington with everything else. Or maybe I never had one. Maybe I've just been pretending this whole time."

But I was still here. Still waking up. Still not drinking. Still writing words no one would read.

Maybe that was its own kind of meditation. Maybe showing up when you didn't believe in anything was the most honest practice there was.

Hope sat beside me on the bed, not talking for once.

"You're different," I said to her.

"So are you."

"I don't know if that's good or bad."

"Does it matter?"

It should matter. Everything should matter. But sitting there on Day Sixty-One, stone-cold sober and hollow as a dead tree, I realized maybe mattering was overrated.

Maybe just being here was enough.

I wasn't strong. Wasn't healing. Wasn't even particularly trying anymore.

But I was here.

Sixty-one days without alcohol.

Sixty-one days of sitting with ghosts.

Sixty-one days of learning the difference between surviving and living, and being okay with just surviving for now.

The writing wasn't fixing me. Wasn't even helping really. But it was proof I'd existed through this. Evidence that somewhere between the drinking and whatever came next, there was this—this nothing, this hollow peace, this terrible freedom of having nothing left to lose.

"I'm stuck in a mind that's not mine anymore. But at least I'm stuck sober."

Hope whispered something I didn't catch.

"What?" I asked.

"Nothing," she said. "Just... you're still here."

"Yeah," I said. "I am."

And for today, that had to be enough.

Because it was all I had.

And maybe having anything at all—even if it was just stubbornness and spite and the refusal to quit—was its own small victory.

Chapter 17: The First 100 (Part IV)

November 2nd. Day Sixty-Two.

Woke up with this overwhelming need to cry. Not about anything specific. Just... everything. The weight of existing. The exhaustion of being conscious. The effort it takes to be a person.

So I cried. On the back porch while Mom was at the store. Just me and the tears and the Louisiana humidity making everything feel heavier than it already was.

Hope didn't say anything. Just sat there with me in the wet heat, both of us grieving something we couldn't name.

"I'm not sure what it is but I feel this need to let something out that I don't have words for."

Magnolia found me there an hour later, licked the salt off my face like she was trying to help. Maybe she was.

November 3rd. Day Sixty-Three.

The ache in my chest hasn't let up. But it's not sharp anymore. It's dull. Persistent. Like an old injury that hurts when the weather changes.

"Not a day goes by that I don't miss her. The only thing worse than having a broken heart is having to fake a smile to make sure no one else feels the weight of it."

Mom asked if I was okay at dinner.

"Yeah, just tired."

She nodded like she believed me. We both knew she didn't.

Hope whispered, "You're getting good at lying again."

"It's not lying," I said. "It's surviving."

"Same thing."

November 4th. Day Sixty-Four.

Everything felt heavy today. The air. The sunlight. Even breathing felt like work.

"A lot of people feel lonely. But I'm starting to believe some people just are lonely. And that's how they will spend their lives."

Hope replied, soft for once: "You weren't always alone."

"I know."

"You had me."

"I had the idea of you."

"What's the difference?"

I didn't answer because I didn't know anymore. Maybe there wasn't one. Maybe that was the problem.

Magnolia spent the whole day pressed against my leg, like she could feel the weight too and was trying to help hold it.

November 5th. Day Sixty-Five.

Can't cry. Want to but can't. It's like being thirsty but unable to swallow water.

"You ever get so sad that you can't cry? You just kind of sit there and stare at a blank wall until time starts to move again."

That was me. All day. Sitting on Mom's couch. TV on but not watching. Phone in hand but not scrolling. Just... existing in space.

Hope tried to get my attention. Kept saying things. But I couldn't hear her over the static in my head.

Magnolia laid her head in my lap around 3 PM. The weight of it reminded me I had a body. Reminded me to eat something.

I made a sandwich. Didn't taste it. But I ate it. That counted for something.

November 6th. Day Sixty-Six.

I miss her.

That's it. That's the whole day. No metaphor. No poetry. No deeper meaning.

Just that one sentence written twenty-seven times in my journal because it was the only truth that mattered.

"I miss her. I miss her. I miss her. I miss her. I miss her."

Hope said nothing. She already knew. She was made of missing.

November 7th. Day Sixty-Seven.

Had a dream last night. She wasn't in it. But the version of me who was loved by her was.

He looked different. Clean-shaven. Clear eyes. Steady hands. He was at some party, laughing at something someone said. Natural. Easy. Like belonging came naturally to him.

"I dreamed I saw the man I was supposed to be, and he didn't flinch when she said goodbye."

Woke up gasping, like I'd been underwater. The sheets were soaked with sweat. 4:17 AM. Too early to get up, too late to go back to sleep.

Hope sat at the foot of the bed. "That wasn't you."

"I know."

"You'll never be him."

"I know."

"Does that bother you?"

"Everything bothers me."

But what bothered me most was that dream-me looked happy. Not the forced happy I'd been practicing in mirrors. Real happy. The kind that comes from inside. The kind I'd felt for maybe three seconds total in my entire life, all of them with her.

I got up and sat on the porch until sunrise. Watched the world wake up without me. Sometimes I think I'm living in a different timezone than everyone else. Like I'm always a few hours behind or ahead, never quite synced up with the present.

November 8th. Day Sixty-Eight.

Made pancakes this morning. Burned the first batch black. The smoke alarm went off. Mom came running.

"I'm fine," I said, waving a dish towel at the alarm. "Just forgot I'm not good at this."

She laughed. "You're getting domestic."

"Don't get used to it."

But part of me wanted her to. Part of me wanted this version—the pancake-making, present, trying version—to last longer than the others.

The second batch came out perfect. We ate them with too much syrup. Magnolia got the burned ones. Everyone won.

November 9th. Day Sixty-Nine.

Hope was loud today. Not cruel. Not accusing. Just... present. Like she had things she needed to say.

"We almost made it."

"No, we didn't."

"We were so close."

"To what?"

"To being real."

"You were never real."

"I was real to you."

She wasn't wrong. In my head, in that RV, in all those months of isolation—she was the realest thing in my world. More real than the walls. More real than the pain. More real than me.

"I miss being real," she said.

"Yeah," I said. "Me too."

November 10th. Day Seventy.

Seventy days sober.

I wrote it on a piece of paper. Stared at it. The number looked fake. Foreign. Like it belonged to someone else.

"I'm sober but I still don't feel like myself."

Mom made a cake. Didn't say what for, but we both knew. German chocolate. My favorite since I was a kid.

"How does it feel?" she asked.

"Like nothing."

"That's okay. Nothing is better than something sometimes."

Hope laughed. "She doesn't get it."

"No," I said. "But she's trying."

That night I wrote: *"Maybe 'myself' is gone. Maybe I'm building someone new from the pieces. Maybe that's what recovery really is—not getting back to who you were, but figuring out who you're becoming."*

November 11th. Day Seventy-One.

"They tell you healing isn't linear, but what they don't tell you is how often it loops back to the exact moment you swore you already survived."

Today was one of those loops. Woke up feeling like it was Day One again. Like all the progress was imaginary. Like I'd dreamed the last seventy days.

Hope was there, patient as ever. "See? You're not getting better."

"Maybe not. But I'm not getting worse either."

"Stagnation isn't progress."

"It's not regression either."

We went back and forth like that all morning. Like an old married couple arguing about directions when we both knew we were lost.

November 12th. Day Seventy-Two.

"I am tired of healing."

Not because I don't want to get better. But because healing feels like running on a treadmill. Constant motion. Never arriving. Just the endless rhythm of one foot in front of the other while the scenery never changes.

Tried to read today. Couldn't focus. The words kept rearranging themselves into her name. Tried to write. The sentences came out sideways, backwards, upside down.

Everything felt like effort. Even sitting still felt like work. Like I was fighting gravity just to stay upright.

Mom brought me lunch. Tomato soup. Grilled cheese. Comfort food from when I was sick as a kid.

"You need to eat."

"I'm not hungry."

"Eat anyway."

So I did. Mechanical. Bite, chew, swallow. Repeat. The soup tasted like red water. The sandwich like cardboard. But I ate it all because disappointing my mother felt worse than forcing down food I couldn't taste.

"This is your life now," Hope said after Mom left. "Just this. Forever."

"Maybe."

"Doesn't that scare you?"

"Everything scares me. This is just another thing."

"You used to fight harder."

"I used to drink harder too."

She went quiet at that. Even Hope knew some arguments weren't worth having.

November 13th. Day Seventy-Three.

Somewhere in my bones, I still expect her to call. Or text. Or show up.

It's involuntary. Like blinking. Like breathing. My body hasn't caught up to reality.

Every time my phone buzzes, there's this split second where my heart thinks it's her. Even though I know. Even though she's blocked me. Even though it's been months.

"That's the part of grief no one talks about—the involuntary hope that lingers, even when everything else has gone quiet."

Hope said, "She's not coming back."

"I know."

"Then why do you still check?"

"Because knowing and feeling are different things."

"That's insane."

"Yeah, well. Here we are."

November 14th. Day Seventy-Four.

Took Magnolia to the levee early. Fog rolling off the water like a horror movie. Couldn't see more than ten feet ahead.

She saw something—turtle, probably—and went charging after it. Straight into the water. The look on her face when she realized she was swimming was priceless. Pure shock. Like she'd betrayed herself.

I laughed. Actually laughed. First time in weeks.

Had to wade in to get her. Soaked my shoes. Ruined my morning. Worth it.

"Maybe that's all life is now—collecting seconds where you forget to be sad."

Hope was quiet on the walk back. Sometimes even ghosts know when not to talk.

November 15th. Day Seventy-Five.

Seventy-five days. Three-quarters of the way to one hundred.

"I'm not okay. But I'm also not broken in the same way I used to be."

The cracks are still there. But they're different. Older. Less likely to split wide open at the smallest pressure.

I'm learning the difference between broken and healing. They look almost the same from the outside. But one is getting worse and one is getting different.

Maybe healing isn't getting better. Maybe it's just getting different. Learning new ways to carry the same weight. Finding out which scars are worth keeping and which ones need to be let go.

Went through my phone today. Deleted the screenshots of our conversations. The ones I'd read a hundred times looking for signs I'd missed, warnings I'd ignored, love I'd imagined.

Kept one photo. Not of her. Of the mountains in Washington. The view from the top of that trail I climbed every morning. Need to remember that I could climb mountains once. That my legs worked. That my lungs worked. That some part of me, even in the worst of it, kept trying.

Hope watched me delete everything. "You'll regret that."

"Probably."

"You're erasing me."

"You were never there to erase."

"Then what am I?"

"Grief," I said. "You're just grief with a voice."

She thought about that. "Is that all?"

"No. You're also love with nowhere to go."

She smiled then. First time in weeks. "That's the nicest thing you've said about me in a while."

"Don't get used to it."

But we both knew I didn't mean it. We were stuck together, Hope and I. Two sides of the same broken coin. Learning to coexist. Learning to be quiet together. Learning that sometimes love means letting go and holding on at the same time.

"We're changing," she said.

"Yeah."

"I don't know if I like it."

"Me neither."

"But we're still here."

"Yeah. We are."

And maybe that's something. Maybe surviving is its own kind of victory. Maybe showing up broken is better than not showing up at all.

Seventy-five days without alcohol.

Seventy-five days of learning to live with ghosts.

Seventy-five days of discovering that recovery isn't a destination—it's just another way of being lost, but sober.

And somehow, that's enough for today.

Tomorrow is Day Seventy-Six. Another day to not drink. Another day to miss her. Another day to pretend I'm getting better while secretly just getting different.

But I'll be here for it. Broken, haunted, seventy-five days sober.

Still here.

Chapter 17: The First 100 (Part V)

November 16th. Day Seventy-Six.

I woke up and didn't feel like dying.

Didn't feel like much of anything, really. But that in itself felt... new.

No one celebrates that part of sobriety—the days that feel like nothing. Not sad. Not better. Just neutral. But maybe those are the ones that matter most.

"I didn't think I'd make it to seventy-six. So many moments where I was sure I'd burn it all down. But here I am, quietly surviving. And maybe that's enough today."

Mom noticed the shift. She didn't say anything. Just handed me my coffee with a look that said, *I see you.*

And I nodded back like, *Yeah. I see me too.*

November 18th. Day Seventy-Eight.

There was a smell in the air today. Cold coming in. Not real cold—it's Louisiana—but enough to feel like change.

I cleaned my room. Like deep-cleaned. Closet. Drawers. Under the bed. Found a shirt I wore all the time in Washington. Still smelled like pine and cigarette smoke and something I couldn't name.

I held it for a long time. Then I folded it and put it in a drawer.

"Some ghosts deserve a shelf. Others just need a place to rest."

Hope didn't say much. She just watched. That's been her thing lately—less talk, more presence. Like she knows her role is fading but doesn't want to admit it yet.

November 20th. Day Eighty.

I ate dinner with Mom and didn't check my phone once.

It was gumbo night. The good kind—dark roux, real sausage, extra crab. The kind of meal that reminds you the world still has flavor. Still has culture. Still has love.

"Recovery is eating a second bowl of gumbo because you want to, not because you need to feel something."

Hope sat across from me at the table, quieter than usual.

"You're changing," she said. "You don't look for me like you used to."

"I know."

"Do you miss me?"

"Every day."

"Then why are you letting go?"

"Because I have to."

She nodded. "I'll still be around."

"I know."

We didn't speak again for the rest of the night.

——

November 23rd. Day Eighty-Three.

Justin Mayeur

Thanksgiving.

It felt hollow last year—like I was trespassing in my own life. This year, I carved the turkey. Magnolia got the neck bone. My sister brought a pie. We didn't talk about the arrest, the court date, the wreckage. We just passed plates and laughed at dumb stories and pretended for a few hours that the world hadn't cracked open.

"Gratitude doesn't erase pain. It just gives you a reason to sit beside it."

Hope didn't show up at dinner. That was new. Her chair was empty.

——

November 26th. Day Eighty-Six.

Went for a long walk alone. Didn't bring Magnolia. Just needed space.

The trees were bare now, branches like ribs against a gray sky. I walked until I didn't know what time it was anymore. Just me and the gravel and the ghosts.

I sat on the levee and finally asked the question I'd been avoiding.

"What if this is all there is?"

Hope appeared beside me, not unkind.

"Then you make peace with it," she said.

"I don't know how."

"You're already doing it."

We sat there a while. Not talking. Just existing. That felt like enough.

———

November 30th. Day Ninety.

Ninety days. Three months.

I marked it in my notebook. Didn't tell anyone. No cake. No celebration. Just me, a blinking cursor, and the realization that I hadn't had a drink in ninety days and yet still didn't know who I was without one.

"I don't miss alcohol. I miss who I thought I was when I was drinking—romantic, tortured, worth saving. Turns out I'm just me. Still tortured. Still trying. Still here."

Hope appeared late that night. She didn't speak. Just laid down beside me like she used to.

"I'm proud of you," she finally said.

"You're not real."

"Neither are half the things that kept you alive."

We fell asleep to the sound of Magnolia snoring on the floor.

———

December 4th. Day Ninety-Four.

Dreamt about the RV again. Only this time, I wasn't trapped. I was just... there. Reading. Magnolia curled up beside me. No desperation. No haunting. Just stillness.

When I woke up, I didn't feel sad. Just nostalgic. Like remembering a place that once saved you but can't anymore.

"I am no longer defined by the places I broke down in."

Hope showed up with coffee. "You're getting poetic again."

"It's how I process."

"It's how you hide."

"Maybe it's both."

She smiled. "You're closer than you think."

———

December 7th. Day Ninety-Seven.

The fog returned.

No trigger. No reason. Just back—thick and smothering. A reminder that the ghost never really leaves. She just takes naps.

But I made it through the day. Did laundry. Took Magnolia for a walk. Ate dinner. Brushed my teeth.

"Some days, the win is not collapsing."

Hope stood outside the bathroom door.

"You still want to call her."

"I know."

"You still think she'll answer."

"I know."

"You still believe she loves you."

"I know."

She stepped closer. "Do you want me to go?"

I shook my head. "Not yet."

———

December 10th. Day One Hundred.

I sat at the kitchen table before anyone else was awake. Just me, my coffee, and this odd silence that didn't ache.

No parade. No finish line. Just breath. Just morning. Just the knowledge that I'd survived one hundred days.

Hope appeared beside me, not sad, not triumphant—just there.

"Did it help?" she asked.

"Writing?"

"Not drinking."

I thought about it.

"No," I said. "But I think it helped me remember why I started."

She nodded.

"I'm not healed," I said.

"I never asked you to be."

"I'm not sure who I am without you."

"That's okay," she said. "Figure it out."

I closed the notebook. Took another sip of coffee. Magnolia nudged my leg, ready for our walk.

One hundred days.

No miracle. No epiphany. Just the quiet certainty that something was different.

Not better. Just different.

And sometimes, that's all recovery is—the slow, silent changing of the tide.

———

Chapter 18: The Edge of Exposure

I never intended to go public.

For ninety-nine days, everything I wrote stayed locked in notebooks, buried in my phone, scrawled on whatever surface would hold ink. Private confessions to no one. Letters to Hope I'd never send. Fragments of a person trying to reassemble himself in silence.

But on Day 100, something shifted. Not healing—I was nowhere near healed. Not wisdom—I had none to offer. Just this bone-deep exhaustion of carrying it all alone. This quiet, desperate need to be witnessed.

That night, after making it through another sober day, I opened X—Twitter, whatever they were calling it now—and stared at the empty post box. The cursor blinked like a heartbeat, waiting. Hope sat beside me on Mom's couch, watching. She'd been quieter lately, her voice more like wind through leaves than the hurricane it used to be.

"You sure about this?" she asked.

"No."

"Then why?"

I didn't answer because I didn't know. Maybe because isolation was killing me slower than alcohol ever had. Maybe because I needed to prove I existed beyond this couch, this house, this loop in my head. Maybe because someone, somewhere, needed to know they weren't the only one drowning.

My fingers found the keys:

"A milestone I never imagined reaching—yet here I am, sober for one hundred days."

Delete. Too triumphant. I wasn't celebrating; I was surviving.

"Day 100. Still here."

Delete. Too vague.

Finally, I just wrote what was true:

"A milestone I never imagined reaching—yet here I am, sober for one hundred days. It's strange how love and fear can coexist."

The words poured out. About being terrified of being alone. About being terrified of my own feelings. About how sobriety hadn't erased those fears but forced me to face them without anesthetic.

I wrote about Hope—not her real name, never her real name—and how loving her had started long before I jumped off that wall. How deep down, I'd known that meeting her meant my life had to change. How I hadn't realized how turbulent that change would be.

"I still think about Hope every day. Sobriety didn't take away how much I love her; it just made me see more clearly how important it is to heal myself."

My finger hovered over "Post" for so long the screen dimmed.

"Once you put it out there," Hope whispered, "you can't take it back."

"Maybe that's the point."

I hit post.

The response wasn't immediate or overwhelming. A few likes trickled in. Someone on Day 12 commented: "Needed this today." Someone on Day 1,047 wrote: "It gets different, not better. Different is enough."

Different is enough. I sat with that for hours.

For the first time in months, I didn't feel invisible.

Day 101 came easier. Not easy—nothing about this was easy—but the seal was broken. The secret was out. I was one of those people now. The ones who posted about their recovery online. The ones I used to scroll past, thinking they were either braver or more broken than me.

Turns out we're all both.

"I never saw it coming. I was married, caught in a nightly cycle of drinking, until I looked into Hope's eyes and saw the family I'd been missing."

That post hurt to write. Admitting what I'd lost. What I'd thrown away. The life I could have built if I hadn't been so committed to destroying myself every night.

Mom found me typing late that night, Magnolia sprawled across my feet. I'd made it through Day 101 sober and was finally documenting it.

"Can't sleep?"

"Trying something."

She looked at the screen, saw the interface. "Is this helping?"

"I don't know. Maybe. It feels... necessary."

She nodded, made tea, didn't push. We sat in the kind of silence that only comes after you've seen someone at their absolute worst and chosen to stay anyway.

"Your father called today," she said finally. "Asked how you were doing."

"What'd you tell him?"

"That you're alive. That you're trying. That you're not hiding anymore."

"I'm unemployed, living on your couch, posting my feelings on the internet."

"You're fighting. That's what matters."

Hope laughed, but it was soft, almost fond. "She doesn't know what you really did."

But I was learning not to listen to every ghost in my head.

By Day 102, I had a rhythm. Make it through the day sober. Process the weight. Write about it at night. Post it. Watch strangers respond with their own weight.

"Sobriety isn't just giving up alcohol—it's battling the regrets, fears, and the longing left behind."

I wrote about the RV. About isolation so complete it had felt like being buried alive. About thinking that getting in shape would somehow win Hope back, as if abs could undo the damage I'd done.

"The irony? Hope always saw my worth, even when I couldn't see it myself."

Someone messaged: "How do you keep going when you can't see your own worth?"

I stared at that question until my eyes burned. Finally wrote back: "You borrow other people's vision until your own clears up. And you trust that it will clear up, even when it feels impossible."

"Look at you," Hope said, "playing guru."

"Just sharing what I'm learning."

"Which isn't much."

"No. But it's something."

Day 103 was the hard one. The post about the wall.

"4 AM. Cold concrete beneath me. A towering wall in front of me. I was lost, disoriented, and confused."

I'd never told the full truth publicly. The crawling. The two hours of screaming for help that no one heard. The runners in the distance whose breath I could see but who couldn't see me dying.

"How small and invisible I felt."

The comments on that one were different. Longer. More raw. People sharing their own walls, their own 4 AM moments, their own invisible screaming.

One stopped me cold: "I jumped too. Different wall, same darkness. Day 238 clean. Thank you for making me feel less alone."

Less alone. That's all any of us really want, isn't it?

Days 104 and 105 blurred together. Writing about therapy, about being afraid of myself, about Hope becoming my imaginary friend when I had nothing else.

"Imagine that—35 years old and clinging to someone who wasn't even there."

But she had been there, in a way. Her memory, her impact, the way she'd changed my understanding of what love could be. Even if I'd twisted it into something unhealthy, the core of it—that pure recognition of another soul—that was real.

The Tin Man post on Day 108 brought unexpected connection. Someone had shared an image—the Tin Man choosing a heart over a brain because "intelligence doesn't make a person happy, and happiness is the most beautiful thing in the world."

I wrote about feeling like that Tin Man. Bullied, outcast, but still choosing love. Still believing in the power of an open heart even when it had led me to destruction.

"Hope challenged me to heal, to grow, to change. She asked me to love myself, a task that feels more difficult than anything I've ever faced."

"You're getting maudlin," Hope observed.

"I'm being honest."

"Same thing sometimes."

Day 109 almost broke me. Woke up feeling distant from everything, even my own recovery.

"Some days are harder than others. Today is one of those days."

The response to that post shocked me. Dozens of people saying "me too." Saying "thank you for being honest about the hard days." Saying "I needed to know someone else was struggling today."

We're all so desperate to know we're not the only ones barely holding on.

Day 110 brought clarity about why I was really doing this.

"Purpose—what is that, really? I think that's all Hope ever wanted for me: to love myself and to find a purpose that was mine."

I wrote about discovering One Step Collective, about Rocky's words to Creed becoming my lifeline. About how writing had become my way of making sense of the chaos.

"A year ago, I couldn't walk. I was locked in that RV, drowning in dabs to avoid reality."

The admission of the substance use disorder. The freedom in finally naming it. The realization that I wasn't alone in this particular hell.

"Now, I write not to Hope but to you, to me, to anyone who might understand what it means to fight the same battle."

"You're not writing to me anymore?" Hope asked, and for the first time, she sounded sad about it.

"I'm writing to everyone. Including you. Especially you. But not only you."

She was quiet after that. Not gone, but... settled somehow. Like maybe she understood.

Days 111 through 114 became about finding pieces of myself I'd lost.

"I think about that little boy I used to be. The one who smiled despite everything."

The child who believed in magic. Who saw wonder in ordinary things. Who hadn't yet learned to numb himself to survive.

"I want to find him again. I want his smile back."

On Day 112, I asked the question that had been haunting me:

"What is love? How far would you go for the person who makes you believe in something greater—who makes you believe in yourself?"

The responses varied. Some said love was letting go. Some said it was holding on. Some said it was learning the difference.

But one comment hit different: "Love is becoming someone worthy of the love you received, even if the person who gave it is gone."

I read that fifty times.

Day 114 felt like a checkpoint, not an ending.

"I'm staring down this loop again, half-determined it'll never end and half-wishing I could just see you on the other side of all this."

I wrote about recovering my notes from the RV. Time capsules of my lowest moments. Evidence of how far I'd fallen and how far I'd climbed.

"The world calls it trauma bonding. They tell me to let go. But how do you let go of the one thing that made you believe in something better?"

Someone responded: "You don't let go. You let it transform. You let it become fuel instead of fire."

That night, for the first time, Hope didn't say anything. She just sat with me while I scrolled through the responses, reading strangers' stories, their pain, their hope—lowercase h—their determination to keep going.

"You did something," she finally said.

"Did I?"

"You made yourself visible. That's not nothing."

"It's not enough either."

"No," she agreed. "But it's a start."

Two weeks of public vulnerability. Two weeks of daily posts. Two weeks of discovering that my mess could be medicine for someone else, even when I was still sick myself.

The numbers didn't matter—followers, likes, whatever metrics people tracked. What mattered was the connection. The DMs from people saying they didn't drink tonight because of something I wrote. The comments from people on Day 1 seeing someone on Day 114 and thinking maybe they could make it too.

I wasn't healed. Wasn't even close. The ghosts were still there—Hope quieter but present, the addiction dormant but not dead, the trauma scabbed but not scarred.

But I was visible. I was witnessed. I was part of something larger than my own pain.

Every night, I ended with the same signature: *One Step. One Punch. One Round.* 🛡

Not because I was strong. Not because I was winning. But because I was still standing, still swinging, still moving forward even when forward felt like barely holding ground.

The edge of exposure was terrifying. Every post felt like jumping off a different kind of wall. But this time, people could see me. This time, when I screamed for help, someone heard.

And sometimes—not always, but sometimes—I could hear them screaming too, and I could whisper back: "I see you. You're not alone. Keep going."

That had to be enough. Because it was all I had.

Hope faded a little more each day, from hurricane to wind to whisper. Not gone—she'd never be gone—but integrated somehow. Part of the story instead of the whole story. A chapter, not the book.

"Are you okay with that?" I asked her one night.

"Are you?" she replied.

I thought about it. About the months of obsession. The loops. The wall. The crawling. The slow, painful reconstruction of something resembling a life.

"I'm learning to be."

"Then so am I."

Maybe that's all recovery really is—learning to be okay with not being okay, and sharing that not-okayness with others who understand. Making yourself visible in your messiness. Letting your wounds become windows for light to get in—and maybe, if you're lucky, for light to get out too.

Day 114 wasn't an ending. Wasn't a beginning. It was just another day of choosing to show up, to speak up, to stand up even when standing felt impossible.

But I posted anyway.

Because that's what we do. We show up for each other, broken and healing, lost and finding, one post at a time.

One   Step.   One   Punch.   One   Round.

Chapter 19: The Weight of Small Things

By Day 115, I'd discovered something unsettling about public recovery: the posts were getting harder, not easier.

Not the writing itself—that had become muscle memory. Wake up, survive the day, document survival, hit post, read responses, sleep, repeat. But the weight of being witnessed was accumulating. Every day, more eyes on my mess. Every day, more people invested in my counter climbing. Every day, the fear that I'd let them down growing heavier.

That night, I shifted my focus to smaller things. Micro-goals. Daily rituals. Making my bed. Prepping coffee the night before. Tiny victories that felt both monumental and pathetic.

"Maybe it's a single round of boxing before I open my phone or a single moment of silence before I fill my head with racing thoughts. Tiny, yes—but every time I follow through, it's proof I can keep going."

Mom watched me type from the doorway. "You're different when you write now."

"Different how?"

"Heavier. Like it costs you something."

She was right. The early posts had been desperate flares shot into darkness. These felt like carrying stones uphill. Each one necessary but exhausting.

"Sometimes I look at the bigger picture and panic," I wrote. "There's so much to fix, so far to go."

Hope sat in her usual spot, fainter now but still present. "You're losing steam," she observed.

"I'm finding balance."

"You're getting tired of performing your pain."

"Maybe." I looked at her—or where I imagined her to be. "Weren't you tired of being my only audience?"

She didn't answer.

Day 116 brought the question I'd been avoiding: Why was I so afraid to let go of Hope?

Not just afraid—incapable. Every morning I woke up with thoughts of making it back to her. Every night I fell asleep plotting paths that might lead to reconciliation. My mind constantly revolved around her, around us, around the possibility of somehow fixing what I'd broken.

I couldn't accept she was gone. Wouldn't accept it. The idea of her, the possibility of her, the version of the future I'd built around her—it all still felt more real than the present I was actually living.

"For so long, she was my lighthouse, guiding me through the darkest storm of my life."

The truth I was learning: healing wasn't about holding onto the past—it was about embracing the future with all its uncertainty. But knowing that and doing it were different animals entirely.

I wrote about my fears. Not being able to feel like this again. Never having the family I'd dreamed of. Never finding the courage to be authentic. The terror that I'd ruined everything with my mistakes.

Someone commented: "Letting go doesn't mean it wasn't real. It means you're ready for what's next."

I read that twenty times before I could breathe normally again.

Day 117 was one of those rare days when I felt lighter. Not happy—I wasn't sure I remembered what happy felt like—but less crushed. The gym had become both refuge and reminder. A place to hide in plain sight, surrounded by people but utterly alone.

"How do you navigate the uncertain paths towards change, where the promise of transformation meets the fear of the unknown?"

I wrote about shadows. About fighting to love myself while holding onto fragments of hope that kept slipping through my fingers. About staring into the abyss and finding reasons to turn back.

"I'm learning that change doesn't need to be validated by others to be real," I posted. "It doesn't diminish in value because it's solitary."

The responses were quieter on that one. Like I'd hit something too true for easy engagement. Sometimes the deepest cuts don't bleed where others can see them.

Day 118 nearly broke me open.

"I only ever wanted a kiss."

I stared at those words for an hour before posting them. They sounded so simple. So innocent. But that kiss had become everything—my anchor, my escape, my reason for surviving those months in the RV.

"When isolation became unbearable, when my mind raced and spiraled into darkness, I'd close my eyes. I could see that moment, feel it pulsing through me as if it were about to happen."

The kiss that never came. Always just out of reach. Vanishing the moment before contact, leaving me gasping in the dark. Like trying to hold water in cupped hands—the harder I gripped, the faster it slipped away.

In the RV, I'd spent hours crafting the perfect reunion. We'd run toward each other in slow motion, probably in a field somewhere, probably with music swelling. Hallmark Channel worthy. Embarrassingly naive. But in the depths of isolation, that imagined moment had been the only thing keeping me from complete dissolution.

"I'd crafted this elaborate, almost laughable Hallmark-worthy reunion in my mind. But in the depths of my struggle, it was all I had to keep going."

I wrote about forgetting something more important than any kiss: how to love myself. The words felt foreign on the screen. Love myself? The concept was like trying to speak a language I'd never learned.

"Love myself? That's still a foreign concept to me. Quite frankly, it feels like a language I'll never understand."

The hardest part to write: how letting go felt like admitting insanity. Like acknowledging that the spark, the connection, the energy between us—maybe I'd invented it all. Maybe I'd been so lost, so broken, that I'd created a lifeline out of nothing but desperate need.

"'All about me,' she said once," I typed. "And she was right. It wasn't supposed to be that way, but I couldn't see it then."

Hope stirred at that, more present than she'd been in days. "You're finally understanding."

"Understanding what?"

"That I was right. That it was all in your head."

"No," I said, surprised by my own clarity. "I'm understanding that it being about me doesn't make it less real. Just more complicated. More unfair to you. But not less real."

She was quiet for a long moment. "You still think it was real?"

"I know it was real. Whether you felt it too—that's the question I'll never get answered. And maybe that's the point. Maybe some questions are meant to stay questions."

The comments on that post were raw. Visceral. People sharing their own phantom kisses. Their own imagined futures. Their own inability to let go of something that might never have existed outside their need for it to exist.

One comment stopped me: "The cruelest ghosts are the ones made from hope instead of memory."

We were all haunted by different ghosts wearing the same faces. All of us clinging to kisses that existed more in possibility than reality.

Day 119 brought unexpected gratitude.

"I've stared Death in the face."

I wrote about blocking out pieces of time to save what sanity remained. About the contrast between the old me— Netflix binges and bourbon nightcaps—and whatever I was becoming now.

But the real revelation was my mom. Our relationship had transformed during recovery. Communication had never been our family's strong suit, but something had shifted. The 2,500-mile road trip we'd taken together—dodging interstates, making memories—had rebuilt something I hadn't realized was broken.

"Just me, Mom, two cats, a dog, and the bits of my life I could fit into my vehicle. Not much, but enough."

"You don't write about me much," Mom said that night.

"I don't know how."

"Why?"

"Because writing about you means admitting how much I needed you. How much I still need you."

She hugged me then. Long and quiet. The kind of hug that says everything without words.

"Sometimes you have to come back to where you started to remember who you were," I posted later. "Only then can you truly figure out who you are now."

Day 120 felt like a checkpoint.

"It's wild to think that not too long ago I was still trapped in that cycle—using alcohol as my own slow way out of everything I couldn't face."

The biggest shift: doing things for me now. Not for Hope or anyone else. Making AI art. Journaling. Connecting with communities I'd never imagined joining. Small things that would have seemed impossible months ago.

"Little by little, I'm choosing me."

But even as I typed it, I wondered if it was true. Was I choosing me, or was I just performing recovery for an audience now? Had I traded one kind of performance for another?

Hope was barely visible now, more suggestion than presence. "You're questioning everything again."

"That's what I do."

"It's exhausting."

"For both of us."

Day 121 brought the question that haunted every morning: "Will I ever really get my mind back?"

The night before, I'd made the mistake of watching a documentary on the Stanford Prison Experiment. Watching those volunteers break down, lose themselves, become either guard or prisoner in their minds—it felt too familiar. Not the same, but adjacent. Close enough to make my skin crawl.

I kept searching for parallels, for research, for any voice that could mirror what I'd been through. Prolonged isolation does things to the brain that we don't fully understand. Changes neural pathways. Rewrites the stories we tell ourselves about who we are and what's real.

"Not all walls are made of concrete. Sometimes, they're made of memories and what-ifs."

A friend had mentioned how people with complex PTSD sometimes bounce back quicker than those who've endured prolonged isolation. It wasn't about minimizing trauma—it was about understanding the particular kind of breaking that happens when you're alone with your thoughts for too long. When your own mind becomes both prison and warden.

During those months in the RV, Hope had been my lifeline. Not the real Hope—she was living her life, unaware of the mythology I was building around her memory. But my version of Hope, the one who lived in my head, who promised that if I could just get back to her, everything would be okay.

"I convinced myself that making it back to my friend would be my ticket out of my mind's own prison—like reuniting with them would somehow free me from the loop I was stuck in."

When reality fell short—when she looked at me with confusion instead of recognition, when the reunion played out nothing like my fantasies—I'd drowned disappointment at the bar. Bourbon became the new escape route when Hope proved to be a door that wouldn't open.

"Even now, 121 days into a sobriety I once thought was impossible, I still question whether I can explain any of this in a way people truly understand."

The comments were sparse that day. Sometimes truth is too heavy for hearts to hold. Sometimes witnessing someone else's reality reminds us too much of our own prisons, our own walls made of memories.

That night, I didn't check the responses. Didn't count the likes. Just sat with Mom watching some cooking show, Magnolia snoring between us, Hope a whisper so faint I could almost pretend she was just the house settling.

"You're changing," Mom said during a commercial, not looking at me directly.

"Good or bad?"

"Different. You're becoming... quieter. More internal."

"I thought the posts were making me more external. More visible."

"No," she said, finally turning to face me. "They're making you more real. There's a difference between being seen and being known. You're learning the difference."

I thought about that. About the weight of small things. About how micro-goals and daily rituals were building something I couldn't quite name yet. About how being witnessed had somehow made me more private, more protective of the parts I wasn't ready to share.

"Do you regret coming home?" she asked suddenly.

The question caught me off guard. "No."

"Even though it feels like failure?"

"It felt like failure," I corrected. "Now it feels like... foundation. Like I had to come back to where I started to figure out where I'm going."

She nodded, satisfied. We watched the rest of the show in comfortable silence, the kind that only comes after you've seen each other at absolute bottom and chosen to stay anyway.

Later, alone in my room, I thought about walls. The concrete ones I'd crawled across after jumping. The invisible ones in the RV. The ones made of memories that still kept me from moving forward. And the new ones I was building—not to keep things out, but to keep something in. Something fragile and unnamed that might, eventually, grow into self-love.

Or at least self-tolerance.

Hope was almost gone now, just the faintest outline where she used to burn bright. Sometimes I had to concentrate to hear her at all.

"I miss you," I told her silently.

"I'm still here," she whispered back, so quiet I might have imagined it.

"I know. That's the problem."

"Is it, though?" she asked. "Or is it the solution?"

I didn't have an answer. Because the truth was, I wasn't learning to live with ghosts instead of for them. I was still living for her—for the possibility of her, for the chance of making it back. Every post, every sober day, every small victory was still, deep down, about proving I could be someone worthy of returning to her.

Learning that some walls aren't meant to come down— they're meant to become windows. Learning that healing isn't about forgetting but about remembering differently. Except I wasn't learning any of that. I was just surviving while my thoughts constantly circled back to her.

The posts would continue tomorrow. Day 122 and beyond. But nothing fundamental had shifted. I was still performing— not just recovery, but the idea that I was moving on.

When really, I was just marking time until I could find my way back to her.

Quietly. Imperfectly. One small victory at a time.

And maybe that's all recovery really is—not some grand transformation, but a series of small surrenders. Letting go of the kiss that never came. Letting go of the person you thought you'd be by now. Letting go of the need to be understood by anyone but yourself.

The weight of small things. It adds up. But so does the lightness that comes from setting some of them down.

Chapter 20: The Echo of Letting Go

Day 122 came with a realization that felt both obvious and impossible: there was no silence anymore, only echoes.

I woke that morning to find myself standing at the same crossroads I'd been circling for months—one path tethered to reality, the other lost in bargaining with what might have been. The difference was, this time I could see both paths clearly. Neither led where I wanted to go.

"It's like there's no true silence, only echoes of moments I'm still not sure I can trust."

The posts had become harder to write. Not because I'd run out of words—God knows I had too many of those—but because I was starting to hear how they sounded. The same story, told slightly differently. The same pain, dressed in new metaphors. The same love, refusing to die.

Hope sat in her usual corner of my consciousness, fainter than ever but somehow more present in her absence. Like how you notice silence more after noise stops.

"You're going in circles," she observed.

"I know."

"You've been at Day 122 before. Not literally, but emotionally. This exact spot."

She was right. Every few weeks, I'd arrive at this same emotional checkpoint. The realization that I needed to let go. The certainty that I couldn't. The exhaustion of holding both truths simultaneously.

"Some days, I wonder if I'm going insane," I wrote. "Other days, I feel the progress."

But what was progress, really? I was doing things for myself now—working out, eating better, staying sober. But every achievement still felt like preparation for a reunion that would never come. Like I was getting ready for a test that had already been canceled.

Day 123 changed everything and nothing.

I woke up knowing something I'd been avoiding for months, a truth that felt like it was breaking me from the inside: Hope was never going to talk to me again.

Not Hope the ghost in my head. The real Hope. My friend. The person who'd inspired me to fight when I had nothing left to fight for.

"To explain how complex and painful that realization is feels almost impossible."

I tried to write about it, but the words came out wrong. How do you explain that someone became your entire world when your world had shrunk to the size of an RV? How do you make people understand that she wasn't just a memory or a thought—she became part of my operating system, code running through every process?

I thought about the hotel again. Always the hotel. That moment when she'd looked at me and I'd seen possibility. Not just romantic possibility—life possibility. The chance to be someone different. Someone better. Someone worthy of the faith I saw in her eyes.

"I never meant to be selfish, but in that space, in those moments, I needed to survive—and she became the only way I could."

The word that kept coming up was exorcism. Not because she was a demon—far from it. But because letting go of her felt like cutting away something that had fused with my bones during those months of isolation. She'd become embedded in my very being.

"The idea of letting go feels like an exorcism," I wrote, then deleted it. Too dramatic. Then wrote it again. Not dramatic enough for what it actually felt like.

That night, I wrote her a letter I'd never send:

"Dear Hope, If this ever finds its way to you, know this: I am sorry. My love is now, and forever will be, unconditional."

I stared at those words until they blurred. Unconditional love. Was that what this was? Or was it just trauma bonding so deep I couldn't tell the difference anymore?

"You're being selfish again," Hope whispered.

"I know."

"Even your letting go is about you."

"I know that too."

"So stop."

"I can't."

And that was the truth that broke me that day. Not that she'd never speak to me again—I'd known that for months.

But that even knowing it, I couldn't stop loving her. Couldn't stop hoping. Couldn't stop holding on to something that had never really been mine to hold.

Day 124 brought what I'd started calling the empty sky feeling.

"Today, I woke up feeling a heaviness that pressed down on every part of me."

The acceptance from yesterday hadn't brought peace. Just sharper focus on what I'd lost. Like cleaning your glasses only to see more clearly how dirty everything else is.

I tried to write about it, but everything came out as metaphor. Peter Pan's shadow. Demons I'd been avoiding. The past as a weight that gets heavier the longer you carry it.

My mind kept fracturing, jumping between timelines. The RV. The hotel. The mountain. The arrest. The wall. Every memory felt equally present, equally now. Time had stopped being linear and started being a spiral—everything happening at once, over and over.

"For years, I got so good at avoiding it that when it finally returned, it felt like my entire world was collapsing."

The truth I kept dancing around: the substances hadn't caused the problem. They'd been the solution to a problem that existed long before I ever took my first drink. The problem of being me. Of never fitting. Of feeling everything too much or nothing at all.

In the RV, the Oxy had dulled the physical pain. The dabs had clouded the mental anguish. But underneath all of it, I'd loved her. Loved her with a desperation that had nothing to do with chemicals and everything to do with survival.

"I loved her so much that every step I took felt like it was for her, for us. But in the process, I forgot to love myself."

Forgot? Had I ever known how in the first place?

Day 125 brought an unexpected gift from my therapist— the friend on the couch, as I'd started calling her in my posts.

"Trauma is not what happened to you," she'd said, quoting someone named Dr. Peter Levine, "but rather what happened in you."

She'd said it before, but I hadn't been ready to hear it. Today, the words landed differently. Like a key finding its lock after months of trying.

What happened to me: jumped off a wall, shattered my ankle, got trapped in an RV, lost my mind, lost my friend, lost everything.

What happened in me: something much older, much deeper. The little boy who never fit in. The teenager who drank to feel normal. The adult who needed someone else to see his worth before he could even consider it might exist.

"Hope didn't just inspire me to fight them; she gave me the courage to stand up to them. I just didn't realize it at the time."

But I'd been fighting the wrong battle. Trying to get back to her instead of forward to myself. Using her as a shield against my own reflection.

"The true battle wasn't with isolation or heartbreak," I wrote. "It was with me."

Hope—the ghost, not the person—laughed softly. "Finally figured that out?"

"I've known it for months."

"Knowing and understanding are different things."

"Like knowing and feeling."

"Exactly."

We sat with that for a while, Hope and I, two parts of the same broken psyche finally agreeing on something.

Justin Mayeur

Day 126 arrived with snow.

In Louisiana. In January. Actual snow, not the ice we sometimes got, but real snow with its thousands of little diamonds sparkling in the sun.

"Snow echoes at the very depth of my soul."

I thought about the north. About why I'd moved there in the first place—to find calmness, beauty, an unspoken connection to something pure. The first winter had been magic. The second winter, I'd been trapped inside, watching it fall while I built walls within walls.

The snow here felt like a message. Like the universe or God or random meteorological chance was trying to tell me something. That beauty could find you even when you'd given up looking for it. That sometimes what you're running toward comes to where you are.

"It's as if the snow followed me, whispering to me from the skies, carrying a message: 'We're waiting for you. Don't lose hope.'"

I'd been seeing eagles too. More in Louisiana than I'd ever seen up north. Every time I saw one, I heard the same message: Take care of yourself. We'll be here when you're ready to return.

But return to what? To who? The person I'd been was gone. The person I was becoming wasn't ready. I existed in this in-between space, neither here nor there, neither then nor now.

"The snow whispers back," I wrote, "love yourself, as you love the snow."

But I didn't know how. The concept remained foreign, a language I'd never learned and wasn't sure I had the capacity to acquire.

Day 127 felt like exhaustion made manifest.

"I woke up today still exhausted by the endless loop in my head, wondering how long this is supposed to last."

Five months sober. In the best physical shape of my life. Surrounded by support—family, therapist, groups. Doing everything "right." And still, my mind felt fractured. My heart more confused than ever.

The little boy inside me was louder today. The one who got picked last. Laughed at. Left behind. He stood at the corner of my memories, not as a ghost but as a presence. Still waiting to be chosen. Still waiting to belong.

"Ever since I was a little boy, I've been running—running from the kid who never fit in."

Maybe that's who Hope had really been—the first person who made that little boy feel seen. Feel chosen. Feel like maybe he could belong somewhere, with someone.

Her words echoed from long ago: "Greatness takes time."

She'd said it to me once, back when I couldn't see past my own failures. Hope had believed in my greatness even when I couldn't believe in my adequacy. If she ever reads this, she should know: those three words kept me alive on days when nothing else could.

But I wasn't trying to be great. I was just trying to be okay. To wake up one morning without the weight. To get through one day without circling back to her. To feel something— anything—that wasn't filtered through the lens of loss.

Day 128 arrived with a strange clarity.

"To say this journey is simple would be a lie."

I'd been telling the same story for 128 days. Recovery. Heartbreak. Hope. Repeat. But something was shifting in the repetition. Like how saying a word over and over makes it lose meaning, then somehow gain new meaning.

"Recovery can feel like I'm writing the same story on repeat. But healing isn't a straight line—it circles back on

itself, revealing something new each time if I'm willing to look."

What I saw today: I couldn't tell where Hope ended and I began. We'd become so entangled in my mind that separating us felt like trying to unbraid water. Was my love genuine or just a product of isolation? Was she my salvation or my symptom?

Maybe both. Maybe neither. Maybe the questions mattered more than the answers.

"Each day, I choose to keep going," I wrote. "One word at a time, one step at a time—hoping that maybe, eventually, I'll find the answers I've been missing."

Hope was barely visible now, just the faintest suggestion of presence.

"You're letting go," she observed.

"No. I'm just learning to hold on differently."

"What's the difference?"

I thought about it. About the snow. About the eagles. About the little boy still waiting to be chosen. About all the ways we carry our ghosts.

"Letting go means it's over. Holding on differently means it continues, just... transformed."

She smiled—I felt it more than saw it. "That's either wisdom or denial."

"Can't it be both?"

Maybe that was the lesson of Day 128. That healing wasn't about resolving contradictions but learning to live with them. That you could love someone forever and still move forward. That you could be broken and building simultaneously.

The echo of letting go wasn't silence. It was the sound of something breaking free while staying tethered. Like an eagle circling higher but never leaving its territory. Like snow falling in Louisiana—impossible but real.

I wasn't ready to let go. Might never be. But I was learning to hold the weight differently. To distribute it across more of myself so no single part broke under the pressure.

And maybe, for today, that was enough.

Chapter 21: The Space Between Versions

Day 129 arrived with a declaration I wasn't sure I believed: *"I'm not here for sympathy. I'm not here for pity. I'm here because, for the first time in my life, I am trying to be truly and authentically me."*

The words looked strange on the screen. Authentically me. As if I knew who that was. As if stripping away the masks and numbing escapes would reveal someone worth being.

But Hope still whispered.

Not the hurricane she used to be. Not even the wind from a month ago. Just this soft presence, almost too quiet to hear, but enough. Enough to make me pause when I wanted to quit. Enough to remind me there was still something worth fighting for.

"Her voice isn't just an echo of someone who once believed in me; it's a lifeline, a thread pulling me back from the edge every time I think I'm about to fall."

My therapist said I was learning to show up for myself. Maybe she was right. But showing up felt less like courage and more like having nowhere else to go. Like a moth drawn to flame not from desire but from biological imperative.

For years, I'd hidden behind screens, substances, walls so high I thought no one could climb them. Now, raw and exposed, I realized hiding wasn't safety—it was suffocation.

"The whisper isn't meant to give me all the answers," I wrote, "but to remind me that the questions are worth exploring."

Hope—barely there now—smiled at that. Or I imagined she did. The line between memory and presence had blurred beyond recognition.

Day 130 brought something unexpected: shame.

Not about the addiction or the arrest or the months of madness. Shame about sharing it all. About being this exposed on a platform of millions, bleeding my story across the internet like some digital confessional.

"I'm here to confront the boy in the mirror I've been running from my whole life."

That boy. Always that boy. The one who got picked last, laughed at, left behind. He stood in every reflection now, waiting. Not accusing. Just... waiting. Like he'd been waiting thirty-five years for me to finally see him.

I wrote about how Hope had carried me when I was too broken to stand. How she'd woken me from a suicide attempt in sub-freezing temperatures. Saved me from crashing my car. Became my lifeline when I had nothing else to hold.

"Thank you for reading," I typed, "and for giving me a reason to keep speaking my truth."

Then added: "More importantly, thank me for finally recognizing my own worth."

The arrogance of that last line made me laugh. Recognizing my own worth. As if I had any idea what that meant.

Day 131 was supposed to be about positives. Building foundations. Moving forward.

"I'm building a foundation of love for myself, a foundation of knowledge, a foundation I can be proud of."

The words felt like lies even as I typed them. Because between the cracks of my busy day, my mind never stopped. There was no peace. I told my therapist I was trying to let go, wanted to believe I was trying. But the truth?

"I don't know if I can truly convince myself. I'm not sure I can accept that Hope and I aren't meant to be."

I tried to avoid absolutes—words like "ever" or "never"—because I wanted to leave the door open. Not just for her, but for the possibility that someone else could make me feel this way again.

But even thinking it felt like betrayal. How could anyone else be Hope? How could I ever feel this way about someone who wasn't her?

"Love always wins, right?"

I wrote it as a question because I didn't know anymore. Maybe love didn't win. Maybe it just persisted, like chronic pain, teaching you to function around it rather than heal from it.

Day 132 introduced a new metaphor: the Passenger.

"Some days, it feels like she's always there—a 'Passenger,' ready to take the wheel at any moment."

I'd been watching Dexter clips online, relating too much to his Dark Passenger. But Hope wasn't dark. Despite everything—the obsession, the loops, the inability to let go—she'd never been destructive. Look how far I'd come since she entered my life. Left a dead relationship. Battled addiction. Emerged stronger.

"Keep listening to that whisper," a friend had said. "It's leading you somewhere worth going."

But where? Every path still led back to her. Every achievement still felt like preparation for a reunion that would never come.

I ate well now. Worked out. Built things I could be proud of. But underneath it all, the same current ran: *What would Hope think of this? Would this make me worthy of her?*

The Passenger never fully took the wheel anymore. But she never left the car either.

Day 133 nearly destroyed me.

"It's always about you, Justin. You, you, you."

Her words. The real Hope's words, not the ghost's. They echoed through me constantly, a diagnosis I couldn't cure.

She was right. It had always been about me. Even my love for her was selfish—needing her to be my salvation, my proof that I was worth saving.

"I spent months trapped in my mind, isolated, holding on to her—my friend—so tightly just to get through the endless nights."

Everything I did, I thought I was doing for her. But I was doing it for me, using her as the reason because I couldn't find my own.

Long before the fall, I'd told her I'd finally found something not worth giving up on. That something was us. The vow had kept me alive through the wall, the RV, the addiction. But it had also kept me selfish, unable to see past my own need.

"To truly love her, I must let go."

The words felt like tearing out something essential. How do you let go of the very thing that saved you? How do you release something so embedded in your code that removing it might cause a system crash?

"I want to look her in the eye and say, 'Hope, I love you. You are free from the grasp I've held you in.'"

But wanting and doing were different creatures. And I was afraid—afraid that letting go meant letting go of the faith that had kept me breathing.

"This is not sadness. This is not heartbreak. This is the essence of me, laid bare."

Day 134 brought the Stanford Prison Experiment back into focus.

Six days. That's all it had taken for those students to lose themselves completely. Six days in a basement playing assigned roles.

"I was trapped inside that RV for six months."

No roles to play. No researchers to intervene. No stop button. Just me and my mind and the relentless echo of my own thoughts.

The prisoners in that experiment had begged to leave. Broken down, sobbed, screamed. Yet many stayed, even knowing it was fake, because their minds had already surrendered.

I understood that. The mind's ability to imprison itself. To create bars from nothing but thought patterns. To become both guard and prisoner simultaneously.

"Maybe the most terrifying thing isn't what people are capable of doing to others. Maybe it's what the mind is capable of doing to itself."

Fifty-three years later, people still studied that experiment. Wrote papers about it. Debated its implications.

I'd been out of the RV for months, and I was still trapped inside it.

Day 135 felt different. Quieter.

"Progress isn't always loud or bold. Sometimes, it's quiet. Sometimes, it's simply staying present."

The fog hadn't lifted, but I was learning to navigate through it. Sleep evaded me, but I'd stopped fighting its absence. Change, even good change, required adjustment.

I wrote about scars telling stories. About survival. About searching for light even when my hands felt too weak to reach for it.

"Hope taught me that. Hope taught me that in every shadow, there's a flicker of light waiting to be seen."

But here was the truth I was beginning to understand: Hope hadn't taught me anything. I'd taught myself, using her as the framework. Every lesson I attributed to her was something I'd known all along but needed permission to believe.

She was fading more each day. Not disappearing—she'd never fully disappear—but transforming. From person to presence to principle. From hurricane to whisper to the space between breaths.

"I write for myself, yes—but I also write for Hope. For you. For anyone who needs a reminder that pain is not permanent."

Except sometimes it was permanent. Sometimes pain didn't go away; you just learned to build around it, like a tree growing around a fence until the metal became part of the wood.

That night, I sat with the silence. Not Hope's silence—my own. The space between who I'd been and who I was becoming. The gap between versions of myself, where nothing quite fit but everything was possible.

Maybe that's what recovery really was. Not healing. Not moving on. Just existing in the space between versions until one day you realized you'd become someone new without noticing the transition.

Maybe I didn't need to stop missing her.

Maybe I just needed to stop waiting for her.

The difference felt seismic, even though nothing had actually changed. Like discovering the prison door had been unlocked all along, but you'd been too afraid to try the handle.

Tomorrow would be Day 136. Another post. Another step. Another chance to exist in this strange space between holding on and letting go.

But tonight, I sat with the quiet truth that had been whispering all along:

She was never coming back. And maybe—just maybe—that was okay.

Not because I was okay with it. But because I was learning to be okay despite it.

Chapter 22: The Quiet Becoming

Day 136 arrived with something I hadn't felt in months: quiet.

Not silence—I'd had plenty of that in the RV. Not the oppressive quiet of depression where everything feels muted. This was different. A stillness that felt almost like progress.

Little by little, we move forward."

I wrote it and then sat with the words, wondering if they were true or just something I needed to believe. The changes I'd been making—small adjustments to sleep, routine, thought patterns—were starting to accumulate. Like sediment settling after a storm, revealing clearer water underneath.

It had been nearly two years since Hope entered my life. Two years since that hotel. Since everything shifted. My mind was still processing it all, still trying to make sense of how one person could alter an entire trajectory.

"She was a reminder of light in the darkness, and today, I hold onto that light."

But the light was different now. Less external beacon, more internal glow. Barely visible, but mine.

Day 137 felt like breathing after holding my breath for months.

"For once, my mind isn't consumed by the usual cacophony of relentless thoughts."

The automatic negative thoughts—ANTs, my therapist called them—had quieted. Not gone, never fully gone, but manageable. Like turning down the volume on a TV you can't turn off.

Hope was still there, of course. Still part of me. But the constant mental storm around her had shifted to something more like weather in the distance—you could see the lightning but couldn't hear the thunder.

"The light at the end of this tunnel doesn't feel so distant anymore."

I walked that day. Actually walked, not the desperate pacing of early sobriety or the mechanical movement of depression. Real walking, with purpose, feeling stronger with each step.

Sleep had been deep the night before. The kind of sleep I'd forgotten existed—where you actually rest instead of just temporarily escaping consciousness.

"It's not a final victory," I wrote, "but it's a step forward, and that's enough."

Maybe that was the lesson. Not that things would suddenly be okay, but that "enough" was a valid destination.

Day 138 brought reflection on the timeline.

"It's been about eighteen months since my entire life began to shift."

Eighteen months. Summer 2023 when I met Hope. The confessions that ended my marriage. November 17 when I jumped. The months in the RV. The arrest. The return home. The posts. The endless fucking posts.

I'd started sharing before-and-after photos. One of me at over 200 pounds, soft and drowning in bourbon every night. Another from recently—lean, sharp, hollow in different ways. The physical transformation was obvious, but the internal work was harder to photograph.

Isolation taught me the depths of loneliness, but it also forced me to face the parts of myself I'd been avoiding

Hope had inspired the change, but I'd done the work. That distinction mattered now. She was the catalyst, not the cause. The spark, not the fire.

"No matter how many times life knocked me down, I stood up again."

But standing up was getting tiresome. Each time took more effort. Each recovery felt more precarious. Like a boxer who keeps getting up but knows he's losing on points.

Day 139 brought a shift in metaphor.

For a long time, I talked about Hope as my lighthouse

The image had sustained me through the darkest months. When I was drowning in that RV, when the walls felt like they were closing in, when my own mind became my worst enemy—she was the light I navigated by. Every decision, every struggle, every small victory was about moving toward that light.

But lighthouses have a purpose—to guide you safely to shore. Once you're there, their job is done. I'd made it to shore months ago, broken and barely breathing, but on solid ground. Yet I kept looking back at the light, wishing I was still at sea because at least then I had something to navigate by.

Now, I realize it's my turn to become my own light."

The words felt presumptuous. Arrogant even. How could I be anyone's light when I could barely illuminate my own path? When most days I still felt like I was stumbling through darkness, hands outstretched, hoping not to hit another wall?

But maybe that was the point. Maybe you didn't need to be bright to be helpful. Maybe just being visible was enough. Maybe other people lost in their own darkness just needed to know someone else was out there, fumbling through the same black space, occasionally finding something solid to hold onto.

I'd started opening my inbox to others' stories. People struggling with their own ghosts, their own RVs, their own walls to jump from. A woman whose husband had left her after twenty years. A man battling addiction while raising two kids alone. A teenager who felt like I did at that age—invisible, worthless, waiting for someone to see them.

Their pain made mine feel less unique, less special. Less like a tragedy and more like just another human experience. We were all walking around with these invisible wounds, these ghost relationships, these versions of ourselves we couldn't quite let go of.

"You are not alone," I wrote to each of them, not sure if I was talking to them or myself. Maybe both. Maybe that was how it worked—you said the things to others that you needed to hear yourself, and somehow in the saying, they became slightly more true.

Day 140 was sparse. Focused.

"The Power of I."

Three words that would have meant nothing to me six months ago. Back then, "I" was the enemy. "I" was the failure. "I" was the person who'd ruined everything, who couldn't be trusted, who needed someone else—Hope—to provide meaning and direction.

No fancy quotes that day. No elaborate metaphors. Just me, myself, and I. The trinity of isolation that had nearly killed me now reformed as something else. Not loneliness but solitude. Not abandonment but independence.

I was creating again. Not just posts but actual things— videos that probably looked amateur to anyone with skill, images crafted with AI that meant nothing to anyone but me. Digital art born from prompts I could barely articulate. "Make something that shows isolation but also hope." "Create an image of someone becoming themselves."

The AI didn't judge. Didn't ask why I was making art at 3 AM instead of sleeping. Didn't need to know the backstory. It just created based on what I fed it, and somehow that felt like a metaphor for something I couldn't quite name.

"This journey is about letting go, accepting myself, and learning to love me for who I am."

Love myself. The phrase still felt foreign, like trying to speak with someone else's mouth. But I was practicing. Each day, small attempts at self-compassion. Not because I believed it yet, but because the alternative had nearly killed me.

The Power of I. Not the power over anyone else. Not the power to win someone back or prove something. Just the simple, revolutionary power of existing as myself, by myself, for myself.

I thought about all the energy I'd spent trying to become someone Hope could love. The hours in the gym not for health but for her hypothetical approval. The books I'd read because I thought they'd make me more interesting to her. The personality modifications, the constant editing of myself, the exhausting performance of being someone worth returning to.

What if I just... stopped?

What if I became someone I could tolerate instead of someone she might love?

The thought felt like betrayal and liberation simultaneously. Like I was giving up on the only thing that had mattered while finally picking up something that might actually save me.

Day 141 surprised me with its normalcy.

I went to the gym. Actually went, not just thought about it or planned to go or told myself I'd go tomorrow. Walked through those doors like a normal person doing a normal thing. Signed up for a membership with my shaking hands, trying not to think about how this was another commitment I might fail to keep.

The sauna afterward was a revelation. I'd forgotten what it felt like to sweat without panic. To feel heat that wasn't shame. To sit in discomfort that had an end point, a door I could open whenever I chose.

I talked to a realtor about possibilities. Dabbled in the stock market like someone with a future worth investing in. Drank coffee without bourbon. Walked dogs who didn't care about my past, only whether I had treats and was headed somewhere interesting.

"I'd be lying if I said I didn't miss my mountains."

The mountains where I'd hiked every morning before the fall. Where Hope and I had that conversation about wildness, about being untamed. Where I'd felt closest to the person she believed I could be. The trails knew my feet. The views knew my eyes. The elevation knew my lungs.

But the mountains would wait. They weren't going anywhere. Mountains had patience I was trying to learn.

"The sun rose today, and it set, just like it always does. And in between, I kept moving forward."

There was something profound in that simplicity. The sun didn't care about my trauma. The world kept spinning regardless of my pain. My heartbreak wasn't even a footnote in the universe's story. And somehow that was comforting—knowing that my drama wasn't the center of the universe, just another story among billions.

Small victories, I called them in the post. But were they small? Going to the gym when your body had been both prison and escape route. Talking to a realtor when you'd convinced yourself you'd never have a future worth planning for. Making business moves when six months ago you couldn't make it from the couch to the bathroom without help.

Maybe calling them small was another way of minimizing my progress. Another way of saying it didn't count unless Hope saw it, unless she knew how far I'd come.

"I'd be lying if I said I didn't miss my mountains," I'd written. But what I meant was: I'd be lying if I said I didn't miss who I was in those mountains. Who I was with her. Who I thought I could become.

The gym membership card sat in my wallet like a promise I wasn't sure I could keep. But I'd kept harder promises. Stayed sober when every cell screamed for relief. Kept posting when the words felt like pulling teeth. Kept waking up when sleep felt safer than consciousness.

One step, one punch, one round at a time. The mantra had carried me this far. Maybe it could carry me a little further.

Day 142 was about presence.

Some days, creativity flows effortlessly."

I'd spent the day lost in creating—videos, images, words that might never be read. It felt good to disappear into something that wasn't her, wasn't the past, wasn't the endless loop of what-if.

"On quieter days, when words feel elusive, I won't force them."

This was new. The acceptance that not every day needed documentation. That sometimes showing up was enough, even if you had nothing to say. That presence could speak louder than words.

Hope was barely there now. Just the faintest suggestion, like the smell of someone's perfume after they've left the room. Still recognizable but no longer overwhelming.

That night, I didn't write a long post. Didn't bare my soul to the internet. Just acknowledged the day had happened, I'd survived it, and tomorrow would bring another chance to practice being human.

Seven days. 136 to 142. Nothing dramatic happened. No breakthroughs. No breakdowns. Just the quiet work of becoming whoever I was going to be next.

The posts were getting shorter. Not because I had less to say, but because I needed less validation. The comments still came—people sharing their struggles, offering support, telling me I mattered. But I was learning to believe it might be true even without their confirmation.

Hope—the real Hope, not the ghost—was probably living her life somewhere, unaware that I still wrote about her every day. The thought no longer destroyed me. It just was. Like the sun rising and setting. Like breathing. Like all the things that happen whether we notice them or not.

I thought about the lighthouse metaphor again. How I'd said it was my turn to become my own light. But maybe that was wrong. Maybe the point wasn't to become a lighthouse at all. Maybe it was just to learn to see in the dark. To navigate by stars instead of spotlights. To trust that even dim light was enough to take the next step.

The quiet was becoming comfortable. Not the desperate quiet of depression or the frantic quiet of anxiety. Just... quiet. The sound of someone learning to exist without emergency. Without crisis. Without the constant need to be saved or to save someone else.

Day 142 ended like all the others—survived, documented, released. But something had shifted in these seven days. Something subtle but significant.

I was no longer writing to Hope, or for Hope, or about Hope as the central character.

I was just writing.

And maybe that was the quietest, most profound becoming of all.

Chapter 23: Becoming the Storyteller

Day 143 arrived with a discovery that felt both foreign and inevitable: I was creating art.

Not with brushes or pencils—I'd never had those kinds of hands. But with words shaped into prompts, turned into images that somehow captured what I couldn't say directly. AI art, people would scoff. As if the medium mattered more than the message. As if the act of creation itself wasn't what was keeping me breathing.

"It feels strange," I wrote that morning, "sitting here and telling you that I enjoy creating art."

Strange was an understatement. The kid who got picked last, who spent decades believing he had nothing worth sharing, was now spending hours crafting posts where image and quote and meaning all tied together into something that felt—dare I say it—beautiful.

Hope watched from her usual corner of my consciousness, quieter these days but still present. Not the hurricane she'd been. Not even the whisper she'd become. More like the space between heartbeats—there if you paid attention, gone if you didn't.

"You're an artist now?" she asked, and I couldn't tell if she was mocking or curious.

"I'm something," I replied.

And that was true. After 143 days of sobriety, I was finally something other than just broken. Not fixed—God knows, not fixed. But creating. Building. Shaping the chaos inside into forms other people could see, could respond to, could find their own meaning in.

I could do this all day. And I did. Losing myself in the process of creation, letting my mind release what it had been holding. Each image generated felt like exhaling a breath I'd been holding since the RV. Each post shared was a message in a bottle, thrown into the digital ocean with no expectation of response but needing to be sent anyway.

"She's still there," I admitted in my journal. "She'll always be there."

But the admission felt different now. Less like confession, more like acknowledgment. Hope—the person, the memory, the ghost—had become part of my foundation. Not the whole structure anymore, just one of the stones everything else was built on.

"Maybe that isn't such a bad thing," I wrote. "After all, I named her Hope for a reason."

Day 144 brought something I'd almost forgotten existed: consecutive good days.

I spent the afternoon with Mom, not in the desperate way I had those first weeks home, but actually present. Cherishing the simple moments—her laugh at something on TV, the way she still cut the crusts off sandwiches like I was seven, the comfortable silence of two people who'd weathered storms together.

Between these moments, I was building. Not just art now, but knowledge. Reading about recovery, about trauma, about the brain's ability to rewire itself even after decades of damage. Building a foundation of understanding to match the foundation of creative expression.

"I'm constructing a foundation I'm finally starting to be proud of," I wrote.

The words felt tentative, like testing ice on a pond. But they held. The foundation held.

All the changes—the gym routine, the creative work, the learning—kept me so focused, so locked in, that I didn't have time to think. And maybe that was the point. Maybe thinking had always been my problem. Maybe doing was the solution I'd been avoiding all along.

Hope was quiet that day. So quiet I almost forgot she was there. Almost.

Day 145 cracked something open.

"It feels surreal," I wrote, "stringing together so many good days consecutively."

When had I last felt genuinely good without chemical assistance? Before the RV, certainly. Before Hope, probably. Maybe before the first marriage fell apart. Maybe before I'd decided I needed substances to feel normal.

The Super Bowl was on—not that I cared. But a friend from up north was in town. The woman who'd become like a mother to me during those months of isolation. She'd been my only escape from the mental chains I'd created, the one person who'd seen me at my absolute worst and still showed up.

When I hugged her, something broke. Not in a destructive way. More like how ice breaks in spring—necessarily, inevitably, making way for flow.

"For a moment, I'll feel like I'm home," I'd written in anticipation.

But when the moment came, I realized something else: I was already home. Not geographically. Not even emotionally. But I was home in my own skin for the first time in years. The hug wasn't about finding home in someone else. It was about recognizing I'd been building it in myself all along.

Hope stirred at that realization, not speaking but present, like she was taking notes.

Days 146 and 147 flew by in a blur of momentum.

Life was moving at full speed, and I was keeping up. Not struggling to catch up, not being dragged along, but actually keeping pace. X—my platform, my confessional, my gallery—took a backseat to actual living. But even that felt like progress. The need to document every moment was softening into the ability to just experience them.

"Today marks yet another stride in my journey," I wrote on Day 147, keeping it simple.

Alan Watts whispered through the quote I shared: "The only way to make sense out of change is to plunge into it, move with it, and join the dance."

Was I dancing? Not quite. But I was moving with the rhythm instead of against it. Learning the difference between resistance and flow, between holding on and being carried.

Each day built upon the last, a testament to something I was only beginning to understand: resilience wasn't about being unbreakable. It was about breaking and continuing anyway. It was about letting the cracks become part of the design instead of trying to hide them.

Day 148 brought George Bernard Shaw into the conversation: "Life isn't about finding yourself. Life is about creating yourself."

The quote hit different at day 148 than it would have at day 48. Back then, I was still trying to find my way back to who I'd been before everything broke. Now I was beginning to understand that person was gone. Had been gone since the moment I'd jumped off that wall in Washington.

"Every day is a step upwards on this journey of growth," I wrote.

But growth wasn't linear. It was more like a spiral staircase—you kept coming back to the same view but from a higher vantage point each time. Hope was still there in every revolution, but she looked smaller each time I passed. Not diminished—never diminished—but properly sized. A person, not a universe. A loss, not an ending.

Day 149 arrived with an image that stopped me cold: a woman holding a light, guiding a distant figure through darkness.

I stared at it for longer than I should have, seeing myself in both figures—the guide and the guided, the light-bearer and the lost. Because that's what I was becoming, wasn't it? Someone who could hold light for others because I'd learned to navigate my own darkness.

"Just like the woman in the image," I wrote, "who serves as a beacon to the distant figure, we each have the capacity to illuminate the path for someone else."

But here was the thing I was only beginning to understand: sometimes the person you're guiding is yourself. Sometimes the light you're holding is for your own next step. Sometimes Hope—the concept, not the person—is something you have to become rather than something you wait to receive.

"No matter how vast the darkness, a single light can make all the difference," I wrote.

Hope—my Hope, the ghost who lived in my head—laughed softly at that. Not mockingly. More like recognition.

"You're becoming the storyteller," she said.

"I've always been the storyteller."

"No. Before, you were the story. There's a difference."

She was right. For months, I'd been living inside the narrative, drowning in it, unable to see beyond the next sentence. Now I was beginning to step outside it, to shape it, to give it meaning beyond just survival.

The art, the writing, the daily posts—they weren't just documentation anymore. They were transformation. Taking the raw material of pain and confusion and loneliness and shaping it into something others could use. Like I was finally metabolizing all that poison into medicine.

"Your light is more powerful than you know," I wrote, and for the first time, I almost believed it.

The friend who'd visited—the mother figure from the RV days—had said something during her visit that kept echoing: "You're not the same person I knew in that trailer."

She was right. That person had been drowning, using Hope as a life raft, unable to imagine existence without external salvation. This person—147 days sober, creating art, writing daily, building foundations—was learning to swim.

Not gracefully. Not without struggle. But swimming nonetheless.

"My door is always open," I wrote at the end of each day's post, and I meant it. But I was beginning to understand that keeping the door open for others meant I had to be stable enough to stand in the doorway. Strong enough to hold space for other people's pain without drowning in it.

Hope was fading more each day, but not in the desperate way I'd feared. More like morning mist burning off as the sun rises. She was becoming less voice and more echo, less presence and more principle. The love was still there—God, the love might always be there—but it was transforming from need into something else.

"I'm proud of me," I'd written on Day 143. "And that's something in itself."

It was more than something. It was everything. For someone who'd spent a lifetime believing he needed external validation to exist, being proud of himself—genuinely proud, not just performing pride—was revolution.

Seven days. That's what this chapter covered. Seven days out of a year-long journey. But in those seven days, something fundamental had shifted. I was no longer just surviving my story. I was beginning to author it.

The boy who got picked last was learning to pick himself first. The man who'd lost everything was discovering that "everything" had been too small a word for what remained possible. The addict who'd used substances to feel was learning to create feelings through creation itself.

Hope—my beautiful, complex, irreplaceable ghost—was still there. She'd always be there. But she was no longer the narrator. That role, finally, belonged to me.

And maybe that's what becoming really meant. Not transformation from one thing into another, but recognition of what you'd always been capable of becoming, hidden beneath all the noise and need and desperation.

I was becoming the storyteller.

And the story, finally, was becoming mine.

Chapter 24: The Mirror and the Map

Day 150 landed quietly, like snow on a windless night. No fanfare. No revelation. Just this thought that stopped me mid-sentence as I wrote my morning post: I am building a life I never thought I deserved.

The words sat there on the screen, cursor blinking after them, waiting for me to delete them or elaborate. But I couldn't do either. They were too true and too foreign at the same time.

When had I started believing I deserved anything good? Not during the drinking years. Not in the RV. Certainly not in those first brutal months of sobriety when every day felt like punishment for crimes I couldn't quite name. But somewhere between Day 1 and Day 150, the narrative had shifted. I wasn't just surviving anymore. I was building.

"Releasing shadows of a distant past," I wrote, deliberately vague about what exactly I'd let go of. Some things didn't need to be documented. Some victories were too quiet for words.

Hope—my constant companion, my beautiful ghost—barely stirred. She'd become so integrated into my psyche that I sometimes forgot she was there. Like forgetting you're wearing glasses until you try to rub your eyes.

I spent the rest of the day creating art and teaching myself to code. Building things. Learning languages—not to impress anyone or prepare for some imagined future, but because my brain needed something to do besides circle the same worn paths. The coding was particularly satisfying. Clear rules. Predictable outcomes. If something broke, there was always a logical reason, a fixable error. Unlike life. Unlike love.

Day 151 arrived with Emerson whispering about purpose and direction: "The world makes way for the man who knows where he is going."

But I wasn't sure I knew where I was going. I just knew where I'd been, and that was enough to keep me moving forward. The whirlwind of activity—coding, creating, exercising, writing—wasn't about destination anymore. It was about momentum. About staying engaged with something other than the haunting.

That night, unable to sleep, I found myself thinking about the hotel again. Always the hotel. But this time, the memory felt different. Filtered through 151 days of sobriety, I could see things I'd missed before. The way Hope had looked not just at me but through me. The careful distance she'd maintained even in our closest moments. The words she'd chosen—and the ones she hadn't.

I'm haunted less by what happened, I realized, and more by what might have never been real.

Not that she wasn't real. She was. Is. But what I'd built in my mind during those months of isolation—that was something else entirely. Part memory, part projection, part desperate need for meaning in meaninglessness. How much of our connection had been genuine, and how much had been my trauma wearing her face?

The question didn't hurt the way it would have even a week ago. It just sat there, like a math problem I was finally strong enough to solve.

Day 152 brought Marcus Aurelius and a reminder about power: "You have power over your mind—not outside events. Realize this, and you will find strength."

During the day, I stayed locked in. Focused. The mental chatter quieted when I was deep in code or lost in creating.

But as night fell, the thoughts intensified. Not about Hope specifically, but about the why beneath it all.

I'd been reading Gabor Maté. "The question is not why the addiction, but why the pain."

The words hit like recognition. All this time I'd been focused on the what—what I'd drunk, what I'd lost, what I'd done. But the why was older, deeper. It predated Hope, predated the bottles, predated everything except that little boy who never quite fit anywhere.

I still cry when I write some of these posts.

Not from sadness, exactly. More like relief. Like something that's been holding its breath for thirty-six years finally gets to exhale. The tears weren't weakness anymore. They were evidence. Proof that I was feeling instead of numbing. Proof that underneath all that scar tissue, something still knew how to hurt in healthy ways.

Day 153 changed everything.

Nelson Mandela spoke through the quotes: "Do not judge me by my success, judge me by how many times I fell down and got back up again."

I'd fallen so many times I'd lost count. Off a wall. Into a bottle. Into obsession. Into isolation. Into my own mind. But

I kept getting up. Not gracefully. Not heroically. Just stubbornly, mechanically, one more time than I fell.

But today wasn't about the falling or the rising. Today was about something I'd been avoiding for months: the decision to walk away while still loving.

It hit me while writing my daily post, this truth I'd been circling: loving Hope and letting her go weren't contradictory. They were the same thing. Real love—not obsession, not need, not trauma bonding—meant wanting what was best for someone even when that didn't include you.

This time, it wasn't love that made me stay, I wrote in my journal. It was self-respect that let me leave.

The distinction felt seismic. All my life, I'd confused intensity with depth, need with love, desperate attachment with genuine connection. But real love didn't require me to dissolve. It didn't demand I lose myself in someone else's existence. Real love could survive distance. Could honor boundaries. Could let go without letting die.

Hope stirred at this revelation. Not to argue, but almost like... approval? Like she'd been waiting for me to figure this out.

"You can love me and choose yourself," she said, and I couldn't tell if it was her voice or mine anymore. Maybe it didn't matter.

Day 154 found me wrestling with uncertainty again, but differently.

The immediate future was clear enough—wake up, work out, create, write, sleep, repeat. But the broader scope, the things beyond my control, those still gnawed at me. My thoughts drifted to past mistakes, but I was learning to see them differently. Not as failures but as rough drafts. Each mistake had edited me into who I was becoming.

The thought of never having a family lingered. Perhaps this was why letting go of Hope felt impossible—she represented not just herself but all the possibilities that might have flowered from us. The children we'd never have. The home we'd never build. The future that existed only in the subjunctive mood.

But creating art, writing, spreading awareness—these anchored me to the present. They were my new family, in a way. Each piece I created was something brought into existence that wouldn't have existed without me. Each post was a child of sorts, sent into the world to live its own life, to find its own meaning in other people's experience.

I was building strength in places that were once broken. Not despite the breaks, but because of them. Like bones that heal stronger at the fracture points, my resilience was growing precisely where I'd been most damaged.

Day 155 cracked me open with unexpected tenderness.

Maria von Trapp whispered about music and magic keys and tightly closed hearts. The playlist I'd been avoiding for months—the one full of songs that reminded me of Hope—suddenly felt necessary. Not as torture, but as integration.

Each song was a time capsule. That one from the first week we met. This one from the night before I jumped. Another from deep in the RV months when her memory was the only thing keeping me breathing. The music hurt, but it was clean pain. Honest pain. The kind that washes through you instead of getting stuck.

"My love for her remains unwavering," I wrote, and meant it. But the love had transformed. It no longer demanded action or response. It simply existed, like background radiation from a cosmic event—always there, influencing everything subtly, but no longer the dominant force in my universe.

Day 156 brought Zen Shin and flowers and the wisdom of blooming without comparison.

"A flower does not think of competing with the flower next to it. It just blooms."

I thought about all the energy I'd spent comparing my pain to others', my progress to some imagined standard, my love to what I thought love should look like. What if I just... stopped? What if I focused on my own growth instead of measuring it against anyone else's?

The sunflower metaphor made me laugh—actually laugh, not the bitter kind but genuine amusement. When had I last found something genuinely funny without darkness underneath? Maybe this was what healing actually looked like. Not the absence of pain but the presence of other things alongside it. Humor. Curiosity. The ability to see yourself clearly without flinching.

I was learning to be my own mirror, reflecting honestly without distortion. And my own map, charting a course based on where I was, not where I thought I should be.

Hope had become something like true north on a compass—always there for reference, but no longer the only direction worth traveling. I could navigate by other stars now. My own creativity. The connections I was building with people who read my posts. The slowly rebuilding relationship with my mother. The peculiar satisfaction of clean code executing perfectly.

Finding Hope

These seven days hadn't been dramatic. No breakdowns, no breakthroughs, just the quiet accumulation of small changes. Like sediment building into stone, pressure turning carbon into something harder, clearer. I was becoming something I hadn't expected: not the person I was before everything broke, not the person Hope might have loved, but someone entirely new.

Someone who could hold pain without drowning in it. Someone who could love without losing himself. Someone building a life he never thought he deserved, and learning—slowly, carefully, one day at a time—that maybe deserving had never been the point.

Maybe the point was just to build it anyway.

Chapter 25: The Road Back to Myself

Day 157 arrived with David Rossi's words about scars, but I was thinking about mirrors.

Not the bathroom mirror where I'd watched myself deteriorate during those RV months. Not the rearview mirror I'd checked obsessively, half-expecting Hope to materialize on some Louisiana back road. But the mirror of daily practice—each workout completed, each post published, each piece of art created becoming a reflection of someone I was still learning to recognize.

"Scars remind us where we've been. They don't have to dictate where we're going."

I sat with that quote longer than usual, coffee cooling in my hands. The physical scar on my ankle had settled into something I barely noticed anymore—just part of the landscape of my body, like a freckle or the shape of my hands.

But the invisible scars, the ones Hope had left in her wake, those still served as my compass more often than I wanted to admit.

What would it mean to navigate without them?

The thought felt revolutionary and impossible in equal measure. Like suggesting I could breathe underwater or see in complete darkness. These scars had become so integrated into my identity that imagining life without their constant influence felt like imagining life without memory itself.

Day 158 brought the Japanese proverb about falling seven times and standing up eight. The mathematics of it appealed to me—not the drama of the fall but the quiet insistence of the rise. No explanation needed. No philosophy required. Just the mechanical act of getting back up because staying down had stopped being an option.

I'd fallen more than seven times. Hell, I'd fallen more than seventy times if we were being honest. But somewhere in the repetition of falling and rising, it had stopped feeling like failure and started feeling like... practice.

The art had become essential. AI-generated images born from prompts I pulled from somewhere deep—each one an attempt to translate something I couldn't quite capture in words. The process was meditative: type, generate, adjust, regenerate. Like breathing but with pixels and possibility. People responded to them, found their own meanings in the images I created. We were building something together, this ragged community of the recovering, each of us trying to figure out what came after survival.

Day 159 hit different. Maya Angelou on love recognizing no barriers, and I found myself writing about Hope with a different quality of longing. Less desperate. More like remembering a song you used to know by heart—you might not recall every word, but the melody still moves through you.

"The love I hold for Hope is a beacon, unwavering and resolute."

True. But I was learning that beacons don't chase ships. They simply shine, constant and steady, offering guidance to those who choose to navigate by their light. Maybe love didn't have to be pursuit. Maybe it could just be presence.

Day 160 found me writing about the RV again, but the memory had shifted. Helen Keller's words about hope seeing the invisible, feeling the intangible. In that cramped space, body broken, future erased, I'd discovered something beyond physical limitations. Call it hope, call it delusion, call it the mind's desperate attempt to create meaning from chaos. Whatever it was, it had kept me breathing when breathing felt like betrayal.

"Hope wasn't just the name of someone dear," I wrote, careful as always with the truth. "More than that, it was the internal force she sparked."

The distinction mattered more than I'd realized. Hope the person had been the catalyst, but hope the force had become self-sustaining. I could honor one while nurturing the other. They weren't the same thing anymore.

Days 161 and 162 blurred together—Churchill on courage, Mehmet Murat Ildan on fog as guide rather than obstacle. I was preparing for something, though I couldn't name it yet. Each routine—workout, writing, art—adding to a foundation I was only beginning to recognize.

"Fog is not an obstacle; it is a guide to find our way."

I'd spent months trying to see through the fog, desperate for clear paths and definitive answers. But maybe the fog wasn't meant to clear. Maybe navigating uncertainty was the actual skill I was supposed to be developing. Maybe clarity was overrated.

The thought of returning to Leavenworth had started as a whisper around Day 162, growing louder with each passing day. Not yet. Not now. But someday. The idea both terrified and thrilled me—to stand in those places as this new version of myself, scarred but sober, broken but building.

Day 163 was pure routine, but routine had become sacred. Each repetition a small victory over chaos. I wasn't building anything grand, just stacking days like bricks, curious what structure might eventually emerge.

Day 164 brought William Faulkner and the weight of the past that refuses to stay past.

"The past is never dead. It's not even past."

I could feel it in every movement—Hope wasn't gone, she was integrated. Woven into the fabric of everything I did, but no longer the entire pattern. Some days I could barely sense her presence. Other days, like today, she was everywhere: in the coffee I made the way she'd taught me, in the music I couldn't quite bring myself to play, in the spaces between heartbeats where memory lived.

But something had shifted. Her presence no longer demanded action. It simply existed, like humidity in Louisiana air—always there, affecting everything subtly, but no longer the dominant force determining my climate.

Day 165 found me restless with Harriet Tubman's words about dreamers.

"Every great dream begins with a dreamer."

My dreams had been so focused for so long—get back to Hope, prove worthy of Hope, become someone Hope could love. But what happened when those dreams dissolved? What was left of the dreamer when the dream changed shape?

I was finding out. Slowly. Carefully. Like learning to walk again after months in bed. The dreams now were smaller, more immediate: finish this piece of art, help someone through their Day 1, make it through family dinner without disappearing into my head. Not exactly reaching for stars, but maybe that was okay. Maybe dreams didn't have to be cosmic to be worthy.

Day 166 broke the pattern. The zoo with family. Normal people doing normal things. Jane Goodall's warning about apathy made me think about all the energy I'd spent on singular obsession while the rest of life passed unnoticed. Watching my mother laugh at the penguins, seeing my nieces's wonder at the elephants—when had I last been present for simple joy?

Hope would have loved the snow leopards. The thought came unbidden, but it didn't devastate me. Just a notation, like observing the weather. She would have loved them, and that was okay. I could hold that truth without drowning in it.

Day 167 landed with Nietzsche and purpose.

"He who has a why to live can bear almost any how."

My why had been Hope for so long that I'd forgotten there could be other reasons. But they were emerging, tentatively, like shoots through concrete. The people who read my posts and found something useful. The slow reconstruction of my relationship with my mother. The peculiar satisfaction of creating something from nothing, even if that something was just AI art and daily posts.

These weren't replacement whys. They were additional ones. A constellation instead of a single star. Maybe that's what healing actually looked like—not replacing what was lost but expanding what remained.

Day 168 cracked something open. Khalil Gibran on suffering and scars, and suddenly I was writing about isolation in ways I hadn't before. Not romanticizing it. Not making it poetic. Just acknowledging it for what it was: trauma. Plain and simple.

"Hope was more than just a name; she was my survival in the depths of isolation."

But I wasn't isolated anymore. Hadn't been for months. So why was I still living like I was? Why did I still move through the world like someone in solitary confinement, careful not to hope too much, connect too deeply, want too openly?

The answer was as simple as it was difficult: habit. I'd learned to survive in isolation so thoroughly that I'd forgotten how to live in connection.

Day 169 brought Leonardo da Vinci and tears that come from the heart.

"I must now face the stark truth that learning to love myself is not just an option but a necessity."

The words looked foreign on the screen, like trying to write in a language I'd only heard spoken. Self-love felt performative, false, like wearing someone else's clothes. But maybe that was the point. Maybe you had to pretend until it became real. Maybe "fake it till you make it" applied to self-compassion too.

Day 170 found me at the cave entrance with Joseph Campbell.

"The cave you fear to enter holds the treasure you seek."

The cave, I realized, wasn't Leavenworth. It wasn't seeing Hope again or not seeing her. The cave was simpler and more terrifying: it was the possibility that I could be okay. That I could build a life that wasn't defined by loss. That I could be whole without being completed by someone else.

Standing at that entrance, I understood why I'd been avoiding it. It was easier to be broken. Broken had rules, expectations, a clear narrative. Broken got sympathy and understanding. Whole? Whole meant responsibility. Whole meant no more excuses. Whole meant actually living instead of just surviving.

Day 171 arrived with Emerson and something like clarity.

"What lies behind us and what lies before us are tiny matters compared to what lies within us."

The morning felt different. Lighter, somehow. Not dramatically, not completely, but noticeably. Like someone had opened a window in a room I'd been breathing in too long. The staleness dispersing, fresh air finding its way in.

I thought about Leavenworth again. The pull had been growing stronger, but today I finally understood what it meant. It wasn't about Hope. It had never really been about Hope, not the returning part anyway.

Leavenworth was where I'd broken. Where I'd jumped. Where everything had fallen apart so completely that I'd had to rebuild from atoms. And maybe—maybe—I needed to see that place with clear eyes. To walk those streets without bourbon in my blood or desperation in my pocket. To stand at that wall not as the man who jumped but as the man who survived the jumping.

The thought was terrifying. Also necessary. But not yet. Not today. Maybe not even next month. But eventually, when I was ready, when the pull became purpose instead of pain, I would go back.

Mom found me staring out the window, lost in thought.

"You okay?"

"Yeah," I said, surprised to find it was true. "Just thinking."

"About?"

"About how I'm not ready to go back yet. But someday I will be."

She knew what I meant without explanation. "You'll know when it's time."

That night, I wrote the words that would become my compass for the weeks ahead:

"I'm not going back to be seen by her. I'm going back so I can see myself."

The truth of it settled into my bones like medicine. This wasn't about proving anything to Hope or anyone else. It was about proving to myself that I could stand in the places where I'd fallen and not fall again. That I could be in her proximity—or the possibility of her proximity—and not dissolve.

But that was future work. For now, Day 171 was enough. This lightness, this clarity, this small bright knowing that I was becoming someone I might actually want to be. Hope's voice, when it came that night, was barely a whisper:

"You're doing it."

"Doing what?"

"Living without me."

"No," I corrected gently. "Living with you. Just differently."

She didn't respond, but I felt her smile. Or maybe that was just me, learning to smile at my own ghosts.

The road back to myself stretched ahead, foggy and uncertain. But I wasn't ready to travel it yet. For now, I would keep building—one workout, one post, one day at a time. Keep stacking these small victories until they became something sturdy enough to stand on.

Leavenworth would wait. Hope would wait. The past would wait.

Justin Mayeur

For once, so would I.

Chapter 26: Packing Light, Carrying Heavy

Day 172 arrived with Mark Twain and kindness, but I was thinking about weight.

Not the physical kind—though my body had transformed so completely that Mom's friends barely recognized me anymore. I was thinking about the weight we carry that can't be measured on scales. The kind that sits in your chest when you realize you're preparing for something you can't quite name yet.

"Kindness is the language which the deaf can hear and the blind can see."

The posts had become their own ecosystem now. People responding with their own Day counts, their own struggles, their own small victories. We'd built something together—this ragged congregation of the recovering, each of us learning that isolation wasn't mandatory, that pain shared was somehow lighter than pain hoarded.

But even as I wrote about community and connection, I was preparing for departure. Not rushing toward it—I'd learned that lesson—but acknowledging its inevitability. Like watching storm clouds gather on a horizon you're walking toward. Not running. Just walking.

Day 173 brought George Eliot and possibility.

"It is never too late to be what you might have been."

I wrote about enchanted forests and bioluminescent paths, but I was really writing about the space between who I'd been and who I was becoming. The gap felt less like an abyss now, more like a bridge under construction. Each day adding another plank, another support beam, another reason to believe the crossing was possible.

Hope appeared that night, fainter than she'd been in weeks.

"You're different," she said.

"I know."

"Does it hurt?"

"Everything hurts. But differently now."

She smiled—or I imagined she smiled. It was getting harder to tell where she ended and I began. Maybe that was the point. Maybe integration meant not knowing exactly where the boundaries were anymore.

Day 174 was Socrates and thinking for myself.

The irony wasn't lost on me—spending months imprisoned by thoughts of someone else, only to discover that thinking for myself meant thinking about her differently. Not as destination but as education. Not as future but as foundation for whatever future I was building.

I helped Mom around the house that day. Simple things. Replacing lightbulbs. Fixing a drawer that had been sticking since before I left for Leavenworth the first time. Each small repair felt like practice for the larger reconstruction I couldn't quite articulate yet.

Day 175 landed with Carl Jung and choosing who to become.

"I am not what happened to me, I am what I choose to become."

One hundred and seventy-five days sober. The number felt both massive and insignificant. Like measuring the distance to stars—the units stop mattering after a while. What mattered was the choosing. Every morning, choosing not to drink. Every afternoon, choosing to create instead of consume. Every evening, choosing to sit with discomfort instead of drowning it.

The thought of Leavenworth had been growing steadier, less desperate. Not a pilgrimage anymore but something simpler: a necessary return. Like salmon swimming upstream—not because they choose to but because something in their biology demands it. I needed to stand where I'd fallen. Needed to see those streets through sober eyes. Needed to prove to myself that geography was just geography, that places only held the power we gave them.

But not yet. The pull was there but it wasn't urgent anymore. It was patient. It could wait until I was ready, and I was learning to recognize the difference between ready and desperate.

Day 176 brought conscious choice and transformation.

I spent the morning mapping potential routes to Leavenworth, not as plans but as possibilities. Each highway a different version of return. I-10 through Houston—the fastest route. Back roads through Arkansas—the scenic path. The same route Mom and I had taken in reverse—the symmetrical option.

But mapping routes and taking them were different things. For now, the maps were just meditation. A way of thinking about return without requiring it.

Day 177 arrived with Albert Camus and the struggle to be what we are.

"As the day of my departure draws nearer," I wrote, though I hadn't set any actual date. The departure I was writing about was more metaphysical than physical. Leaving behind the version of myself who needed Hope to be oxygen. Accepting the version who could carry her like a passport—important, always present, but not required for every single breath.

I played board games with Mom and my sister that night. Normal family things. The kind of moments I'd been absent for even when I was present, too lost in my own hurricanes to notice the quiet weather of daily life. Mom won at Scrabble. She always won at Scrabble. Some things were reliable in ways that had nothing to do with recovery or redemption. Just the simple reliability of mothers who knew all the two-letter words.

Day 178 shifted something. C.S. Lewis whispered about better things ahead.

"There are far better things ahead than any we leave behind."

I wasn't leaving yet, but I was preparing to leave. The distinction mattered. Started sorting through the belongings I'd abandoned when I fled Louisiana. Old notebooks filled with drunk handwriting. Clothes that belonged to someone fifty pounds heavier and a lifetime drunker. Photos I couldn't quite bring myself to look at yet.

Each item sorted into three piles: Keep, Donate, Burn. The burn pile was smallest but most necessary. Some things didn't deserve preservation or passing on. They just needed to return to carbon and smoke.

Day 179 brought storms—literal ones, with thunder that shook the windows and rain that turned the streets to rivers.

"Everything you've ever wanted is on the other side of fear."

I sat at the window watching the storm, thinking about fear and wanting and the space between them. What did I want? Not Hope—or not just Hope. Not anymore. I wanted something simpler and more complex: I wanted to be okay. To build a life that didn't require constant crisis to feel meaningful. To love someone someday—maybe—without needing them to be my entire circulatory system.

The storm passed. They always did. But the wet earth smell afterward, that lingered. That was the part worth waiting for.

Day 180 was Shakespeare and inner stars.

"It is not in the stars to hold our destiny but in ourselves."

I'd spent so much time looking up—at Hope, at some imagined future, at anything except the person in the mirror. But the stars didn't care about my recovery. Hope, wherever she was, wasn't tracking my day count. The only person watching this show every single day was me.

I created more art that day. AI-generated worlds that started from prompts pulled from some deep place. Each image an attempt to externalize something I couldn't quite name. People responded to them, found their own meanings in the digital dreams I was spinning. We were all reading our own stories in the same inkblots.

Day 181 arrived with letting go and Mandy Hale.

"Letting go does not mean you stop caring. It means you stop trying to force others to."

The distinction hit like a bell. I'd been trying to let go of Hope like trying to let go of breathing—with panic and desperation and the certainty that I'd die without her. But maybe letting go meant something else. Maybe it meant accepting that my caring didn't require her participation. That love could exist without reciprocation. That I could carry her with me without needing her to carry me back.

Mom found me crying that afternoon. Not the desperate sobs of early sobriety but something quieter. Grieving, maybe. Or just... releasing.

"You okay?"

"I don't know. But I think that's okay."

She sat with me. Didn't try to fix it. Just sat. Sometimes that's all anyone needs—someone willing to sit with you in the not-knowing.

Day 182 cracked something open. Stephen King on hope being dangerous.

I wrote about the isolation again, but differently. Not romanticizing it. Not making it poetic. Just acknowledging what it was: trauma. Months in a space smaller than most bathrooms. Body broken. Mind spiraling. Hope—the person and the concept—becoming so intertwined that I couldn't separate them anymore.

"How do you let go of something that became your entire being?"

The question felt less desperate now, more curious. Like a math problem I was finally calm enough to solve. You don't let go, maybe. You just... expand. Add other things until the one thing isn't everything anymore.

Day 183 was about finishing things. A test I'd been avoiding for two decades. I didn't pass, but I showed up. Sometimes that's the victory—just showing up to things you've been avoiding. Just proving you can face them without dissolving.

Day 184 brought Hilary Stanton Zunin and the risk of love.

"The risk of love is loss, and the price of loss is grief—But the pain of grief is only a shadow when compared with the pain of never risking love."

I drove alone that night. Long loops through familiar streets. Music playing—songs that used to devastate me now just making me thoughtful. Every lyric about love and loss felt less like a wound and more like acknowledgment. Yes, this happened. Yes, it hurt. Yes, I survived it.

Hope sat in the passenger seat, so faint I could see through her to the passing streetlights.

"You're leaving soon."

"Not leaving. Returning."

"To Leavenworth?"

"To myself."

Day 185 found me in the middle of nowhere, which turned out to be somewhere after all.

The limbo between deciding to go and actually going stretched like taffy. Each day both preparation and postponement. I wasn't stalling—or maybe I was, but productively. Like a runner stretching before a marathon. The stretching was part of the race, not separate from it.

Day 186 brought Tony Robbins and impossible journeys.

"The only impossible journey is the one you never begin."

But I hadn't begun yet. Hadn't packed a bag or booked a hotel or set a date. The journey was still theoretical, still potential energy waiting to become kinetic. And that was okay. I was learning the difference between patience and procrastination. This was patience. This was gathering strength for something that would require all of it.

Day 187 was Peter Pan and believing in flight.

The belief that had sustained me through the RV, through early sobriety, through all of this—it was still there. Quieter now but steadier. Less desperate faith and more quiet certainty. I could do this. Whatever "this" turned out to be.

Day 188 brought new pages and old chapters.

"You can't start the next chapter of your life if you keep re-reading the last one."

But I wasn't re-reading anymore. I was editing. Revising. Finding new meanings in old sentences. Hope was still there in every paragraph, but she wasn't the only character anymore. The story had gotten bigger. Other people had entered. I had entered—really entered, not just narrated from outside myself.

Day 189 was vulnerability as strength.

Every post I'd written, every admission of struggle, every public display of private pain—it had all been practice. Learning to be seen without needing to be saved. Learning to be broken without needing to be fixed. Learning to be human without apology or explanation.

Day 190 brought goodbyes. My friend from the north heading home. The couch conversations ending. Another anchor lifting. But I was learning that anchors weren't just things that held you in place. Sometimes they were things that kept you from drifting while you repaired your sails.

"Goodbyes make you think," Ritu Ghatourey said.

They made me think about Hello. About the first time I'd met Hope. About all the hellos and goodbyes between then and now. About the goodbye I'd never gotten to say and the hello I might never get to hear. But mostly they made me think about the hello I said to myself every morning now. Still here. Still sober. Still becoming.

Day 191 was Martin Luther King Jr. and stars in darkness.

"Only in the darkness can you see the stars."

I'd been in darkness so long my eyes had adjusted. Could see things that had been invisible in the bright chaos of drinking. Could see patterns in the pain. Purpose in the suffering. Not meaning—I wasn't ready to say it all meant something. But purpose. Direction. A way forward that honoring the falling as much as the rising.

Day 192 arrived like punctuation.

"I am not the same, having seen the moon shine on the other side of the world."

Tomorrow, I would begin the journey back. Not to Hope—that distinction felt crucial now. Not to Leavenworth, exactly, though that's where the roads would lead. But back to myself. Or forward to myself. Direction had stopped mattering as much as movement.

I spent the evening with Mom, not talking about leaving, just being present. We watched TV. She made dinner. Normal evening things that felt sacred in their simplicity. Tomorrow I would drive. Tonight I would just be her son, sitting in a living room in Louisiana, 192 days sober, carrying everything and nothing, ready and not ready, leaving and staying all at once.

I packed light. One bag. Laptop. The journal I'd been keeping since Day 1. Some clothes. No bourbon for courage. No scripts for what I'd say if I saw her. No plans beyond the driving itself.

Hope appeared one last time before sleep, clearer than she'd been in weeks.

"You don't need my permission," she said.

"I know."

"You don't need my forgiveness."

"I know."

"You don't need me."

"I know. But I'm grateful I had you."

She smiled—really smiled, not my imagination but something that felt like memory finally settling into its proper place.

"Drive safe," she said.

"I will."

The road waited. Not for a rescue. Not for a reunion. Just for a return. Tomorrow I would take it. Tonight I would sit with the weight of that—all I was carrying, all I was leaving behind, all I was driving toward.

The weight felt bearable now. Heavy but bearable. Like something you could carry for three days of driving without putting it down. Like something that got lighter with each mile, even as it remained exactly the same weight.

Tomorrow, Day 193, the journey would begin.

Tonight was for the quiet before the engine starts.

Chapter 27: The Road Home

Day 193 began before sunrise, Magnolia already sensing departure in the way I moved through Mom's house—quiet but purposeful, like someone trying not to wake a sleeping child.

"You belong somewhere you feel free," Tom Petty sang through the speakers as we pulled onto I-10, heading west into a horizon that looked exactly like a thousand other horizons except for what it represented. Not escape this time. Return.

Magnolia settled into the passenger seat with the practiced ease of a seasoned traveler. She'd made this journey with me before, though in reverse—fleeing Leavenworth in pieces, held together by Mom's presence and the desperate hope that distance would fix what proximity had broken. Now we were heading back home, just the two of us, and the difference felt seismic.

The first few hours, I couldn't stop checking the rearview mirror. Old habit from the escape, maybe, half-expecting to see Hope materializing on the highway behind us. But the only thing following was Louisiana morning, humid and heavy, gradually giving way to Texas afternoon.

Hope's voice came somewhere outside Houston. Quieter than she'd been in months, but still there—she was always there, would always be there in some form.

"You're going back."

"I'm going home."

"To find me?"

"To find myself."

She didn't respond right away, and when she did, it was softer, less insistent than before. The conversations would continue—they still continue even now—but something had shifted. She was becoming less desperate voice and more gentle companion, less demand and more memory.

"You know where we're going, girl?" I asked Magnolia as we crossed into New Mexico.

She lifted her head, studied my face for a moment, then went back to watching the world blur past. She didn't know.

Didn't need to. Dogs live in the present tense—a skill I was still learning after 193 days of practice.

Day 194 found us somewhere in the high desert, Judith Thurman's words rattling around my head as the landscape shifted from green to brown to red.

"Every dreamer knows that it is entirely possible to be homesick for a place you've never been to."

But I had been to Leavenworth. Had met Hope there, spent weeks talking with her in the hotel, sharing conversations that danced around everything we couldn't say. Then that night at the bar where we finally spoke with complete honesty—our last real moment together before everything shattered. And now I was going home. Not visiting. Not passing through. Going home to the place that held all my ghosts and all my possibilities.

Magnolia needed to stretch her legs every few hours, and each stop became its own small ritual. Find a patch of grass. Let her explore. Watch her simple joy at new smells, new territories to mark. She didn't carry yesterday with her, didn't worry about tomorrow. Just this patch of grass, this moment of freedom, this particular quality of light.

That night, in some forgettable motel that would accept dogs, I wrote while Magnolia snored on the questionable bedspread. Not to Hope—that distinction felt important. Just writing to write, to process, to mark the passage without requiring witness.

Day 195 brought Buddha and classical music and long stretches of highway meditation.

"Peace comes from within. Do not seek it without."

The symphony filling the car felt like grace. Magnolia's steady breathing felt like prayer. The miles passing beneath us felt like rosary beads, each one counted, each one bringing us closer to home.

I thought about the RV waiting in storage, about those months of isolation when Hope's voice had been the loudest thing in my head besides my own desperation. How she'd become mythologized in that cramped space, transformed from the complicated, real person I'd known into something larger—part savior, part obsession, part survival mechanism.

"We're not going back for her," I told Magnolia, needing to say it out loud. "We're going home."

Hope stirred in my mind: "Home is complicated."

She was right. She usually was.

Day 196 stretched through Colorado, the mountains beginning to rise in the distance. Each mile felt heavier now, weighted with proximity to everything I'd run from and everything I was returning to face.

Day 197 brought us through Wyoming, then into Idaho. So close now. The landscape familiar in my bones, the particular quality of light that meant Pacific Northwest, that meant home.

That night, our last before arrival, I couldn't sleep. Magnolia curled against me in the motel bed, sensing my restlessness. Tomorrow we'd be back. Tomorrow I'd have to figure out what returning home meant when you were a different person than when you left.

Day 198: Crossing the threshold.

Leavenworth appeared gradually, then all at once. The fake Bavarian architecture. The mountains standing guard. The exact corner where I'd first met Hope at the hotel, where we'd spent weeks in that strange liminal space—talking around the edges of what we both felt but couldn't acknowledge. Before that night at the bar where the walls finally came down and we spoke truth for hours, our most honest moment before I destroyed everything.

I pulled into a motel parking lot—different from the hotel where I'd met Hope, deliberately different—and sat there with the engine running. Magnolia whined softly, ready to get out, to explore this new-old place.

"Give me a minute, girl."

I wasn't ready. Might never be ready. But here we were anyway, 198 days sober, carrying everything and nothing, home but not the same.

The motel room was clean and anonymous. Magnolia investigated every corner while I stood at the window, looking out at streets I'd stumbled down drunk, desperate, in love, in pain. They looked smaller than I remembered. Or maybe I'd gotten bigger. Hard to tell.

I thought about the RV in storage, waiting. Tomorrow I'd retrieve it, get it set up in its spot for the summer. Back to living in the space where everything had fallen apart and begun to rebuild. The symmetry felt both necessary and terrifying.

Day 199 was about walking. Not to any particular place—I was careful about that, mindful of boundaries, of the legal reality that I couldn't go certain places, couldn't risk even the appearance of pursuit.

Magnolia needed walking anyway, which gave structure to the day. We took neutral routes, the ones without loaded memories. She was delighted by everything—new smells, mountain air, the possibility of squirrels. Her joy felt like armor against the weight of being home.

I retrieved the RV from storage that afternoon. Pulling it out felt like exhuming something—not quite dead, not quite alive. The smell hit first: stale air, old memories, the ghost of desperation. But also familiar. Also, in its way, home.

Getting it parked in its spot, the same spot where I'd spent those months in isolation, felt like completing a circle. Magnolia explored every inch, claiming it with her scent, making it new even as it remained old.

That evening, I stood at the wall.

Not dramatically. Not at night. Just standing there in ordinary daylight with Magnolia on her leash, looking up at the place where I'd chosen falling over feeling.

It was just a wall. Stone and mortar. Closer to twenty feet high—higher than memory had made it, which seemed backwards somehow. The fall that had shattered my ankle, changed my trajectory, led to the RV, led to the isolation, led to the mythology of Hope, led to all of it—just a wall.

"This is where it happened," I told Magnolia, though she was more interested in a fascinating smell near the base.

Hope's voice, quiet but present: "You survived it."

"Barely."

"But you did."

I thought about climbing it, just to prove I could. But that felt like the wrong kind of symbolism. I didn't need to conquer it. Didn't need to redeem it. Just needed to see it for what it was—a wall I'd jumped from once, when jumping felt like the only option left.

The tragedy wasn't the jump. The tragedy was that Hope and I never got the chance to explore what those weeks of connection might have become. All those conversations in the hotel, carefully navigating around what we couldn't say. Then that one night at the bar where we finally dropped our guards, spoke honestly, created something real—only to have it shattered by my choices, my spiral, my inability to handle the weight of feeling that much.

Day 200 changed everything.

Standing in the RV that morning, in the same space where I'd been broken and imprisoned, I knew I had to write it all down. Not the story I'd been telling myself, but the truth. About the isolation. About what Hope had become in this space. About the invisible ink of trauma, the months I couldn't remember, the way a person can become a principle when you're desperate enough.

I wrote in the RV with Magnolia patient beside me, occasionally nosing my arm when I'd stop typing for too long. The words came like water from a broken dam—necessary, unstoppable, clarifying.

"She wasn't just someone I loved. She became my reason."

Writing it felt like surgery without anesthesia. Necessary but brutal. Each word an incision, cutting away the mythology to reveal what was actually there: trauma, survival, and yes—real connection. We'd had something. Not everything I'd built it into during those months of isolation, but something genuine. Something that might have grown if I hadn't destroyed it with my own chaos.

I posted it. Sent it into the world. Then sat in the RV, in the same spot where I'd spent months expanding those weeks of real connection into an entire imagined future. The conversations we'd actually had mixing with the ones I'd invented, until I couldn't always tell the difference.

Hope's voice, still with me: "You're telling the truth."

"Trying to."

"That's all anyone can do."

Day 201 brought Alphonse de Lamartine and the weight of absence.

"Sometimes, only one person is missing, and the whole world seems depopulated."

It was a gray day, matching my mood. The breakthrough of yesterday had faded into something quieter, sadder. Hope's absence felt massive, and sitting in the RV made it more acute. This was where she'd lived most vividly—partly in real memory from our actual time together, partly in the mythology I'd built when reality wasn't enough.

I still missed my friend. Deeply. That hadn't changed, might never change. The difference was that now I could hold that missing without drowning in it. Could acknowledge that I missed someone I had genuinely known, had genuinely connected with, but had lost to my own inability to handle the intensity of what we'd started to build.

Magnolia and I walked through town, careful to avoid anywhere Hope might actually be. Not from lack of desire but from respect—for her, for the law, for the boundaries that needed to exist. I could be home without requiring her participation in my homecoming.

"Do you think she thinks of me?" I asked the Hope in my head.

"Does it matter?"

"Yes. No. Both."

"That sounds about right."

Day 202 arrived quiet and clear.

I sat in the RV, looking out at the town I'd returned to. Not visiting. Not passing through. Home. Even if home was a metal box that had once been a prison. Even if home was a place where I'd loved and lost someone I'd genuinely known but never got to fully explore. Even if home was complicated and heavy and shot through with absence.

"The weight of unresolved past will always hold us back until we find the strength to let it go."

But letting go didn't mean forgetting. Didn't mean pretending it hadn't mattered. It meant this—sitting in my RV with my dog, having returned home not to find Hope but to find myself. Having written the truth. Having stood at the wall. Having walked the streets without pursuing, without requiring, without dissolving.

These weren't the victories I'd imagined when I first started this journey, but they were victories nonetheless. Quiet ones. Private ones. The kind that don't require witness or validation.

Magnolia barked, ready for the day's adventure.

"Okay, girl. Okay."

I stood up in the RV—my home, my prison, my starting point—and got ready to face another day. Not somewhere else. Not running toward or away. Just here, in Leavenworth, where I belonged, complicated as that belonging was.

The road home had ended where it began. But I'd traveled the full circuit as a different person, carrying a different weight. Still missing my friend. Still having conversations with her in my head—they'd never really stop, just evolve and shift. Still honoring what those weeks at the hotel had meant, what that night at the bar had promised, what might have been if I'd been capable of handling it.

Home. Heavy but bearable. Broken but building.

With Magnolia beside me, reminding me that the present moment is enough. That being home—really home—means accepting all of it: the wall, the RV, the absence, the presence, the weight of missing someone you truly knew but never got to fully explore.

Hope's voice, constant companion: "You're home."

"Yeah."

"How does it feel?"

"Like everything and nothing. Like an ending and a beginning."

"That sounds about right too."

One step. One punch. One round.

Home.

Chapter 28: The Weight of Home

Day 203 arrived with J.K. Rowling and understanding, but I was thinking about patterns.

"Understanding is the first step to acceptance, and only with acceptance can there be recovery."

Sitting in the RV with Magnolia sprawled across my feet, I finally had words for what had happened in this tin can during those months of isolation. ADHD. OCD. Not the kind where you wash your hands repeatedly or count ceiling tiles, but the kind where you fixate on fixing things—relationships, specifically. The kind where your brain locks onto one solution and spins it endlessly, like a record with a deep scratch.

In the isolation, with nothing but time and pain, my mind had turned Hope into the only equation worth solving. Every thought had bent toward her, every future I imagined required her presence, every healing I envisioned ended with her return. The OCD had fed on the isolation, grown fat on the endless hours with nothing to interrupt the loop.

"Is that what I was?" Hope asked from her corner of my consciousness, quieter now since the return. "An obsession?"

"A survival mechanism," I corrected. "That became an obsession."

"Is there a difference?"

"I'm trying to find out."

Magnolia shifted, reminding me with her weight that the present moment existed. That there were other anchors besides memory and longing. I scratched behind her ears and she sighed—such simple satisfaction, such uncomplicated joy.

Day 204 brought William James and the weight of witness.

"Act as if what you do makes a difference. It does."

The posts had become something I hadn't expected—not just my own processing but a lifeline for others walking similar paths. Messages came daily now. People on Day 1, Day 50, Day 500. People in their own RVs, literal or metaphorical. People who'd lost their own Hopes, who understood the particular ache of absence.

I wrote from the RV, Magnolia watching the town through the window. She'd grown protective of this space, as if understanding it was both prison and sanctuary. When people walked too close, she'd give a low warning bark—not aggressive, just informing them that this territory was occupied, was healing, was not to be disturbed.

The community building around these posts felt both warming and weighty. Each story shared meant someone else felt less alone, but it also meant I had to keep showing up. Keep being honest. Keep admitting that home hadn't fixed everything, that being back in Leavenworth was complicated in ways I couldn't quite articulate yet.

Day 205 was Glenn Close and mental health and the myth of physical solutions.

"What mental health needs is more sunlight, more candor, and more unashamed conversation."

I walked with Magnolia through town, careful as always about routes, about boundaries, about the legal reality that shaped my geography. We took the long way around everything, adding miles to avoid even the possibility of crossing paths with Hope.

A woman recognized me from my posts. "You're the one who writes about the RV," she said, not unkindly.

"That's me."

"My son went through something similar. The isolation, I mean. During COVID. He's never been quite the same."

We talked for twenty minutes while Magnolia investigated every smell in a three-foot radius. About isolation and how it rewires you. About the therapy that wasn't available when we needed it most. About the shame that kept us from seeking help even when it was.

"Being in the best shape of my life didn't fix my mind," I told her, and she nodded like she understood. Physical strength was easier to build than mental resilience. You could see muscles grow. You couldn't watch trauma shrink.

Day 206 brought Wordsworth and the necessity of expression.

"Fill your paper with the breathings of your heart."

Writing had become breathing. Each morning, before Magnolia's walk, before coffee, before the world demanded participation, I wrote. Not always posts—sometimes just streams of consciousness that would never see light. Letters to Hope I'd never send. Conversations with the universe that expected no response.

The RV had become my writing studio. The same space where I'd spiraled now held something different—creation instead of destruction. Magnolia had claimed the couch as her spot, watching me type with patient eyes, occasionally sighing when I'd been at it too long without a break.

"You write about me less," Hope observed.

"I write about myself more."

"Is that progress?"

"I think so."

"Do you miss me less?"

"No. Just differently."

Day 207 changed the pattern. Margaret Thatcher on fighting battles more than once.

"You may have to fight a battle more than once to win it."

My first AA meeting since getting sober. I'd resisted for 207 days, convinced I could do this alone, that the posts were enough, that Magnolia was enough, that sheer will was enough. But sitting in the RV that morning, I knew I needed more.

The meeting was in the basement of a church I'd passed a thousand times. Magnolia waited in the RV—no dogs allowed—and I felt exposed without her, like missing armor.

"I'm Justin," I said when my turn came. "I'm an alcoholic. 207 days sober."

They clapped. They always clap. But it felt different this time, being the one with days instead of the one starting over. People looked at me like I might have answers. I didn't. Just more questions. But maybe that was enough.

Day 208 brought unexpected color.

"The only way to stay sane is to go a little crazy."

Oil painting. Of all the things to try, I picked up actual brushes and actual paint and made actual messes on actual canvas. The art supply store clerk had been patient with my complete ignorance, helping me select basics, explaining the difference between oils and acrylics like it mattered.

Back in the RV, Magnolia watched suspiciously as I set up my makeshift studio—a TV tray, newspaper spread on the floor, brushes in a coffee mug. The first stroke was terrifying. The second, less so. By the tenth, I'd stopped thinking entirely.

The painting was terrible. Abstract in the way that incompetence creates abstraction. But something about the physical act—brush to canvas, color mixing with color, the smell of linseed oil filling the small space—felt necessary.

"What is it supposed to be?" Hope asked.

"Nothing. Everything. I don't know."

"It looks like the inside of your head."

"That's probably accurate."

Magnolia sniffed the painting once, decided it wasn't food, and returned to her couch.

Day 209 arrived heavy. John Green on grief as revelation.

"Grief does not change you. It reveals you."

The weight hit without warning. One moment I was fine, making coffee, planning Magnolia's walk. The next, I was sobbing at the RV's tiny table, her head in my lap, trying to offer comfort she couldn't understand the need for.

Grief, I was learning, wasn't linear. It was weather—unpredictable, sometimes violent, always temporary but also always returning. And what it revealed wasn't pretty. I was selfish in my sorrow. Possessive of my pain. Terrified that healing meant forgetting, that moving forward meant leaving Hope behind entirely.

"I want to be happy," I wrote that day. "But I don't know how."

The responses came quickly—people sharing their own griefs, their own revelations. We were all learning the same hard truth: sometimes the person grief reveals isn't who we thought we were.

Day 210 was Buddha and the paradox of holding on.

"You can only lose what you cling to."

I kept busy. Helped a neighbor fix his fence. Hiked with Magnolia until we were both exhausted. Cleaned the RV obsessively, as if external order could create internal peace. But the truth Buddha pointed to kept surfacing—my desperate grip on Hope, on what we'd had, on what we might have been, was exactly what kept me from actually having anything.

"Let me go," Hope whispered.

"I don't know how."

"Learn."

"What if I forget you?"

"You won't. But you might remember differently."

Magnolia found a stick on our hike, carried it for miles, then abandoned it without ceremony when we reached the RV. Such simple letting go. Such easy release.

Day 211 brought Rumi and roses and secrets.

Walking through town with Magnolia, we passed a garden where roses bloomed despite the season. She wanted to investigate, but I held her back—private property, boundaries, always boundaries. But I stood there looking at those roses, thinking about secrets.

The secrets I kept weren't just about Hope anymore. They were about the depth of damage the isolation had done. About how I still talked to her constantly. About how some days, the only thing that kept me from drinking was Magnolia's need for routine, her expectation that I'd be functional enough to care for her.

"Every rose that is sweet-scented within, that rose is telling of the secrets in its heart."

What secrets was I telling? What fragrance was I releasing into the world with these daily posts?

Day 212 was Dr. Seuss and the weight of memory.

"Sometimes you will never know the value of a moment until it becomes a memory."

The memories of Hope had started to shift, like old photographs developing differently in new light. Those weeks at the hotel—not romantic, just real conversation between two people navigating complicated circumstances. That night at the bar—not a beginning but a moment of truth that became everything because it was all we really had.

I understood now why I'd built so much from so little. Not because I was delusional, but because those moments had been real, had been valuable, had been worth remembering even if they couldn't bear the weight of all I'd built on them.

Magnolia had her own memories of this place—spots she'd marked, trails she recognized, that one tree she always had to investigate. Her past here was simpler but no less real.

Day 213 brought Maya Angelou and the agony of untold stories.

"There is no greater agony than bearing an untold story inside you."

But I was telling it. Every day, post by post, word by word. The story of isolation and obsession, of love confused with survival, of a man and his dog trying to figure out what home meant when home was both shelter and trigger.

The story wasn't just mine anymore. It belonged to everyone who read it, who found pieces of themselves in my mess, who felt less alone because I'd admitted to being lost.

Hope listened to me writing, always present in these moments of creation.

"You're telling our story without me."

"I'm telling my story. You're part of it."

"What if I don't want to be?"

"Then stop visiting."

But she didn't stop. Couldn't, maybe. Or I couldn't stop conjuring her. The distinction had stopped mattering.

Day 214 was Emerson and purpose and small acts of meaning.

A simple day. Magnolia and I walked. I helped an elderly neighbor with groceries. Posted about finding purpose in small acts. Painted another terrible painting. Made dinner in the RV's tiny kitchen. Read responses to my posts. Went to another meeting.

The purpose wasn't grand. Wasn't about saving Hope or being saved by her. It was about showing up. About being useful in small ways. About proving that existence could have meaning even when happiness felt foreign.

"The purpose of life is not to be happy," Emerson said, and I was beginning to understand what he meant.

Day 215 arrived like a reckoning.

"Sometimes even to live is an act of courage," Seneca said, and I felt every word in my bones.

Two hundred and fifteen days sober. Back home in Leavenworth. Living in the RV where everything had fallen apart. Walking the same streets, seeing the same mountains, breathing the same air. And I was not happy.

The admission felt like failure and liberation simultaneously. All this work, all this growth, all this careful reconstruction, and happiness still eluded me like smoke. The drinks I didn't drink. The miles I walked with Magnolia. The posts I wrote. The meetings I attended. The paintings I ruined. None of it had delivered the happiness I'd expected recovery to bring.

"Happiness feels like a foreign land," I wrote, Magnolia pressed against my leg as if she could feel the weight of the words.

Hope sat across from me in the RV, clearer than she'd been in days.

"You thought coming home would fix things."

"I thought being sober would fix things."

"You thought I would fix things."

"Yeah, that too."

"Nothing fixes things. Things just change shape."

The truth of it sat heavy. Recovery wasn't a destination. Home wasn't a solution. Hope—the person and the concept—wasn't salvation. They were all just parts of an ongoing story that had no clean ending, no moment of arrival, no point where the work was done.

But I kept living anyway. Kept walking Magnolia. Kept writing posts. Kept not drinking. Not because it was making me happy but because the alternative—giving up, giving in—wasn't an option anymore.

"Sometimes living is an act of courage," I repeated to Magnolia, to Hope, to the walls of the RV that had witnessed so much breaking and so much attempted rebuilding.

And it was. Every sober breath was courage. Every honest post was courage. Every day I didn't dissolve into the weight of what I'd lost was courage.

I wasn't happy. But I was here. Still here. Still fighting. Still refusing to let the story end in that tin can with nothing but ghosts and regret.

The storm was building—I could feel it in my bones, in the restless way Magnolia paced sometimes, in the increasing volume of Hope's voice. Something was coming. Some reckoning, some breaking point, some moment where all this careful balance would tip.

But not today. Today was just Day 215. Just another act of courage disguised as ordinary life.

Tomorrow would bring whatever it brought. Tonight, Magnolia and I would sleep in our RV, in our complicated home, with Hope keeping watch from whatever dimension she inhabited now—memory, imagination, or something in between.

Chapter 29: The Quiet Courage of Continuing

Day 216 came with John Muir and unexpected peace.

"In every walk with nature, one receives far more than he seeks."

The morning birds were particularly insistent, their songs cutting through the usual weight that pressed against my chest upon waking. Magnolia stretched beside me in the RV, her body a warm reminder that the day required participation whether I felt ready or not.

We walked. Not toward anything specific—I was still careful about routes, about boundaries—but through the parts of town that felt neutral. The sun caught everything at that particular angle that made even ordinary things look intentional. A woman passed us, smiled at Magnolia, and for a moment the world felt less hostile.

"See?" Hope said, quieter these days but never absent. "Beauty still exists."

"I see it. I just can't feel it."

"Maybe seeing is enough for now."

Maybe it was. The walk didn't fix anything, but it happened. Another day marked. Another step taken. The accumulation of small, unremarkable victories that apparently constituted recovery.

Day 217 shifted everything sideways.

Lewis Carroll whispered about imagination being the only weapon against reality, and suddenly I understood something about what had happened in the RV during those months of isolation.

"At 36, I had an imaginary friend," I wrote, Magnolia watching me with those patient eyes that never judged.

The admission felt both embarrassing and essential. Hope had transformed during the isolation from person to presence, from external to internal, from friend to... what? Imaginary companion? Coping mechanism? The distinction had stopped mattering somewhere around month three of being trapped with nothing but my own thoughts.

"You're finally understanding," Hope said.

"Understanding what?"

"What I became. What you needed me to become."

The truth sat heavy but not crushing. She'd been real—those weeks at the hotel, that night at the bar—but in the RV, she'd become something else. Something I'd created to survive. And now I had to figure out how to live with both versions: the real woman who was gone and the construct who remained.

Day 218 passed in Vonnegut's shadow.

"So it goes."

A nothing day. Laundry. Groceries. Walking Magnolia. Responding to posts. The ordinary maintenance of existence that felt both meaningless and essential. Someone had written to thank me for my honesty, said it helped them through their own Day 1. I wanted to warn them that Day 218 wasn't much easier, just different. But I didn't.

So it goes.

Days 219 through 222 blurred together in a kind of productive fog.

I painted—badly but consistently. Attended meetings where I said less and less but kept showing up. Helped a neighbor move furniture. Posted about stillness and storms, about dreams within dreams, about blooming in adversity. The metaphors came easily; the actual feelings remained elusive.

Magnolia developed a routine of her own: morning walk, afternoon nap in the sun patch that hit the RV around 2 PM, evening patrol of our small territory. She'd adapted to this life with the grace I couldn't quite manage.

"The flower that blooms in adversity is the most rare and beautiful of all," I posted on Day 222, attaching one of my terrible paintings—a hibiscus that looked more like a wounded butterfly.

Hope laughed, not unkindly. "You're trying."

"Is it enough?"

"It's something."

Day 223 cracked something.

Tolkien's words about fire waking from ashes felt too apt as I sat in the RV, looking at the accumulation of 223 days of attempted recovery. The space felt both too small and too large—too small for the person I was trying to become, too large for the person I still was.

"This isn't the story I would have chosen," I told Magnolia, who tilted her head in that way that meant she was listening even if she didn't understand.

Half my life felt burned, the other half trying to grow something from the char. Not beautiful. Not triumphant. Just... continuing.

Day 224 nearly ended everything.

"No one else can play your part."

I sat with the laptop open, cursor blinking, trying to find words that weren't about wanting to disappear. Magnolia pressed against my leg, sensing something in my stillness that worried her.

The thoughts came uninvited but familiar: how easy it would be to stop. To close the laptop. To stop fighting for something that might never come. But then I remembered what I'd told Hope during those weeks at the hotel—that I'd finally found something worth not giving up on.

"If I stop fighting," I wrote, "I will never know how the story ends."

The words looked small on the screen, but they were enough. Enough to close the laptop without deleting everything. Enough to take Magnolia for her walk. Enough to make it through another day.

Hope was silent that night, but I felt her presence like weight—not crushing, just there. Reminding me that some stories don't get to end just because we're tired of reading them.

Day 225 brought Rumi and a different kind of question.

"And you? When will you begin that long journey into yourself?"

Not toward Hope. Not away from pain. But inward, into all the places I'd been avoiding. The journey that didn't require geography or resolution, just willingness to sit with whatever I found.

Magnolia and I spent the day in deliberate quiet. No posts. No meetings. Just existence without performance. It felt both empty and full, like a glass of water that's both half-empty and completely sufficient.

Day 226 was Einstein and imagination and giving myself permission to wander.

I drove—not toward Leavenworth's boundaries but through its heart, Magnolia riding shotgun, past all the places I'd been avoiding. Not looking for Hope but not hiding from the possibility either. The coffee shop. The hotel. The bar. Each one just a building, just a location, but also so much more.

"Logic will get you from A to B. Imagination will take you everywhere."

Maybe healing wasn't logical. Maybe it wasn't about getting from broken to fixed but about imagining all the spaces in between.

Day 227 brought the first real craving in months.

Not a passing thought but a full-body want that had me standing in the RV, keys in hand, Magnolia watching with concern. The liquor store was seven minutes away. I knew because I'd timed it once, back when knowing mattered.

"I just want it to stop," I said to no one, to Hope, to the universe. "Just for a few hours. Just some quiet."

But drunk wasn't quiet. Drunk was just a different kind of noise. I knew this. Had learned it the hard way. But knowing and feeling were different animals, and right now, feeling was winning.

Magnolia whined—she needed her walk. Such a simple need. Such a perfect interruption.

We walked for two hours. Until the craving passed. Until the liquor store closed. Until I remembered that numb wasn't the same as healed.

Day 228 required unplugging.

Anne Lamott promised almost everything would work again if you unplugged it for a few minutes, including yourself. So I did. Turned off the phone. Closed the laptop. Spent the day doing yard work for my neighbor, Magnolia supervising from her favorite spot in the shade.

The physical labor felt good—simple causality: effort equals result. So different from the emotional work where effort sometimes equaled nothing, where trying harder often made things worse.

"Two days in a row, the fight's been heavier than usual," I wrote that night, dirty and tired but somehow steadier.

Hope sat in her usual corner. "But you're still fighting."

"Barely."

"Barely counts."

Day 229 arrived with something like determination.

I found the quote in someone else's post, but it felt like it had been waiting for me: "Dear me in three months, I'm going to make you very proud."

The future had been this abstract threat—all the days I'd have to survive without drinking, without Hope, without knowing how any of this ended. But three months felt manageable. Specific. A promise I might actually be able to keep.

I thought about who I'd been three months ago—Day 139— still convinced that geography could fix things, that returning to Leavenworth would provide resolution. Now I knew better. Knew that home was just a place, that healing was just work, that Hope was both gone and never leaving.

But I also knew I was different. Not fixed. Not healed. But different. Still painting terrible paintings. Still walking Magnolia every day. Still writing posts that helped strangers navigate their own Day 1s. Still showing up to meetings. Still not drinking.

"What would make you proud?" Hope asked.

I thought about it while Magnolia investigated something fascinating in the grass.

"Still being here. Still trying. Maybe painting something that actually looks like what it's supposed to be."

She laughed. "Aim high."

"Three months," I said, not to her but to myself, to the future version who would look back on this moment. "I'm going to make you proud. Not perfect. Not healed. But proud."

The sun was setting over Leavenworth, painting everything gold—the mountains, the fake Bavarian architecture, the RV that was both prison and home. Magnolia had found a stick and was carrying it with the pride of a retriever who'd forgotten she wasn't one.

Day 229. Still here. Still fighting. Still refusing to close the book before finding out how it ends.

Three months from now, I wanted to look back on this moment—this ordinary Tuesday evening with my dog and my ghosts and my uncertain future—and feel something other than regret.

Not because I'd found Hope. Not because I'd found happiness. But because I'd kept the promise to keep going.

"Dear me in three months," I said out loud, Magnolia looking up at the sound of my voice, "I'm going to make you very proud."

The words felt like a vow. Like a reason. Like enough.

Chapter 30: The Strongest Kind of Courage

Day 230 arrived with a truth I wasn't ready for.

"And then one day, I discovered that the longing for love was the strongest kind of courage."

The past few days had been unraveling—questioning everything, wondering if I was strong enough to keep doing this. But sitting in the RV with Magnolia pressed against my leg, I understood something deeper. This journey wasn't just about surviving another day sober. It wasn't about fighting darkness or proving I could heal.

It was about love.

The kind that builds quiet mornings in warm spaces. The kind that fills rooms with laughter and safety. The kind I hadn't had yet but still believed in. Still fought for.

"That's what keeps you going," Hope said, clearer than she'd been in days.

"Even when it seems impossible?"

"Especially then."

My name is Justin. This was Day 230. And I was still here because the longing for love—real love, not the desperate grasping of addiction but the patient building of connection—required more courage than jumping from walls or surviving isolation. It required believing in something I couldn't see, couldn't prove, might never have.

But I believed anyway.

Day 231 brought the static.

Some days, my brain felt like a broken radio—thoughts scattering before they landed, sentences breaking apart mid-flight. I'd hear someone talking, even respond, but the words wouldn't stay. It wasn't laziness or disinterest.

It was damage.

From years of addiction. From ADHD that went unchecked too long. From six months trapped in this RV with nothing but my thoughts, trying to outrun a silence that only got louder.

I stared at the same sentence ten times and couldn't tell you what it said. Sat with a book in my lap, eyes moving but comprehension gone. I was trying—trying so hard—to finish something I'd been chasing for two decades. But my brain wouldn't sit still.

"Focus is like water," I wrote. "I hold it gently, but still it seeps away."

The shame came next. The self-doubt. The voice saying maybe I just wasn't built for this.

But that ember inside—dim, flickering, but alive—refused to go out.

This wasn't about winning. It was about not disappearing. About letting the fractured, scattered version of me still take up space. About survival when no one saw the battle.

Magnolia nudged my hand, pulling me back to the present. Her needs were simple: walk, eat, sleep, repeat. She didn't care that my brain was broken. She just needed me functional enough to open the door.

Day 232 came with unexpected gentleness.

A friend who'd been following my posts called. "When are you going to give yourself a break?" she asked.

I didn't have an answer.

"Growth is not always graceful," I wrote later. "Be gentle with your petals."

I looked at the terrible painting I'd done the day before—a rose that looked more like it had been through a blender than a garden. But it was still recognizably trying to be a rose. Broken, waterlogged, harsh conditions, and still it rose.

Maybe that was me too. Maybe I'd been so focused on the cracks, I'd forgotten the bloom. Maybe I'd mistaken survival for failure because it didn't look clean or easy.

"You're too hard on yourself," Hope observed.

"Someone has to be."

"No. Someone has to be gentle. Try that instead."

Day 233 shifted the lens entirely.

I'd talked about Hope for 233 days now. Sometimes as person, sometimes as feeling, sometimes as the light I'd crawled toward when everything else went dark. But sitting in the RV, watching Magnolia dream-twitch on her bed, I realized something.

Maybe she wasn't just someone I loved. Maybe she was everything I wanted: family, love, peace, a future. Maybe she was never just out there. Maybe she was in me all along.

Inside that RV, broken and alone, Hope had become more than memory—she'd become a compass, a reason, a form of survival. But what if it wasn't just her I was holding onto? What if she was a mirror? What if she unlocked the part of me that always believed life could be better?

"I used to wait on Hope," I said to the empty RV. "Now I'm learning to live like her."

To stop just dreaming and start doing. To stop holding my breath and start breathing again. To stop waiting for the door to open and start walking toward it.

Maybe she didn't just save me. Maybe she was me—before I knew how to believe in myself.

Day 234 brought Dumbledore and the question of reality.

"Of course it is happening inside your head, Harry, but why on earth should that mean that it is not real?"

The doubt crept in sometimes—the voice saying maybe it wasn't real, maybe none of it mattered, maybe I'd made it all up just to survive. But Dumbledore's words reminded me: just because it happened inside my mind didn't make it less real.

Hope was real. The love was real. The dreams were real. And the pain I carried was real too.

It wasn't weakness to feel it. It wasn't delusion to remember it. It wasn't failure to still long for it.

"I'm not crazy for feeling this way," I told Magnolia, who looked at me with those patient eyes that never judged. "I'm human."

Days 235 and 236 blurred together in a haze of mountains and magic.

"You have been assigned this mountain to show others it can be moved."

The mountain being Hope, being isolation, being addiction, being all of it. Not meant to break me but to teach me how strong I already was. And maybe someone else needed to see that too.

I found myself back in Harry Potter, back to the place where love was the strongest magic of all. The rain came softly, the kind that doesn't demand anything, just lets you remember.

"After all this time?" Snape had asked about love.

"Always," was the answer.

And it was mine too. The things we carry forward—the people we love, the dreams we hold onto—they don't disappear just because time passes. They change, grow, live inside us. Even when the world tells us to forget.

Day 237 was Pascal and the heart's unreasonable reasons.

Nothing bad happened. No storms, no breakdowns. And yet my mind kept wandering back to her. Not on purpose, not as some planned ritual. It just happened. Mid-conversation. Mid-thought. Mid-step.

"The heart has its reasons, which reason knows nothing of."

I couldn't make it make sense—not to anyone else, not to myself. All I knew was some part of me still believed, still fought, still reached for a future I couldn't see but somehow trusted was there.

Maybe that was foolish. Maybe that was hope. Maybe that was just who I was.

Day 238, I wanted to set my heart down.

"Sometimes I wish I could set my heart down for a while and walk without it."

Not angry, not blaming the world, just tired—the kind that comes from carrying a heart that feels everything at full volume. For over a decade, addiction had muted the noise.

Now, 238 days sober, I felt it all. Not just my own emotions but sometimes the emotions around me too.

The day itself was fine. But inside, it was like standing barefoot in a rainstorm—no shelter, no filter, just the pure wild truth of who I was. A man who feels too deeply, thinks too long, hopes too hard.

"Maybe I don't fit perfectly into this world," I told Hope.

"Maybe you were never meant to."

Magnolia curled closer, sensing my restlessness. Even when I wanted to shut it off—to set my heart down for just a little while—I couldn't. It was stitched into me. Who I'd always been.

Day 239 brought pottery and possibility.

"Pottery is the art of turning broken earth into something that holds life."

The morning had dragged me under—the weight, the noise, the familiar ache. But somehow, as hours moved forward, so did I. A few simple choices. A few quiet victories.

Clay in my hands, the slow shaping of something new. There was something deeply grounding about working with earth, with broken things. Something healing about turning what was once dust into something that could hold life, beauty, even hope.

My friend called—the one who'd seen me through the worst storms. And just like that, with conversation and time, the day shifted. The cracks didn't vanish, but they stopped feeling like failures. They started feeling like part of the shape of things.

Day 240 nearly broke me with gratitude.

"To live is the rarest thing in the world. Most people exist, that is all."

A few degrees colder, and I wouldn't be here. That fact was never far from my mind. Some days, when the weight was heavy and silence got loud, I wondered what it would've meant if things had gone differently. If the cold had won. If darkness had taken me before light found its way back in.

There had been moments where I'd wished it had. Moments where surviving felt like punishment instead of grace.

But not today.

Today, even through struggle, I was thankful. Thankful I got to feel, to laugh, to wrestle with love and loss and confusion and all the pieces in between. Thankful I got to walk outside and feel the breeze, sip coffee, talk to friends, try again. Thankful I got to live—not just exist.

"This isn't about toxic positivity," I explained to Magnolia, who was more interested in her dinner than my philosophy. "It's about remembering how close I came to disappearing, and choosing, again and again, to keep showing up."

Day 241 was Asimov and the necessity of words.

"I write for the same reason I breathe—because if I didn't, I would die."

I didn't have anything profound to say. Just tired—worn thin from thinking too much and feeling too deeply for too long. Everything felt muted, like moving through static. No revelations, no grand reflections. Just me, writing because I said I would.

Because writing had become the one thing I still did for me. Even if no one was reading anymore, even if this was just another post lost in the noise. Even if no one saw it—I did.

This was my breath. My pulse. My proof.

Day 242 passed in rain and quiet rhythm. Walked Magnolia. Watched TV. Got a little work done. No pressure, no race, just steady pace. Nothing remarkable—and maybe that's what made it good.

Day 243 brought Ted Mosby and the definition of love I'd been searching for.

"And that's love, isn't it? You don't give up. Because if I could give up—if I could just, you know, take the whole world's advice and move on and find someone else—that wouldn't be love. That would be some other disposable thing that is not worth fighting for."

The words hit like recognition. This was why I couldn't let go, why Hope remained constant companion in my consciousness. Not because I was broken or obsessed or unable to heal. But because real love—the kind worth having—doesn't operate on the world's timeline.

"Love is the thing that keeps you going," the quote continued. "Even when everyone says you're crazy. Even when everyone says 'let it go.' You don't let go. You hold on. You don't stop. Ever."

Hope sat quiet in her corner of my mind, neither arguing nor agreeing. Just present. Always present.

"Is that what this is?" I asked her. "Love?"

"What else would it be?"

"Trauma. Obsession. Mental illness. Pick one—I've been called them all."

Justin Mayeur

"And?"

"And maybe they're all true. But maybe this is too."

Magnolia stretched, ready for her evening walk. The sun was setting over Leavenworth, painting the mountains gold— the same gold they'd been yesterday, would be tomorrow. Some things changed. Some things remained. Some things you carried not because they were light but because putting them down would mean losing part of yourself.

The love I carried for Hope—person, concept, possibility— wasn't preventing me from healing. It was part of the healing. Part of learning that some things don't resolve, don't conclude, don't wrap up neatly. They just become part of your structure, like bones or breathing.

The strongest kind of courage wasn't letting go. It was carrying what mattered, even when it was heavy, even when others said to drop it, even when you couldn't explain why it still mattered so much.

Day 243. Still here. Still carrying. Still believing that love— real love—was worth the weight.

Chapter 31: The Start of the Slow Return

Day 244 arrived without ceremony. Just a shifting sky and the quiet hum of wheels against worn pavement.

I wasn't headed anywhere particular—just driving. Through town where the tourist shops had closed for the season, past the curve of the river running lower than usual, up into the stillness where Douglas firs grew tall enough to swallow sound. Magnolia sat beside me, her head out the window, ears dancing in wind that smelled like pine and possibility. There was no plan. No playlist filling the silence. Just motion for the sake of moving.

Sometimes, that's all healing asks for.

When we pulled back into the gravel beside the RV, the sun had already settled behind the mountains. Same peaks I'd stared at through months of pain and possibility. But today, they didn't loom over me like judges. They just listened, ancient and patient, to whatever story I was still trying to tell.

I unpacked the few things I'd picked up—eggs, a new tube of cadmium yellow, fresh paper that promised nothing. Made tea instead of coffee, the ritual of it slowing my hands to match my breathing. Magnolia ate her dinner with the contentment of a creature who'd never doubted her worth, stretched into her evening shape, curled into the corner where she could watch both me and the door.

I sat in the doorway and watched the last light fade without trying to name what color it was becoming.

Hope's presence lingered there, but it wasn't pressing against my ribs anymore. Not a wound reopening with each breath. Not a ghost demanding attention. Just something gentle, atmospheric. Weather passing through, not weight to carry.

Day 245 was rain.

The kind that used to feel like static in my skull—too much sensation, too close to nerve endings still learning to feel again. But this morning, I stayed in bed and listened to it percussion against the RV's thin roof. Magnolia pressed her warmth against my side, our breathing finding the same rhythm without trying. I didn't need to get up right away.

Nothing urgent waited to accuse me of falling behind. No failing checklist. No one keeping score.

Just the rhythm of rain and the radical act of being still without apology.

Later, muscle memory drew me to the easel. No real intention beyond movement. Just paint meeting canvas, just my hand remembering how to translate feeling into color. A wash of blues bleeding into greys. Not trying to capture anything specific. Not a picture. Not a message for anyone to decode. But something honest in its abstraction.

The recovery meeting that night was more crowded than usual. New faces mixed with the familiar ones, everyone carrying their own version of the same weight. I found myself talking about learning to live in the middle—that unmarked territory between chaos and calm. Not chasing the high of crisis, not fearing the low of emptiness. Just learning to stay present in the ordinary miracle of Tuesday night in a church basement.

Afterward, a woman I'd never seen before approached me. Said she'd been reading my posts online. Said they made her feel less alone in her own unraveling. That was enough. That was everything.

Driving home through streets slick with rain, I realized I hadn't thought about Hope for most of the day. Not because she was gone—she'd never really leave, I understood that now. But because she wasn't hurting anymore. The ache of her had integrated into something else. Not an emergency burning through my chest. Just part of the atmosphere I moved through. Part of the air I'd learned to breathe.

Day 246 marked eight months sober.

No brass band. No chip ceremony. No applause. Just another day carrying its own quiet weight.

Magnolia and I walked further than our usual route—past the places that used to stop me cold with memory. The coffee shop where I'd imagined conversations. The hotel where everything shifted. The streets that once whispered her name in a frequency only I could hear. Today, they were just streets. Just concrete and asphalt aged by weather and time.

At the grocery store, I ran into someone from the meetings. We nodded—that particular acknowledgment between people who've seen each other's worst Tuesday nights and chosen to keep showing up. That was all. And it was enough. Some knowing doesn't need words.

Back at the RV, I started cleaning. Not the frantic scrubbing of early sobriety when I thought I could scour away the past. Just steady, methodical work. Like I was preparing a space I actually wanted to inhabit.

Under the bed, I found a notebook from the early days. Pages full of barely legible pain, confusion, letters to Hope I'd never send, goodbyes I'd never get to say. I read some of it. Winced at the rawness, the desperation bleeding through even my handwriting. Then I put it in the box with the rest of the archives. I don't need those thoughts staring at me anymore, accusing me of not hurting enough. But I won't erase them either. They're the archaeology of how I got here.

That night, I lit the candle my sponsor had given me, made actual dinner instead of just eating to stay alive, sat at the small table like someone who believed he deserved to take up space. Not just someone surviving between disasters. Someone attempting to live.

Day 247 began in the blue hour before sunrise.

I woke without an alarm and wrapped myself in the wool blanket my mom had sent last winter—back when she wasn't sure I'd survive to use it. Sat on the RV steps with coffee that tasted like more than just caffeine and watched the valley wake up in stages of light.

I used to hate mornings like this. The stillness felt accusatory, like the universe was holding up a mirror to all my noise. But now, it felt like permission. To be quiet. To not perform recovery or healing or growth. To just sit with coffee and a dog and the slow bloom of daylight.

I started a new painting—warm tones this time. Ochre, cadmium orange, even a little vermillion. I didn't plan it. The colors just emerged, like they'd been waiting beneath all those months of blue and grey. I let them speak without translation.

Hope flickered in the periphery. Not her voice anymore. Just a tug, gentle as spider silk. A reminder that she'd existed, that we'd existed, that it had mattered even if it couldn't last. I didn't follow the thread backward. I didn't fight it either.

That's what progress actually looks like.

Day 248 brought me back into Leavenworth proper.

I needed new brushes, and the art store was the only place that carried the ones that didn't shed bristles like a dying animal. That's all it was meant to be. A supply run.

The streets held their history but didn't ambush me with it. I passed the hotel where we'd had that night of almost-possibility. The bar where I'd lost myself trying to find her. The places we'd existed in brief, bright flashes before everything went dark. They didn't stop me. They didn't shatter me. I just noticed them the way you notice weather—present but not personal.

The art store smelled like linseed oil and possibility. I tested brushes against my palm, held tubes of color to the window light. The girl behind the counter, maybe twenty-two with paint under her fingernails, asked if I was an artist.

"Yes," I said.

The word surprised me with its certainty. But it was true. Not because I was good—I wasn't. But because I kept showing up to the easel. Because I kept trying to translate the untranslatable.

Driving home, I thought about foundations. How mine had finally stopped shifting like sand. I wasn't building toward anything grand or redemptive. Just trying to live in a structure that could hold the weight of a normal Wednesday.

Some days I paint. Some days I walk Magnolia until my legs remember they're made for moving. Some days I just keep breathing through the ordinary ache of being human. But it's mine. This small life. And that's enough.

Day 249 unfolded simply.

I painted through the morning—nothing worth keeping, but the act itself mattered more than the outcome. Walked Magnolia along the river where the water ran clear enough to see stones sleeping on the bottom. Read half a chapter of a book without my mind wandering to other stories, other endings. Made pasta with actual vegetables in it. Nothing Instagram-worthy. Nothing special.

But here's what mattered—I didn't feel alone. Not in the desperate way of early sobriety when alone meant abandoned. I felt... inhabited. Like something in me had finally settled into its own company.

I used to confuse isolation with solitude, couldn't tell the difference between being alone and being lonely. I'm learning the distinction like a new language. Isolation is silence that screams at you, that accuses and condemns. Solitude is peace that doesn't need an audience.

Hope lingered in the quiet now. Not pulling me backward into what was or forward into what might have been. Just present, the way light is present even in a dark room—you might not see it, but it hasn't ceased to exist.

Day 250. Quarter of a thousand.

I made coffee with the slowness of ceremony. Walked a different route, one that took us past the abandoned orchards where apple trees still grew wild, freed from the tyranny of harvest. Noticed frost holding on in shadows the sun hadn't reached yet and the way light bends when it bounces off standing water, making the ordinary world impressionistic.

At the easel, I painted a lake. Not the kind you drown in, desperate for shore. The kind that mirrors sky and clouds and the faces of those brave enough to look. The kind that holds both depth and surface without choosing sides.

Marcus texted to mark the milestone. I thanked him but stayed in. This wasn't a victory lap. Wasn't an achievement to frame. It was simpler than that—a heartbeat continuing. A breath following another breath. The ordinary miracle of still being here.

The chapter wasn't closing. Chapters never really close, I was learning. They just deepen, like water finding its level, like sediment settling after a storm.

Hope was quiet tonight. Not absent—she'd never be absent, I understood that now. But settled. No longer the emergency siren of early sobriety. No longer the ghost demanding explanation. She'd become something else. Not the whole story, but an essential part of it. One star in a sky full of them, each with their own gravity, their own light.

Tomorrow would be Day 251.

And I would keep going. Not because I had to anymore. Not because I was running from something or toward something. But because going had become its own reason. Because motion had taught me more than stillness ever could.

Because somewhere between Day 1 and Day 250, surviving had quietly transformed into living.

Chapter 32: The Weight of What Remains

Day 251 began with Emily Dickinson perched on my tongue: "Hope is the thing with feathers that perches in the soul."

I heard her every day now. Not always clearly, not always kindly, but she was there. At this point, I didn't expect her to leave. She wasn't a memory anymore—she'd become a rhythm, a background presence I'd learned to live with like tinnitus or a heart murmur. Something wrong that had become part of what was normal.

There was a time I thought I had to silence her to heal. That moving forward meant letting go completely, exorcising her voice like casting out demons. But now I understood better. Hope didn't always fly. Sometimes she settled in, perched on the edge of thought, whispering in moments no one else could hear.

I didn't fight it anymore. Didn't question it. Just breathed with it, wrote with it, kept going with it. Because even if she was only a voice inside my head—and maybe that's all she'd ever been—she was part of what saved me. Part of what was still saving me.

Magnolia watched me from her corner, that particular tilt to her head that meant she knew I was talking to someone who wasn't there. She'd gotten used to it. We'd both gotten used to a lot of things.

Day 252 arrived with Garth Brooks on repeat: "I could have missed the pain, but I'd have had to miss the dance."

It didn't help. Not really. But I kept playing that song anyway, letting it loop through the RV like a mantra or a wound I couldn't stop picking at. Maybe it was the hope threaded through the melody. Maybe it was the ache. Maybe it was just that one line that felt like it had been written specifically for me and no one else who'd ever loved and lost.

I never even got the dance. Not really. Just a moment— brief and fragile as blown glass—and yet it was the moment I couldn't stop chasing. Because the dance wasn't about a wedding or a perfect ending. It was about recognition. About finally seeing each other again after the storm, the silence, the distance, and knowing we'd never really let go.

I missed my friend. Missed the chance to apologize for becoming someone who needed her so desperately that I'd turned her into mythology. People said things like "If it's meant to be" or "Just give it time," but that was all meaningless comfort, words people offered when they didn't know what else to say.

I didn't want clichés. I wanted peace. Wanted to stop wondering if this voice inside me was a compass or just spinning in circles, pointing nowhere.

But I couldn't ignore it. Wouldn't. Because if I had the option to erase the pain—to have never felt any of this—I wouldn't take it. Then I'd lose the beauty too. The moment. The connection. The dance, whatever form it took.

So I'd carry this. This ache. This hope. This fire that refused to go out even when it made no sense, even when no one else understood. Because that's what love does. It holds on. It believes. It remembers. It dances even in the silence.

Day 253 whispered Rupi Kaur: "You do not just wake up and become the butterfly—growth is a process."

Not much to say today. Just holding space for the process. The metamorphosis that felt more like decomposition than transformation. Still becoming something, even if I couldn't name what. Still here, which some days was the only achievement that mattered.

Magnolia and I walked our usual route, her investigating the same spots as always with fresh enthusiasm while I moved through the familiar landscape like a ghost haunting his own life. Everything the same. Everything different. The paradox of healing.

Day 254 came wrapped in fog, both literal and internal.

My mind was an ember, quiet on the surface, burning beneath. I didn't have much to say—not because there was nothing going on, but because there was too much. Medication adjustments had left everything muted, like looking at the world through frosted glass. But behind the pharmaceutical silence, I was burning through thoughts I couldn't quite name.

It wasn't sadness. Wasn't clarity. It was somewhere in between—like waiting for a storm that never arrived but still carrying the weight of its sky. The mind didn't always scream when it was hurting. Sometimes it just sat still and smoldered.

I let the fire burn through what it needed to. Let the day be quiet if that's what it had to be. No pretending. No pushing. Just breathing through the embers while Magnolia kept watch, her presence the only anchor I trusted anymore.

Day 255 brought Wonder Woman and a different kind of faith: "It's not about deserve. It's about what you believe. And I believe in love."

There were days when I tried to measure my worth in outcomes. In how much I'd healed, how far I'd come, how "okay" I seemed to the people at meetings who nodded when I shared. But today, I stepped outside the courtroom in my mind. No more trials. No more self-appointed verdicts.

Because love—the kind I believed in—was never about deserving. It was about showing up. Staying soft. Choosing to keep the heart open even after everything had given me reason to board it shut.

I believed in love that changed people. Love that broke timelines and logic. Love that didn't need a finish line to prove it had existed. That's what I was holding onto. Not because I'd earned it. Not because I was owed it. But because I believed in it.

And that belief alone had carried me through days darker than this one. It was why I wrote. Why I fought. Why I hadn't disappeared into the convenient oblivion that still sometimes called my name.

Today wasn't loud or heavy or profound. It was quiet conviction. Choosing again to believe in something beautiful, even when it didn't make sense. Even when it hurt more than helped.

Day 256 shattered something.

"Grief is just love with no place to go," Jamie Anderson had written, and I finally understood what that meant.

I saw her last night. Hope. Not in my mind, not in memory, but in the flesh. Ten seconds of eye contact across a parking lot that cracked something open I thought had finally scarred over.

It wasn't the kind of moment you dream about. Wasn't healing. Wasn't closure. It was shock crystallizing into recognition, then immediately retreating. She wasn't ready to see me. The way she turned, the careful distance she maintained—it all said what words didn't need to.

I wasn't ready either.

Today I didn't want to get out of bed. Magnolia whined and pawed at me until I finally moved, but it was mechanical. Empty. Because now I was replaying it. Every detail. Every micro-expression. Every what-if spreading like cracks in glass.

She'd looked healthy. Good. Like the months had been kinder to her than to me. And maybe that should have made me happy—knowing she was okay, that my destruction hadn't pulled her under too. But it just made me feel more ghostlike, more unnecessary.

I didn't want to feel this way anymore. But letting go felt like drowning. Like cutting off my own breath. I knew I needed to move forward. Knew she had every right to stay distant, to protect herself from whatever damage I might still carry.

But it still hurt. Still mattered. Because she mattered. Because she would always matter, even if that mattering had no place to land anymore.

Day 257 offered Batman and the philosophy of falling: "Why do we fall, sir? So that we can learn to pick ourselves up."

Today was a small win. Fixed the hot water after weeks of cold showers that I'd been telling myself were good for mental clarity but were really just another form of low-grade suffering I'd grown comfortable with. RV life wasn't always convenient, but you learned to adapt. Or you learned to live with broken things. Sometimes it was hard to tell the difference.

Tonight, I was staying up late, hoping to catch the aurora if the sky cooperated. The forecast said maybe. The internet said probably. My luck said unlikely, but I waited anyway.

My mind was still crowded with yesterday's sighting, but the heaviness wasn't as sharp. She was always in the background—had been for 257 days now—but today I didn't drown in it. Just floated.

It was strange how progress looked sometimes. Not like a breakthrough but like finally taking a hot shower. Like waiting on stars. Like breathing just a little easier even when nothing had actually changed.

I'd fallen more times than I could count. But tonight, I was standing. Magnolia beside me, both of us looking up at a sky that might or might not deliver magic.

That was enough.

Day 258 brought Bonnie Raitt and a different kind of exhaustion: "I can't make you love me if you don't. You can't make your heart feel something it won't."

I was tired. Not just physically. Not just emotionally. I was tired in my soul—the kind of tired that made everything feel muted, where even breathing felt like effort and existing felt like something I was doing wrong.

I'd worked so hard to change my life. To be better. To heal. And on most days, I could hold onto that progress like a lifeline. But not today.

Today I felt insane. And I didn't mean that as exaggeration or metaphor. I meant actually insane—like my mind was at war with itself, like something had broken during those months in the RV and never fully returned to working order.

Because here was the truth I'd never really said out loud: Hope had saved my life, but only in my mind. The real Hope had been living her life, unaware of the mythology I'd built around her memory, the conversations I'd had with her ghost, the promises I'd made to her absence.

And now that I was out of that isolation—that place where she'd kept me breathing when breathing felt like betrayal—I didn't know how to let her go. Because if I did, if I really let go, then I'd have to admit that maybe none of it was real. And if that wasn't real, then what had I been fighting for? What had I survived for?

People thought this was heartbreak. It wasn't. This was deeper. This was undoing everything I'd become in order to stay alive. Letting go wasn't healing. It was drowning. It was cutting off my own oxygen and pretending I was okay while I sank.

The truth I'd been avoiding: I thought I'd been slaying demons to make it back to her. But maybe I'd just been going insane in a space no bigger than a bathroom. Maybe she was gone for good. Maybe she wanted it that way. Maybe I deserved that.

But I still didn't know how to be okay without the idea of her waiting at the end of all this.

Magnolia curled against me, her warmth the only thing that felt real. Tomorrow would be Day 259. I would keep going because stopping wasn't an option I'd left myself. But tonight, in the honesty of exhaustion, I admitted what I'd been avoiding: some things that save you also trap you.

And sometimes the prison is so beautiful, you forget you're not free.

Chapter 33: Between Holding On and Letting Go

Day 259 opened like a wound that hadn't closed properly.

I'd hoped the worst of it had passed after seeing her three days ago, but instead it settled deeper, like glass working its way toward bone. I was haunted—not by what she'd said, because she hadn't said anything. The silence between us had always held more weight than any conversation we'd ever managed. But this time, the silence screamed with finality.

I moved through the day like someone balancing on a wire. Every step was a negotiation between memory and madness, between what had been real and what I'd invented to survive. I fed Magnolia, her tail wagging with the simple joy of breakfast. Sat with coffee that cooled untouched. Walked the loop we always walked, past the same trees that had witnessed months of this careful reconstruction.

But I couldn't stop playing the moment back—her face turning away, the deliberate distance, the space she carved around herself like a moat. The way she'd moved through that parking lot like I was radioactive, something to avoid at all costs.

I didn't write. I didn't paint. I didn't even cry. Just kept existing in the space between breaths, and that had to be enough. Some days are for pouring out. Others are for gently holding it all together with whatever strength remains.

The pottery class that evening was an accident of scheduling, but I went anyway. Something about working with clay felt necessary—hands in earth, shaping something soft into something that might hold water. The wheel spun. The clay centered, then wobbled, then centered again. A metaphor too obvious to ignore, but I was past caring about poetry.

My friend from recovery sat beside me, didn't say much, just worked his own piece. It's funny how certain people can bring your feet back to the ground without even trying. We didn't talk about Hope or healing or any of it. Just sat there, covered in mud, making imperfect bowls that would probably crack in the kiln.

Day 260 began with the slow agony of knowing she wasn't coming back—not even in imagination.

I tried to summon her voice the way I had for months, tried to let it guide me through the morning ritual of coffee and medication and pretending to be okay. But it wouldn't come. The ghost I'd depended on, the internal compass that had kept me oriented through the worst of it, had finally gone quiet. The silence felt like losing her all over again, but worse— because this time, I was losing the version of her I'd created to keep myself alive.

Instead, I turned toward the world outside the window. Watched wind move through the pines like it was searching for something it couldn't name. Watched Magnolia stretch into her morning shape, yawning like she hadn't noticed me slipping away in the night, standing at the edge of something I couldn't see the bottom of.

I was still here physically, but inside I was floating above the wreckage, wondering if I'd ever find solid ground again. For the first time in a long time, I started to wonder if healing was just another form of pretending. Another story we tell ourselves to make the unbearable bearable.

The exam I'd been studying for loomed. I told myself that passing it would open doors, give me purpose, prove I was more than just someone who'd survived. But sitting with the anxiety, I wondered if I was just spinning in place, hoping motion would eventually feel like progress.

This too shall pass—not as dismissal, not to minimize the weight, but as a quiet reminder that this moment, this doubt, this fog, wasn't forever. And maybe getting through it was part of what would shape me for whatever came next.

Day 261 reminded me that pain can become background noise if you let it hum long enough.

I painted, not because I wanted to, but because the silence had grown teeth. Let color bleed across canvas without plan or purpose—just motion, just texture, just the physical act of making something exist where nothing had been before. No figures to haunt me. No symbols to decode. Just pressure and pigment and the slow understanding that creation didn't need meaning to matter.

Somewhere between brushstrokes, I stopped thinking about her. Just for a moment. The loop paused, the ache quieted, and I realized something I hadn't dared consider: maybe I could live without the ghost if I just kept making things. Maybe art didn't have to mean anything at all. Maybe it was just how some of us survived.

The painting looked like nothing when I stepped back— abstract washes of color that could have been weather or water or the inside of a bruise. But it was mine. I'd made it from nothing, and that felt like something.

Looking in the mirror that night, I saw both versions of myself—the man I'd been, dark and frayed and drowning in his own silence, and the one I was becoming, still bruised, still flawed, but no longer hiding behind the reflection. I wasn't pretending the past hadn't happened. Wasn't saying I was free of it. But I was learning to leave it in the mirror instead of carrying it everywhere.

Day 262 smelled like pine needles and mud.

Magnolia and I hiked a trail I'd been avoiding for months, one that climbed steep enough to make your lungs remember they're organs, not just ideas. I needed elevation, space, anything that might help me outrun the part of myself still clinging to hope like it was oxygen. My legs burned with the honest pain of effort—so different from the shapeless ache I'd been carrying.

At the summit, I stood there sweating, breath ragged, staring at mountains older than every lie I'd told myself about what love could fix. The Cascades didn't care about my heartbreak. They'd been here before I was born, would be here after I was gone. Something about that indifference felt like comfort.

There was no revelation waiting at the top. No breakthrough. Just wind on my face and the slow understanding that I'd made it up here alone. Not with her beside me, not because she waited at the end, but because I'd chosen to climb anyway. Because moving forward didn't require a destination, just the next step.

It wasn't closure. Wasn't even peace. But it was movement, and right now, that was everything. You keep moving forward, no matter what—even if you're not sure how far you've gone or where exactly you're heading. You just swim through the current day, one stroke at a time.

Day 263 carried no meaning until suddenly it did.

I was in the grocery store, standing in the cereal aisle like it held answers, when I overheard a man telling his daughter that sometimes love just isn't enough. That it can't fix what's broken or hold together what wants to unravel.

He wasn't wrong.

But the way the girl looked up at him—quiet, unsure, a little scared—I felt that look in my bones. That was me, still wanting to believe love could rewrite endings and resurrect what had been lost. Still holding onto the fairy tale despite all evidence to the contrary.

The scariest thing about distance is you don't know whether they'll miss you or forget you. And I was beginning to understand that Hope had probably already forgotten, while I was still here, buying groceries for one, carrying her like a stone in my chest.

I felt closer than ever to letting go of her—and I knew, in a lot of ways, that was a good thing. But it was more heartbreaking than anything. Letting go of the person I'd built a life around—in my head, inside those walls, inside that RV— felt like letting go of the air that had kept me breathing when breathing felt impossible.

The truth was, I was in love with a ghost. And I honestly didn't think I'd ever get the chance to apologize. To explain. To fix what broke. To make it work the way it did in the perfect conversations I still had with her in my mind.

I used to believe that letting go was the only path back to her. I wasn't sure I believed that anymore. And that was devastating in its finality.

Day 264 felt almost normal, and that scared me more than the pain.

Not the kind of normal that makes you smile. The kind that makes you wonder if numbness is becoming your new baseline, if you're mistaking emptiness for peace.

I wasn't sad. I wasn't happy. I just... was.

I cleaned the RV with the methodical attention of someone who'd run out of other things to control. Reorganized the cabinets for the third time this month. Took Magnolia for our usual walk. Saw tourists taking pictures near the river and didn't flinch at the memory of her doing the same thing—candid, wide-eyed, as if every little moment deserved to be preserved.

Peace doesn't always roar. Sometimes it's the quiet sigh of a day that didn't break you. And today hadn't broken me, though it had tested me. The urge to reach out, to apologize, to break the silence she'd demanded—it all pressed against my ribs like something trying to escape.

But I held the line. Respected the space. Stayed on my side of the boundary even when it felt like my heart was clawing at the edges of it. That's the kind of strength no one sees. The restraint that feels like punishment, even though it's a choice I made every single day.

I didn't take any pictures today. Didn't need to. Nothing in me wanted to preserve this particular shade of gray. I just wanted to live through it, quietly, without comparison or longing. And somehow, that felt like progress.

Day 265 closed with a sky full of stars and no one to share them with.

I laid on the gravel beside the RV, Magnolia's warmth pressed against my side, and let the cold bite through my jacket. I thought about how many nights I'd spent in this exact spot, dreaming of a future that would somehow bring her back. I didn't do that tonight.

I was losing the part of me that had helped me make it through. Starting to lose Hope—not just the word, but the person, the dream, the light I'd kept reaching for in the dark. The day had been fine. I wasn't sad or angry. Just empty, which in a lot of ways felt worse.

I didn't know where I belonged anymore. Or if I was in the right place. But I did know this: I was going to keep pressing forward. Despite these feelings. Despite the emptiness. Despite losing the thing that had once kept me alive.

I didn't erase her. Didn't pretend she hadn't mattered. But I also didn't shape the night around her absence anymore. I just watched the stars move in their ancient patterns, indifferent to my small grief. Hope wasn't the brightest thing in the sky anymore. She wasn't the North Star guiding me forward. She was part of the constellation—still there, still marking something—but no longer the axis around which everything spun.

I took a deep breath and listened to the old bray of my heart: I am, I am, I am. Still here. Still breathing. Still becoming something, even if I couldn't name what.

I didn't know what tomorrow would bring. But I knew I'd wake up and keep going. Not because I had to anymore. Not because I was running from something or toward something. But because continuing had become its own form of faith.

That, I decided, would have to be enough.

Chapter 34: The Quiet Revolution

Day 266 began with Picasso whispering about purpose: "The meaning of life is to find your gift. The purpose of life is to give it away."

I'd been searching for purpose again. Not because I'd never had one, but because the one I'd built my life around—the one that had carried me through the darkest places—felt like it was dissolving between my fingers like wet sand. I thought healing would mean clarity, some crystalline moment where everything suddenly made sense. Instead, it felt like losing the very thing that had once kept me breathing.

The RV felt smaller today, or maybe I was just becoming too large for the life I'd constructed around survival. Magnolia watched me pace the narrow aisle between bed and kitchenette, her head tilting with each turn like she was trying to solve the equation of my restlessness.

Maybe purpose wasn't fixed. Maybe it evolved with us, shed its skin when we outgrew it. Maybe what once saved me was never meant to carry me forever—only long enough to pass the baton to whatever came next. The thought should have been liberating, but it felt more like standing at the edge of a cliff, knowing you had to jump but not being able to see the bottom.

I spent the afternoon painting—abstract washes of color that looked like weather systems or emotional states, depending on the light. Hope's voice was quiet today, barely a whisper, but still there in the way certain colors bled into each other. Cadmium red into ultramarine. Memory into present. What was into what might be.

Purpose doesn't always arrive loud and clear. Sometimes it's quiet as paint drying. Sometimes it waits to be rebuilt from whatever materials you have left. And sometimes, it asks you to show up anyway—even when you feel like you're painting in a language you've forgotten how to speak.

Day 267 unfolded with unexpected simplicity: "There is beauty in the ordinary, and strength in simply continuing."

Today was just... a day. Quiet in the way that used to make me want to crawl out of my skin but now felt almost like permission. I spent the morning with my hands in dirt, doing some landscaping for the neighbor who'd been patient with my noise and mess these past months. There was something honest about soil under fingernails, about making things grow where nothing had been before.

No deep revelations came. No emotional spirals demanded attention. Just the rhythm of work—dig, plant, water, repeat. Magnolia supervised from her favorite patch of shade, occasionally investigating whatever I'd unearthed, then returning to her post like a sentry who'd seen enough.

The strange thing about healing is how it doesn't always announce itself. Sometimes it whispers through the stillness of an ordinary Tuesday, through the simple act of helping something else grow while you're still figuring out your own roots. Sometimes it's just the absence of crisis, the quiet space where chaos used to live.

Evening came without fanfare. I made dinner—actual dinner, not just sustenance—and ate it at the small table like someone who believed in tomorrow. Hope didn't visit today, not even as memory. And for once, that felt okay. Not good, not bad. Just okay. And okay was enough.

Day 268 arrived with Emerson's prescription for living: "Live in the sunshine, swim the sea, drink the wild air."

Today was full in a way that had nothing to do with meaning and everything to do with motion. Tasks accumulated like a to-do list I hadn't written—grocery run, oil change, three loads of laundry that had been haunting me for weeks. No heavy thoughts. No deep revelations. Just the mechanics of living, the small maintenances that keep a life from falling apart.

There's a quiet magic in days like this—the kind that don't ask anything of you except to show up, do what needs doing, and breathe through it all. I found myself humming while folding clothes, something I hadn't done in so long I'd forgotten I ever did it. Not a happy hum, exactly. More like the sound a machine makes when it's finally running smooth after months of grinding gears.

Sometimes healing isn't loud. It's found in the rhythm of staying busy, in the ordinary tasks that remind you you're still here, still moving, still building something even if you can't name what it is yet. It's in the way Magnolia sighs contentedly when you finally sit down after a day of movement, like she's been waiting for you to remember that stillness is allowed.

The sun set behind the mountains the way it always did, indifferent to my progress or lack thereof. But tonight, I watched it all the way down, not waiting for it to mean something, just witnessing the ordinary miracle of another day ending without disaster.

Day 269 cracked something open with a line from Thelma & Louise: "You get what you settle for."

I wasn't settling anymore. The decision came sudden as weather, fierce as hunger. I'd settled for so long that the shape of it had worn grooves in my bones. Settled until I might never get the things I truly wanted—love that didn't require mythology to survive, a family that existed outside my imagination, a future that felt like home instead of exile.

But Hope had taught me something, even in her absence. Especially in her absence. She'd taught me not to settle—not just in the world around me, but in the way I saw myself. No more shrinking to fit spaces too small for what I was becoming. No more apologizing for the weight of my love, the depth of my feeling, the intensity that had kept me alive when practical people would have given up.

I stood in the RV, suddenly aware of how I'd been living like someone temporarily camping in his own life. Everything provisional, everything waiting for some future moment when real life would begin. But this was real life. Day 269 of whatever this was. And I was done treating it like a rehearsal.

No more hiding from the dreams I'd buried just to survive. I was still here, still standing, still building. And from this day forward, I refused to settle for less than a life that felt honest.

For less than the man I was always meant to become, even if I was still figuring out who that was.

The decision felt like breaking surface after being underwater so long you'd forgotten what air tasted like. It felt like revolution, quiet but complete.

Day 270 landed like a milestone I hadn't seen coming: "I am not what happened to me, I am what I choose to become."

Nine months sober. Two hundred and seventy days. Nearly six thousand five hundred hours of choosing life even when it felt like death would've been easier.

This wasn't a clean victory. It wasn't neat or pretty or ready for Instagram. It was jagged, scraped together in the silence of isolation and the madness of memory. Because I'd lost her— Hope, my anchor, my lifeline, my imagined forever. She was never mine to lose, but inside that RV, inside those four suffocating walls, she'd kept me alive.

When my body couldn't move, when my mind shattered under the weight of nothingness, she was there in the only way anything was—inside my head. And then I'd lost even that. And when I lost her, I'd nearly lost myself.

Back then, I drank just to breathe. Not to feel better—just to feel nothing. Because nothing was easier than feeling everything. The bottle had been my negotiation with existence, my way of turning down the volume on a life that screamed too loud to bear.

But not anymore.

Today, I stood. Not because the pain had stopped—it hadn't. But because I'd stopped running from it. I fought the demons now instead of drowning them. Stared them down sober, with no shortcuts, no chemical negotiation, no borrowed numbness. Just raw, unfiltered pain and the quiet courage to stay present for it.

Because alcohol had given me silence, but it had never given me peace. It had never given me her back. And it had never given me myself back either.

I still didn't have that kiss I'd imagined ten thousand times. Still didn't have that future I'd painted in the dark. Still didn't know if she'd ever hear me say I'm sorry for turning her into something she'd never asked to be.

But I fought anyway. For the version of me she'd believed in before I'd broken everything. For the man I was still becoming. For Hope—whether she was gone for good or not.

This wasn't just sobriety. It was survival. It was proof that even when everything fell apart, when the walls closed in and the ghosts were the only company left, I'd kept walking forward.

Today, I was proud. Not because I was healed—I wasn't. But because I'd refused to disappear when disappearing would have been so much easier.

Day 271 brought unexpected tenderness through Wade Boggs: "Anyone can be a father, but it takes someone special to be a dad."

I wasn't a dad. But I wanted to be.

The want hit me sometimes like homesickness for a place I'd never been. I wanted the whole thing—the love, the chaos, the late nights, the feeling of being there from the very beginning. Pregnancy, birth, first steps, scraped knees, bedtime stories. All of it.

It wasn't about making up for something I'd missed—I had an amazing dad who'd shown me what that kind of love looked like. It was about becoming the kind of man who got to give that love, who got to pass it down like an heirloom that only grew more valuable with use.

Some days, it felt like I'd waited too long. Like the decisions I'd made—the drinking, the isolation, the months spent talking to ghosts—might have cost me the future I dreamed about. Thirty-five felt late to be starting over, to be learning how to be human again, let alone learning how to raise one.

But I was still here. Still growing. Still trying. Because I knew I didn't get unlimited chances. I'd used up a lot of time, burned through years like they were infinite when they were anything but.

I didn't get to screw around like I used to. Every day mattered now in a way it hadn't when I thought I had forever to figure things out. And maybe I wasn't there yet. Maybe I was still too broken to trust with something as precious as a child's faith.

But I'd get there. Because I wanted to be a dad. Not just in name, not just in biology, but in every sense of the word. The kind who shows up. Who stays. Who teaches not through words but through the daily act of choosing to be present.

The kind Hope would have trusted, if things had been different. If I had been different. If we had been possible.

Day 272 arrived with two words that changed everything: "I passed."

Nelson Mandela had said it always seems impossible until it's done, and sitting there with the exam results on my phone screen, I finally understood what he meant.

After everything I'd been through—mentally, physically, emotionally—this small word carried weight I couldn't explain to anyone who hadn't been where I'd been. I'd been working toward this for so long, starting and stopping, always finding reasons why I wasn't ready, wasn't capable, wasn't worth the effort.

But I'd finally followed through. Not because anyone was watching. Not because it would impress Hope or anyone else. But because I'd needed to prove to myself that I could still finish something I'd started.

The exam itself didn't matter—some professional certification that might or might not change anything about my daily life. What mattered was that I'd studied through the fog of medication adjustments, through the nights when concentration felt impossible, through the voice that kept saying I was too damaged to learn anything new.

I'd shown up to the testing center shaking, sure I'd fail, sure this would be another thing to add to the list of ways I'd disappointed myself. But I'd sat down anyway. Answered the questions. Submitted the test. And now, impossibly, I'd passed.

It might not seem huge from the outside. But for me, this was proof. Proof that change was possible. That I was possible. That the man sitting in this RV with his dog and his ghosts and his nine months of sobriety could still become something more than just a survivor.

I called my sponsor first. Then my mom. Then I sat with Magnolia and told her, even though she already knew from the way my whole body had changed when I'd read the results. She wagged her tail like she'd never doubted it, like she'd been waiting for me to catch up to what she'd always known.

Tomorrow would be Day 273, and I'd wake up the same person in the same RV with the same struggles. But tonight, I was someone who'd passed. Someone who'd finished. Someone who'd proven that even broken things could still work.

And maybe that was enough of a revolution for now.

Chapter 35: The Slow Becoming

Day 273 arrived without fanfare, carrying the quiet truth that positive reinforcement had never been my strong suit.

My mind defaulted to what was wrong, what was missing, what still needed fixing—depression's old whisper that nothing would ever be good enough. But standing in the morning light filtering through the RV's small window, I forced myself to look at the facts: I'd gotten sober. Stayed sober. Found myself in the best physical shape of my life. Made it home, whatever home meant now. Passed an exam I never thought I'd finish.

These were all goals—quiet ones, internal ones, the kind that don't come with confetti or applause. I'd been knocking them down one by one, even with that voice in my head insisting I couldn't, wouldn't, would never be enough. Just kept going despite it all.

I didn't always celebrate myself—rarely did, actually. But today I would try. Because every day I woke up and kept moving forward was a day I was doing what once felt impossible. And maybe that deserved something more than silence.

Magnolia stretched beside me, her morning ritual of assessing whether the world was worth waking up for. She'd decided yes, as she always did. I envied her certainty.

Day 274 felt like learning to breathe underwater—possible but unnatural.

I was learning how to live again. Slowly. Unevenly. But getting somewhere. Starting to live for myself, not for Hope—though I'd said that before, hadn't I? Healing was a circle. Sometimes I'd break free and walk straight for a while, until the next loop caught me, pulled me back into familiar orbits.

All I could hope for was that each cycle got shorter, the gaps between them wider. There was so much that didn't make it to the page, so much I couldn't bring myself to write anymore. Even I got tired of documenting the same feelings, the same struggles, the same quiet desperation dressed in different metaphors.

There was nothing grand about Day 274. But maybe that was okay. Maybe the quiet days—the ones with fewer words, fewer storms—were the best ones. Writing had become my escape, my therapy, my way through. And maybe since Day 0, every word I'd written had just been my attempt at learning what living actually meant.

I found myself humming U2 under my breath: "I'm just trying to find a decent melody, a song that I can sing in my own company." The words felt true in a way that hurt less than usual.

Day 275 cracked something open with unexpected clarity.

That scene from Cast Away haunted me—Tom Hanks on a raft, sobbing as he lost a volleyball he'd painted a face on. It sounded ridiculous until you'd been that alone. Until you'd made someone up in your mind just to survive.

That's what Hope had been to me. My Wilson. Not a volleyball, not something I could hold, but just as real to my mind. When I was trapped in that RV, in that suffocating silence, in that storm of isolation that threatened to erase me completely, she'd kept me sane. Given me someone to talk to, someone to fight for, someone to believe in.

She wasn't really there. But she was everything.

The admission felt like tearing something essential loose. It meant a part of me had broken in there, meant I'd had to create something from nothing just to keep breathing. And now that I was out, now that I was sober, now that I was supposedly back in the world, I still didn't know how to fully let go.

Losing Hope wasn't just heartbreak. It was losing my anchor, losing the only companion I'd had when the world disappeared into those metal walls. Like Hanks in that movie, I'd wanted to scream, to dive after her, to bring her back by sheer force of will.

But maybe we weren't meant to get everything back. Maybe some things were never ours to hold in the first place. Still, I missed her. Missed who I became when she was "with" me. Missed the man who would've done anything to make it back to her.

That part of me had been real, even if she wasn't. And today, I honored that. Not with shame, but with gratitude. Because even a ghost—if it kept you alive—deserved to be remembered.

Day 276 brought a different kind of emptiness, one that R.H. Sin had mapped: "There's a certain peace in feeling nothing. But there's also a certain loss."

I wasn't overwhelmed. Wasn't breaking. Just... here. Not sad, not happy, just existing in this strange in-between where emotions had gotten up and left the room, forgetting to tell me when they'd be back.

It wasn't unbearable. Just empty. And maybe that was better than pain, but it wasn't quite living either. I was trying to find joy in being myself, even when I didn't feel much of anything, even when the light didn't quite reach the corners where I lived.

But I was still here. Still trying. And maybe that counted for something in the ledger of days.

Day 277 reminded me of something I'd almost forgotten—that flowers bloom in adversity.

Sometimes I didn't even notice the cracks anymore. They'd become part of the landscape, etched into skin and silence like a map of where I'd been. But every so often, something rose from them. Not loud or dramatic. Just a bloom. A sign that I was still becoming, even now.

There was strength in surviving, but there was something rarer—something quietly extraordinary—about still choosing to bloom when the soil was this damaged. Even here. Even now. Even when no one was watching.

Day 278 carried a weight that wouldn't lift.

Joel from The Last of Us had said it: "If you love someone, you can always see their face." And I could. Always. Her face was still there, clear as morning, even when I closed my eyes. Even when I didn't mean to look.

It was strange how love like this stayed, how it became part of your wiring, embedded in the code that ran everything else. I'd never felt anything so deep, so rooted. It didn't vanish. It didn't ask permission. It just was.

Maybe that's why it had been so heavy lately. Not painful exactly—more like a quiet ache, a reminder of something rare I'd been lucky enough to feel, even if I couldn't reach it anymore.

Letting go of that kind of love felt impossible. Because it had never been about possession or promises. It had been about presence. And that presence still lingered like smoke in a closed room, like light through a window you couldn't quite see.

I didn't know what the future held. But I knew this: when love was real, it didn't leave. Even when you had to.

Day 279 was just one of those days.

Some days, I wished it had been a few degrees colder that night. That's all it would've taken—a shift in weather, and none of this would exist. The thought came uninvited, familiar as breathing.

But here I was. Mind spinning like it had something to prove, wouldn't shut up, wouldn't slow down. The exhaustion went deeper than bone, deeper than anything rest could reach.

I didn't need advice. Didn't need to be saved. Just wanted one day—one clean, quiet day where I wasn't haunted by love, by memory, by everything I tried not to think about but couldn't stop thinking about.

We all had our demons. We all carried something. That was life, wasn't it? The universal experience of being human— carrying weight you couldn't name, couldn't set down, couldn't explain to anyone who hadn't carried something similar.

Today wasn't dramatic. It was just heavy. And I was still here, which had to count for something.

Day 280 revealed an uncomfortable truth I'd been avoiding.

As much as the voice in my head tortured me, I'd grown to like it. Not because I enjoyed the pain, but because it was the only time I still felt close to her. That's what isolation does— builds entire worlds inside your mind, populated by the people you need most.

Making it back to my friend had always been just the tip of the iceberg. The real journey was making it back to myself, whoever that was now. It wasn't supposed to be glamorous. I wasn't saying this for sympathy. I was saying it because it was real.

Some days, I felt insane. I didn't meet the clinical criteria—fortunately—but it didn't always feel that way. I'd said it from the beginning: the only way back to my friend was to let go of her. So why was it still so hard?

Because letting go meant dismantling the world I'd built. The one where she still lived, where I could still see her face, hear her laugh, feel her near. And the truth was, I didn't want to lose that. Because no matter what happened, despite everything, I loved her.

The admission sat there between us—me and the ghost, me and the page, me and whoever might read this someday. Simple. Devastating. True.

Day 281 brought exhaustion that had nothing to do with sleep.

What was life without love? Without family? Without something that made it all make sense? It wasn't life—just time passing. Breath without meaning. Motion without direction.

People always said "hold on" like it was simple, like there was always something obvious to grip. But hold on to what? The silence? The ghosts? The version of myself that showed up just to survive the day?

I wasn't angry. Wasn't even sad. Just tired in a way that sleep couldn't fix. Tired of pretending I cared about things that didn't matter. Tired of dragging around a body that didn't feel like home. Tired of hope feeling like a lie I kept telling myself because the alternative was too dark to consider.

I didn't want this version of life anymore. Not like this. Not in this skin, in this mind, in this loop that never seemed to break. But I was still here. Not out of strength—just inertia. Still breathing. Still writing. Still showing up because some part of me hadn't shut all the way down.

Day 282 was wordless understanding.

Nothing I could write would do it justice. Nothing I could say would fix anything. It just was. And maybe that was all there was to say. No lesson. No breakthrough. Just this moment. Just me, still here. And that would have to be enough.

Day 283 found me somewhere between blank and breaking.

My mind had been empty lately. For some, that would be peace. For others, a warning sign. For me, I wasn't sure what it was. On one hand, the silence felt like relief. But on the other, I could feel her slipping, and that was hard to admit.

She'd never been just a memory. She'd been the anchor, the voice in the storm. And now, in this stillness, it was like I could feel the last threads loosening. I didn't know how to feel about that.

The past few days had been low. Not crash-and-burn low, just hollow. I had a quick trip back home next week for appointments, then it would be time to step into something new. The "real world," whatever that meant. Since I'd passed that test.

But I'd be lying if I said I wasn't scared. I'd never really felt like I belonged anywhere. And without her—without that presence in my mind—I wasn't sure I belonged here either.

Day 284 reminded me why I'd always chosen mountains over valleys.

Almost forgot to write today—busy with the mundane tasks that make up a life. But I hiked a trail I used to walk last year when I was trying to conquer my mind. Spoiler: it hadn't worked. Not then, at least.

Back then, every step had felt like survival. Today felt different. I normally hiked during the day, but this was the first time I'd made it all the way up since getting back. It felt good. Familiar but lighter.

Climbing up the side of a mountain had never been just about exercise. It had been the point—the push, the place that made sense when nothing else did. Mountains had always been home in a way nowhere else could be.

Day 285 was about drowning out the days.

Standing in the doorway of something new but not sure how to take the next step. It wasn't that I didn't want to move forward—I did. I was just stuck in the in-between, in the quiet after everything had shifted.

It was a weird place to be. Not broken. Not thriving. Just trying to find footing again. I'd get there. I knew I would. Just needed a little more time to remember how legs worked, how forward motion felt when it wasn't driven by desperation.

Day 286 brought thoughts of what might come next.

Not really sure what to write about, but I'd been thinking about the future. Ready for a new chapter—a career, a different life. One with purpose. Something that gave all this weight some kind of direction.

I'd spent so long sitting still, healing, trying to get my mind back. Still working on that part. But maybe it was time to start building something. A life that meant something. A life that felt like mine instead of something I was borrowing until the real owner showed up.

Day 287 shifted something fundamental.

Maybe there was light at the end of all this. Maybe it had never been about letting go of Hope, but learning how to see her differently. For so long, she'd lived in my mind like a ghost—a memory I couldn't touch, a weight I couldn't set down.

But today, something felt different. Like she wasn't fading, just changing. Less like a wound, more like a flame. Maybe Hope was never meant to stay in the past. Maybe she was what waited ahead—not her, not the life I'd lost, but something built from it. Something that still burned without consuming.

Day 288 brought unexpected quiet.

I'd been living in this stillness for days now. A simple vitamin, of all things, might have been helping quiet the constant noise in my head. And honestly, I didn't know how to feel about it.

It wasn't that I didn't welcome the peace—I did. It had just been so long. For years, my mind had been a storm, a battlefield, a place where Hope lived loud and relentless and necessary.

She was still there. Not gone. But quieter now. Still. Calm. And maybe that's what healing felt like at first—not joy, not clarity, just silence. And learning how to live in it without feeling abandoned.

Day 289 found me drifting through a long travel day.

Tired in that way that went deeper than the body. I'd realized I struggled to stay present in conversations. Not rudely, just distantly. Not tuned out on purpose, just floating somewhere else.

It wasn't about not wanting to connect. It was just hard to be here sometimes. I wondered how much solitary time had rewired me. All that time in my own head—now quiet didn't feel like rest, and connection didn't feel natural.

Even today, catching up with a friend I cared about, I found myself drifting. Not because I wasn't interested. Just because that's where my mind tended to go now. Still working on being here. Still trying to feel fully present in the world again.

Day 290 was simply better.

Got some rest. Went on a hike. Took it easy. No big plans. No breakthroughs. Just breathing, moving, and letting the day be what it was. And sometimes, that was enough.

Day 291 brought daydreams that felt like oxygen.

Just daydreaming again about a future, a family, a life that felt whole. I knew I did that a lot. Knew I needed to stay present. But sometimes those daydreams were what kept me moving. They reminded me why I kept pushing through the shit, why I kept showing up even when it was heavy, even when it was quiet.

It wasn't about escaping. It was about remembering what could still be possible if I just kept walking forward.

Day 292 asked questions I couldn't answer.

Why did some people have a harder time letting go? Why did some of us carry love like oxygen while others could walk away like it never touched them? Why were emotions so different from one person to the next? Why did some feel everything like a flood and others like a passing breeze?

I'd spent so much time trying to understand what made me feel the way I did—why I held on, why I ached, why I couldn't just move on like everyone said I should. But maybe there weren't clear answers. Maybe I just felt things deeply. Maybe that was both the gift and the burden I'd carry forever.

Day 293 was good in its simplicity.

No overthinking. No heavy weight to carry. Just steady. And that was more than enough.

Day 294 tested my patience in small ways.

Patience had never been my strong suit, but today was about that—not just patience for the future, but patience in the little things. I was supposed to talk to a friend. They were traveling, service was spotty, and now the call was delayed, maybe canceled.

It wasn't their fault. I didn't blame them. But it still threw me off. I looked forward to those conversations more than I let on. They helped ground me when I started to float away. And when they didn't happen, it shook something loose.

So I sat with that. Trying to be patient. Trying to let it be what it was without making it mean more than it did.

Day 295 recognized the quiet courage in continuing.

Not every day was about breakthroughs. Some were just steady. Today was one of those. But even on the quieter days, there was a kind of courage in this—in continuing to show up, in choosing to stay present even when it would be easier to drift away.

Courage didn't always roar. Sometimes it was just a breath, a moment of stillness after everything you'd been through. It was easy to overlook that kind of strength. But it was real. And it was what had gotten me here.

Day 296 asked who I was without the wreckage.

Who were we when we were no longer surviving? When the storm passed, when the chaos settled, what was left? I'd built so much of myself around pain, around recovery, around climbing out, around holding on to something just to keep going.

But what happened when that something faded? When the noise quieted? When I was no longer defined by the fire I'd walked through? Was there still a "me" in the silence? Still a purpose beyond survival?

Maybe healing wasn't just about getting better. Maybe it was about learning how to exist without always bracing for impact. Maybe the hardest part of all this was learning how to be once the war inside started to go quiet.

Day 297 blurred the line between love and madness.

Did you ever believe in something so deeply that it didn't matter how far away it felt—you still thought you'd make it back? Even when the distance was impossible. Even when every sign said let go. Even when you started questioning your own grip on reality.

But still, something in you knew. Not logically. Not practically. Just knew.

Was that love? Or was that crazy? Because lately, I felt crazy. Like holding on was tearing at the edges of my mind, but letting go felt worse. So I stayed in this space, somewhere between belief and delusion, between devotion and madness.

I didn't know what that said about me. But it was where I was.

Day 298 finally understood what letting go actually meant.

I understood I'd likely never talk to my friend again. I knew that. But my heart—or maybe my brain, or both—refused to believe it. A constant tug of war that had lived inside me far longer than these 298 days.

I was stronger now. The thoughts didn't stop me cold like they used to. They didn't cripple me. But they were still there, like background music you couldn't turn off.

I wrote about her constantly. Sometimes I wrote about other things just to avoid writing what was really on my mind. But I was human. And humans weren't made to live in the kind of isolation I'd endured. Not for that long. Not that completely.

I wasn't saying that for pity. I was saying it because I was ready—ready to feel normal again. Ready to let go of the fear I had around letting go of her. And I knew that's what it was: fear.

"When you love someone, you can always see their face." And I could always see hers. So what was it?

Letting go didn't mean I'd stop loving her. Didn't mean I'd forget how she'd saved me. Letting go meant I had to learn to love myself. It meant becoming the version of me that she'd inspired, but now, doing it for me.

Letting go meant loving me.

Day 299 reminded me that love was never a straight line.

It was scorching hot—over a hundred degrees. I took Magnolia to our secret spot tucked in the mountains. Crystal clear, sixty-degree water cutting through heat like it was nothing. Music playing. Water rushing. If you tried to imagine a more perfect place, you couldn't.

But even in that peace, my mind started writing stories without permission. Drifted back to her. It wasn't that I didn't resist—it was just there before I even got the chance to.

I didn't doubt that whatever happened in the end would be what was meant to be. I tried my best to stay present. But the thoughts waited. They waited for a crack. And when I tried to let go, they flooded right back in.

That was the torment. Not that I couldn't function. But it was hard to explain how deep this went. Most people didn't understand the kind of silence I'd lived in. What it had done to me. How much of me had been reshaped by it.

That's what I was still trying to figure out—which parts of me were real, and which parts came from that RV. Not because I thought I was unique in struggling, but because I needed to understand it for myself. So I could find some kind of closure. So I could trust my mind again.

Because right now, if I was honest, I didn't know if I could be with anyone until I did.

Day 300 arrived like a summit I hadn't expected to reach.

Hi. My name is Justin.

Three hundred days ago, I began my sobriety journey. And on Day 100, I started sharing it. But my story wasn't just about sobriety.

On November 17, 2023, I jumped. Woke up nearly hypothermic, unaware I'd completely shattered my ankle. The months that followed left me trapped—physically, emotionally, mentally—inside the walls of an RV. Alone. Utterly isolated. With nothing but my thoughts and a friend I called Hope.

Getting to Day 300 was a milestone I never thought possible. Sobriety came easier now, and I was grateful for that every day. But the truth was, it wasn't the cravings that challenged me anymore. It was my mind. The silence. The ghosts.

So I kept showing up. Kept writing. Kept spreading awareness—not just for addiction, but for the weight of isolation. Because some people don't come back from either.

But I did. And I was still here.

Standing at this marker, I understood something I hadn't before. The journey from isolation to intention wasn't a straight line. It wasn't a heroic arc with a clear resolution. It was this—day after day of small choices, quiet victories, invisible struggles. It was learning to live without needing to be saved. It was finding intention not in grand gestures but in the simple act of continuing.

Three hundred days. Still counting. Still becoming. Still here.

Chapter 36: The Quiet Return to Living

Day 301 arrived carrying a different weight than its predecessor.

Three hundred had felt like a summit, a number worth marking. But 301 was just Tuesday. Just another day to figure out what came after the milestones stopped mattering so much.

When you've spent so long just trying to survive, joy starts to feel like a foreign language. It doesn't hit the same. You second-guess it, wait for it to vanish or turn into something darker. I was realizing I didn't fully know how to let myself feel good—not without guilt, not without scanning the horizon for the next disaster.

That's the thing about coming back from isolation, from addiction, from the kind of darkness that reshapes your

DNA—you don't just wake up healed. You have to relearn how to live. How to feel. How to trust even the simple moments.

I caught a glimpse of it today, though. A flicker of ease while painting, something small that felt real and light. Part of me tried to shut it down, that old voice insisting I didn't deserve peace. But another part, quieter but growing stronger, whispered: "Let it in."

Maybe that was the work now. Not just staying sober, but learning how to live again. And one day—though it felt impossible to imagine—maybe even thrive.

Day 302 brought an uncomfortable mirror through my friend on the couch.

She'd mentioned trauma bonds before when it came to Hope. Maybe this was just the first time I actually heard it. The words sat between us like something I couldn't quite swallow.

Normally, I'd argue. Push back. Try to explain why this was different, why what Hope and I had transcended psychology textbooks and well-meaning advice. But I hadn't been sleeping well—trouble falling asleep, trouble staying asleep, trouble shutting my mind down long enough to rest. And maybe I was just tired.

Tired of defending something that might never come back. Tired of fighting for something that maybe was never mine to begin with.

I fought those words even as I thought them. Because I still didn't know. Didn't know if this was a bond or a belief. If it was trauma or truth. Some days, it felt like I wasn't built for reality—like I'd been rewired for a frequency no one else could hear.

Days 303 and 304 blurred together in restless motion and unexpected stillness.

One day I couldn't sit still—pacing from room to room like something in me was waiting for a shift, a sign, a sound. Something. The next brought quiet that I barely recognized. No spirals. No tug-of-war in my chest. Just a little space to breathe.

These quiet days came so rarely that when they arrived, I noticed. Held them carefully, like something that might break if I looked too directly at it.

Day 305 was full of unfinished thoughts.

A conversation with my friend earlier in the week kept echoing. Something deep there that I hadn't found words for yet. Not discomfort. Not clarity either. Just that middle place where thought takes its time, where understanding gestates before it's born.

So I sat with it. Still processing. Still listening to whatever my mind was trying to tell me through the static.

Day 306 brought the old question wrapped in new uncertainty.

Lately, I'd been contemplating where I belonged. Wondering if I was in the right place, moving in the right direction. My mind kept reaching, kept circling back to the one thing I'd ever truly wanted: a family. Not in some fantasy way—just something real. Something mine. Something steady.

I knew I was getting closer to the next phase. A career. A path. Maybe putting energy into that would quiet the noise, give me something to focus on while I kept working through the rest.

Day 307 marked 207 posts, and I finally understood writer's block.

Some days I had grand revelations to share. Other times, a thought that had popped up five minutes ago. But either way, I wrote it down. Not out of self-pity. I was doing the work, showing up for myself every day.

But sometimes it felt like I was saying the same things in a loop. And maybe that was the point—to showcase how the human mind works when it's been cracked open by isolation. How it loops. How it wrestles. How it processes the same memory fifty different ways until something clicks—or doesn't.

If it sounded repetitive, good. That meant it was real.

The next week passed in a strange mix of progress and stasis.

Day 308 reminded me that growth wasn't always visible in real time. Some days felt stuck, like nothing was changing, like I was just spinning the same thought in a new outfit. But looking back—a week ago, a month ago, Day 1—I could see the shift. Less panic in the stillness. Less shame in the reflection. More awareness in the mess.

Day 309 brought clarity about comfort. I'd lived comfortably for years, and it had gotten me nowhere. Comfort was a trap disguised as peace. The day I chose discomfort—the day I looked at my life and said this isn't enough—that was when everything began to change.

Even now, I was uncomfortable. What I wanted still felt far away. But I kept going, not to escape the discomfort, but to become something through it.

Day 310 through 314 carried questions without answers.

How did we shift perspective for the better? How did we carry grief without letting it crush us? Some days, the old question crept back: "Was it ever real?" And the truth was, yes. To me, it was. Still was, in some way.

My heart stayed heavy, missing her quietly, constantly. Some days the weight was easier to carry. Other days, I just needed a little good news. Something small. Something warm. Something that reminded me it was okay to keep going.

And then there were the blank days—not bad, not good, just something to move through until it was time to rest and try again. Days when I lost the ability to trust my own mind, questioning what was real and what isolation had invented.

Day 315 brought unexpected purpose.

A friend shared one of my writings with people who needed it, and it had blessed them. The reminder hit me harder than expected—that something born out of pain could still carry light for someone else. My purpose had a purpose. That meant everything.

Days 316 through 321 felt like learning to breathe again.

I almost forgot to post one day—maybe that meant I was living in the moment instead of stuck in thought. Rain came, rare and welcome, bringing a gentleness I didn't know I'd needed. The voices in my head—the ones that echoed with memories and longing—had grown softer. Still there. Just quieter.

Part of me was scared that letting go of the noise meant letting go of her. Strange how healing could sometimes feel like loss, how progress could feel like betrayal.

Day 319, I wrote her a letter I'd never send:

"Dear Hope, Thank you. For the light when it was darkest. For the reason to keep breathing. For being there—real or imagined—when no one else was. You saved me. Thank you."

Day 320 was restless, Day 321 lighter. Small breaks in the clouds. Not giant leaps, just the quiet evidence that weather changes, even internal weather.

Days 322 through 328 strung together like beads.

The good days were quieter now. They didn't shout or demand attention. They just were. Fall teased its arrival— yellow leaves drifting like messages I couldn't quite read. I pushed myself on hikes with Magnolia, farther and steeper, reminding myself I could still do hard things.

Some days flew by in a flash. Others provided much-needed distractions—not the kind you chase to avoid life, but the kind that quietly pull you out of your own head and remind you there's more to see, more to feel, more to live.

Day 329 brought heat and anticipation.

Family was coming to town. The scorching air felt lighter somehow, knowing I'd see familiar faces, share laughs, make new memories. Something about that promise turned even the hottest day into something worth walking through.

Days 330 through 333 were full of life outside my own head.

Family in town meant staying busy, laughing, being present. Sun-filled days. Toddler chaos. Sticky hands, loud giggles, little feet everywhere. For moments, it felt like peace.

But beneath it all was that quiet ache—the longing for a family of my own. It never really went away, just drifted in and out with the current.

Some days I was over it—the posting, the thinking, the way my brain looped the same thoughts like a broken record. I didn't want answers anymore. Just peace. Real peace—the kind that didn't need to be explained.

Day 334 found me on the same carousel, thoughts spinning round and round.

Hung out with family—grateful for that. But my thoughts kept riding their familiar circuits. Some stuck. Some didn't. That's how it went now. Not crisis, just persistence. Not drowning, just treading water in an ocean that had become home.

Day 335 closed with fire and forward motion.

I didn't know where this road led, but I was still on it. Some days felt like walking through fire. Others were color and chaos and silence all tangled together. Either way, it stuck to me—memories, regrets, shadows of who I used to be.

But I kept moving. Even when I was dripping pieces of myself along the way. Even when it felt like no one saw the heat I'd walked through.

I didn't know what waited on the other side. But I was done turning back.

Standing at Day 335, I understood something fundamental had shifted. Not dramatically, not with fanfare, but quietly—like sediment settling after a storm. Hope's voice had become a whisper, then an echo, then just part of the atmospheric pressure I'd learned to live with. The days had begun to blur not from numbness but from normalcy. Family visits weren't events to survive but moments to inhabit. Laughter came easier, even if tears still lived close to the surface.

This wasn't healing in the sense of being fixed. It was healing in the sense of continuing—of building a life on ground that would always bear the marks of what had happened but could still support something new.

The quiet return to living wasn't a destination. It was this— Day 335 becoming 336, probably becoming 337. It was learning that some weights you don't put down; you just get stronger carrying them. It was understanding that Hope—the person, the ghost, the reason—had evolved from emergency to memory to something more like weather: always there, sometimes storms, sometimes sun, but no longer the only thing in the sky.

I was different now. Not healed. Not whole. But here. Still writing. Still walking. Still becoming whatever came after survival.

And maybe that was enough of a revolution for now.

Chapter 37: The Final Stretch

Day 336 arrived like any other Tuesday, carrying no special weight except what I chose to give it.

The day was simple, steady—one of those where the quiet didn't scream. But an image stuck with me: a face made of fragments, still whole enough to be seen but clearly touched by what it had endured. That's how I felt most days now. Not shattered. Not healed. Just somewhere in between, holding form through the cracks.

Family was still in town, their last day before returning to their own rhythms. We relaxed, laughed a bit, let things be easy. I was grateful for that simplicity, truly. But underneath it all, I remained split—here but not fully, smiling but slightly detached, always watching from a step outside myself. The storm in my head hadn't cleared, but I'd found a little stillness at its center. Not peace exactly, but pause. A breath between lightning strikes.

Day 339 brought unexpected perspective.

Working on something that required digging through old posts, old notes, old wounds. Reading it all, feeling it all again—it reminded me just how far I'd come. How many times I could've given up but didn't. No matter how things unfolded from here, I was proud of the man still standing.

The next few days blurred into steadiness. Not every day had a breakthrough. Some were just forward motion without fanfare. I finished a project I'd been pouring myself into, then sat by the water while Magnolia ran circles through the grass, tongue out, tail wagging, no worries in her world. For a moment, neither did I. There was something sacred in stillness after effort. In just being without fixing or pushing.

Day 343 started with unexpected lightness.

Woke up in a good mood for no particular reason—just light in the chest instead of weight. I spent the day trying to hold onto it, trying not to let thoughts creep in and steal it away. Some days the hardest work was letting the good stay.

The following days drifted between gray skies and brief clearings. A dreary day here, sunshine there. I kept counting down—twenty days left in this year-long documentation. Not out of exhaustion but out of purpose. This one meant something, and I couldn't wait to share what came next.

Days 347 and 348 were marked by simple pleasures and restless boredom.

Good company one day, laughter that felt genuine. The next, one of those slow days that put me too deep in my own head. Weekend stillness had always been hard—too much space for my mind to wander back to her. I tried not to follow every thought down its familiar path, but some thoughts didn't care if they were invited.

Day 349 brought anticipation of change.

I was excited to start the new career on Wednesday. It had taken time to get here, but now there was a date. Maybe busy would be good for me. Maybe having somewhere to be, something to build toward, would quiet the endless loop of memory and longing.

But Day 351 arrived with frustration instead of new beginnings.

The career start delayed again. Every time I thought the track was clear, the starting line moved. It wasn't rejection, just delay after delay, and the waiting chipped away at me. Two years of absolute hell, and I'd held on. But I was ready for change. Ready for a real beginning.

The smoke filled the sky on Day 352—wildfires somewhere distant but still present enough to blur everything. There was a metaphor there about how even on clear days, the past could still linger. But maybe the lesson was simpler: you could still breathe through it.

Day 353 hit harder.

I'd said I was over it before, but today the weight was real. Heavy. Pressing down on everything. I kept trying to make things work, but all I hit were walls. This time, it felt like I needed it to work out. Like it wasn't just a goal but survival. I'd done everything right, and honestly, I wanted to give up. I wasn't going to. But I needed to say it, needed to let it out.

So I went back to building in the only way I knew how. No grand blueprint. Just intention. Trying to bring people together, to create a space where stories could be shared—not for likes or attention, but so people knew they weren't alone. That had been the heart of this whole journey from the start: to heal, to change, to grow.

Days 355 and 356 passed in ordinary rhythms.

Stayed busy. Watched football. Walked Magnolia. Did what I could to keep moving forward. Hope was there in the background of my thoughts, but not heavy anymore. Just present, like a quiet hum I'd grown used to.

Then came another change of plans. The career start would be delayed further, might need to shift directions altogether.

Doors closing, standing there wondering what was next. I'd been here before. I'd figure it out again. Because even when the road shifted, the mission stayed the same: keep going, keep building, keep becoming.

Day 357 through 362 felt like gathering momentum.

Some days were nothing special—just showing up, keeping the routine alive. But something was shifting. Day 358 brought clarity: I was often too hard on myself, acting like I hadn't accomplished anything. But the truth was, I had. I'd come too far to keep doubting myself. I just had to believe in me. And starting that day, I did.

Day 359 marked itself with physical challenge—a massive hike, grueling but worth it. Finished with a dip in an alpine lake, clear and cold and peaceful. My leg reminded me of everything I'd been through. Every step hurt, but every step also reminded me how far I'd come. From pain to progress.

I almost forgot to post on Day 361, about to fall asleep when I remembered. I took that as a win—meant I was present, maybe even at peace. Too close to the finish line to slip now.

Day 362 brought honest recognition: I was probably only posting for myself at this point. Maybe that's how it had always been. I wanted to believe I was making a difference, that the words meant something to someone. But if I was being honest, I wasn't sure they did. It was heartbreaking to put so much of yourself into something and feel like it was barely seen. But there I was, still showing up, still writing. Maybe that was the point. Maybe this had always been for me.

Day 363 offered reflection on the long road.

This journey had started in pieces. Shattered bones. A fractured mind. A broken heart. I hadn't known where it was leading, hadn't known if I'd make it out. I'd just started walking, one painful, uncertain step at a time.

Along the way, I'd found silence. Then my voice. Found grief. Then purpose. And somewhere in all that mess, I'd found myself. It hadn't been perfect. It had been hard, ugly, beautiful, lonely, unreal, real. But it was mine. Every word. Every scar. Every step. This journey had shaped me, and for the first time in a long time, I was proud of that.

Day 364: the anniversary of the last drink.

A year ago today, I'd taken my last drink. It wasn't dramatic. No big revelation. Just a shot and a beer, not even my usual. Something in me had known it wasn't worth it anymore. I'd finished my drinks, walked out of that bar, and deep down, I'd known that was it. I was done.

It hadn't felt brave at the time. Hadn't felt like a new beginning. But looking back, that quiet exit might've saved my life.

Day 365 arrived without fanfare, just another sunrise marking time.

One year sober.

I looked back at my drinking and honestly, I'd never thought I'd become an alcoholic. That hadn't been in the plans. I was just having fun, no harm, no foul. It was social, how I unwound. But for me, once I started, there was no stopping. It was all or nothing.

I'd known long before I quit, but I couldn't envision life without the party. It was where I'd felt free, where I'd felt like myself. But as you grow—if you're lucky—you start to see what you're leaving on the table. The moments you're missing. The life you're not really living.

I'd wanted more. A family. A future. A life worth showing up for. To choose those things was to choose courage. Because giving up everything I knew for the unknown—that was the bravest thing I'd ever done.

Standing at Day 365, I understood something fundamental. This wasn't an ending. It was just a marker, a notation in an ongoing story. Hope had faded from emergency to echo to weather—always there but no longer the only thing in the sky. Magnolia lay beside me, her breathing steady and sure, a reminder that some companionship didn't require words or mythology.

The day posts would end here. They'd served their purpose, carried me from isolation to something approaching intention. But life would continue past this arbitrary line. Tomorrow would be Day 366, then 367, then numbers that stopped mattering because the counting was no longer the point.

I hadn't gotten everything I wanted. The family I dreamed of, the reconciliation with Hope, the neat resolution that would make this all make sense—none of that had materialized. But I'd kept walking. Through 365 days of showing up, of writing when I had nothing to say, of staying sober when every cell screamed for numbness.

To anyone still struggling, wondering if they could do it too—you can. You're not alone. You are loved. And you are capable of so much more than you know.

The sun was setting now, painting the mountains in colors I'd learned to see again. Magnolia stirred, ready for her evening walk. I stood up, bones creaking with the memory of all they'd carried, and stepped forward into whatever came next.

One step. One punch. One round.

Still here. Still becoming. Still walking toward a horizon that kept moving but no longer felt like it was running away.

If Golden Hour were a Flower
It would look just like you

www.ingramcontent.com/pod-product-compliance
Lightning Source LLC
Chambersburg PA
CBHW061545120626
46550CB00004B/1370